THE WICKED + THE DIVINE

VOL. 9, "OKAY"

GILLEN

MᶜKELVIE

WILSON

COWLES

KIERON GILLEN
WRITER

JAMIE McKELVIE
ARTIST

MATTHEW WILSON
COLOURIST

CLAYTON COWLES
LETTERER

SERGIO SERRANO
DESIGNER

CHRISSY WILLIAMS
EDITOR

DEE CUNNIFFE
FLATTER

THE WICKED + THE DIVINE, VOL. 9, "OKAY"
First printing. October 2019.
ISBN: 978-1-5343-1249-4
Published by Image Comics Inc.
Office of publication: 2701 NW Vaughn St., Suite 780, Portland, OR 97210.

For information regarding the CPSIA on this printed material call: 203-595-3636.
Representation: Law Offices of Harris M. Miller II, P.C. (rights.inquiries@gmail.com).

This book was designed by Sergio Serrano, based on a design by Hannah Donovan
and Jamie McKelvie, and set into type by Sergio Serrano in Edmonton, Canada.
The text face is Gotham, designed and issued by Hoefler & Co. in 2000. The paper
is Orion 60 matte.

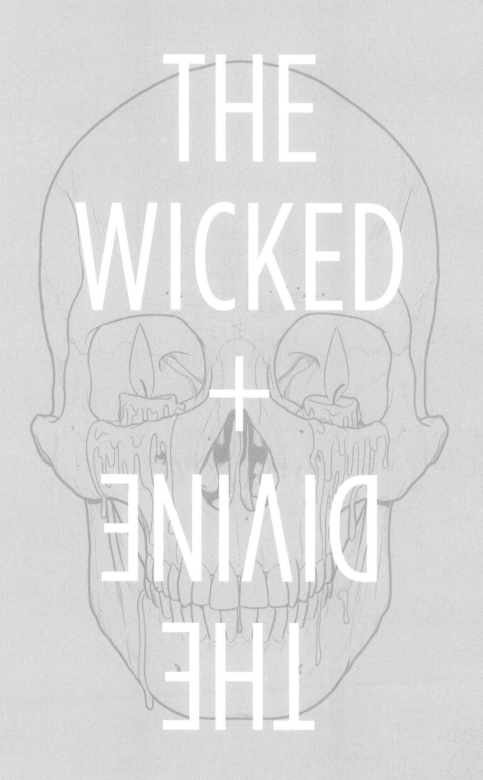

GILLEN MᶜKELVIE WILSON COWLES

THE
WICKED
+
DIVINE
THE

VOL. 9, "OKAY"

THE
WICKED
+
THE DIVINE

PREVIOUSLY...

Every ninety years twelve gods return as young people. They are loved. They are hated. In two years, they are all dead. It's happening now. It's happening again.

Many gods are already dead. Persephone has somehow abandoned her divinity, and escaped into seclusion. The manipulated forces of Minerva think her an irrelevance... but it seems she can still create fire with a finger click. Hmm.

But the question of The Great Darkness looms...

Laura. Descended god. So the question is... what is she?

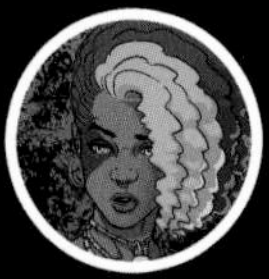

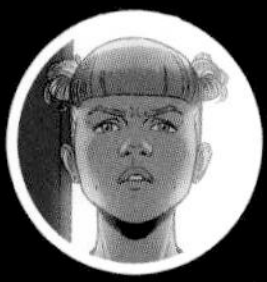

Minerva. Or Ananke. 6,000 death-phobic years of lying and murder. Shows no sign of stopping.

THE PANTHEON

Lucifer. Underworld god. Framed for murder. Apparently killed, actually living head.

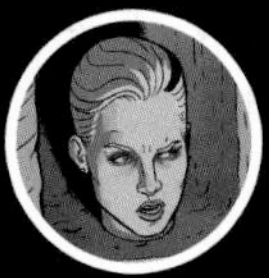

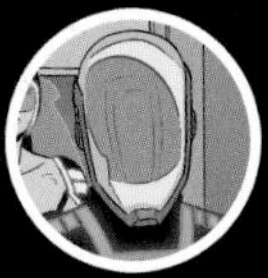

Woden. Shithead 'god'. Gains abilities from his son, Mimir. Thinks he's the big baddy.

The Morrigan. Triple-formed underworld god. Murdered Baphomet then killed herself to bring him back.

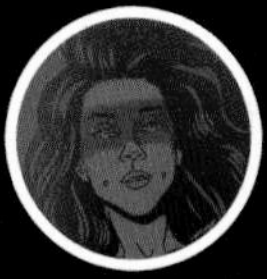

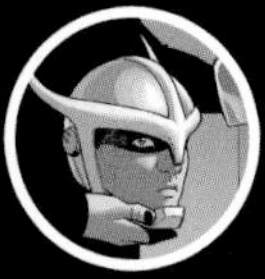

Mimir. Knowledge god. Living head decapitated by father, Woden. Forced to construct for things for him.

Nergal. Punderworld god. Previously Baphomet. Continues to build temple to abusive Ex.

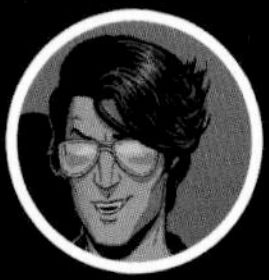

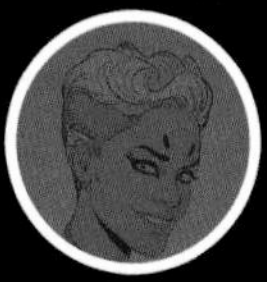

Sakhmet. Feline war god. Ate her dad. Went on rampage. Was killed by Minerva.

Dionysus. Hivemind dancefloor god. Doesn't sleep. Burned out powers. Now brain dead in hospital.

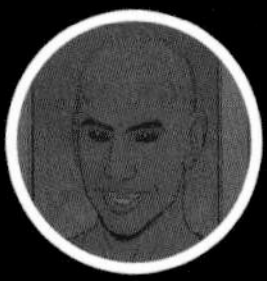

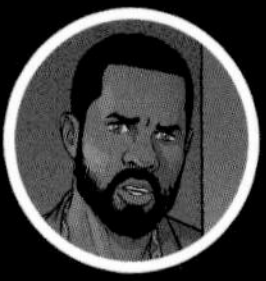

Baal. Fire god posing as a storm god. Ex-lover of Persephone and Inanna. Sacrificing kids for the greater good.

The Norns. Cynical journo Cass and crew wanted to tell world the truth. Locked up as no one believed them.

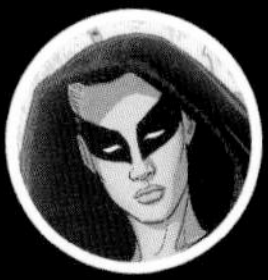

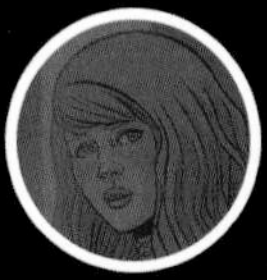

Amaterasu. Sun god. Accidentally prompted Sakhmet's killing spree. Eventually killed by Sakhmet.

Inanna. Queen of heaven. Ex-lover of Baal. Seemingly murdered, actually living head.

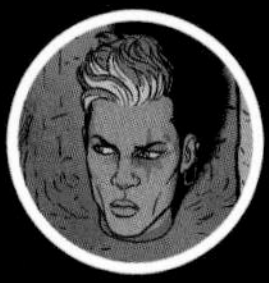

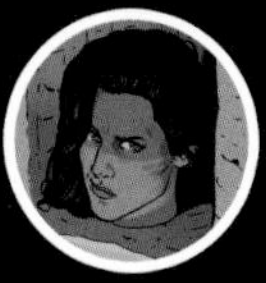

Tara. Apparently secretly killed by Ananke in assisted suicide, actually a living head.

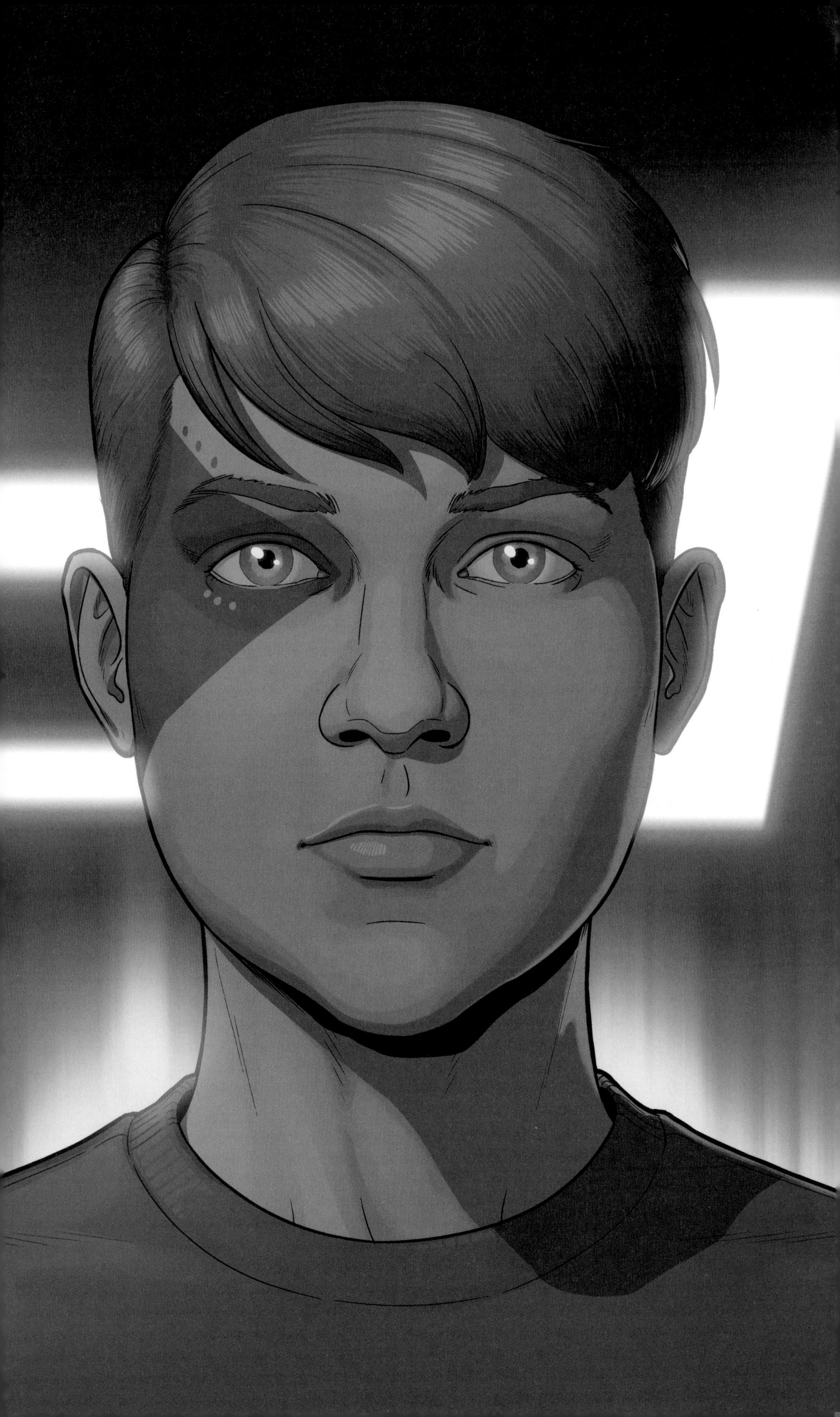

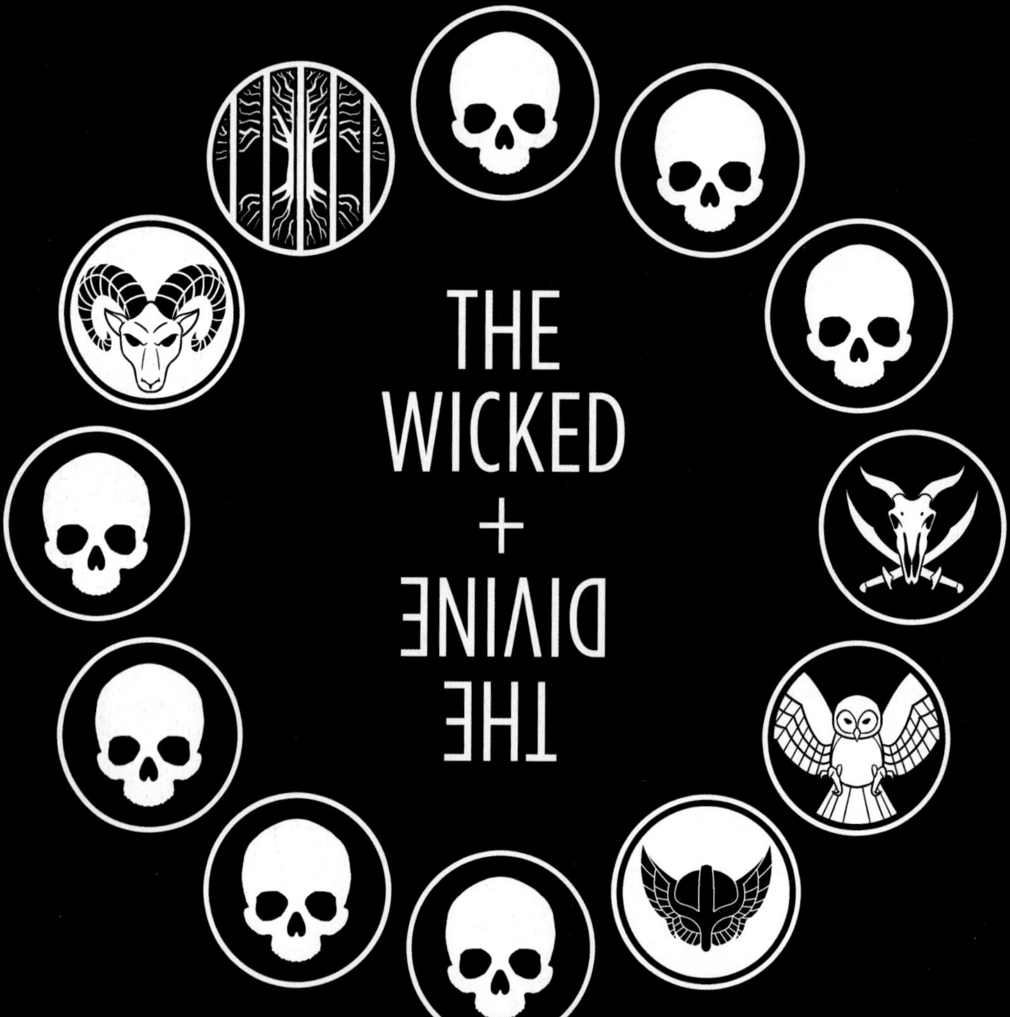
THE
WICKED
+
DIVINE
THE

Footage recorded surrounding the events
of the O2 disaster of 1st May 2015.

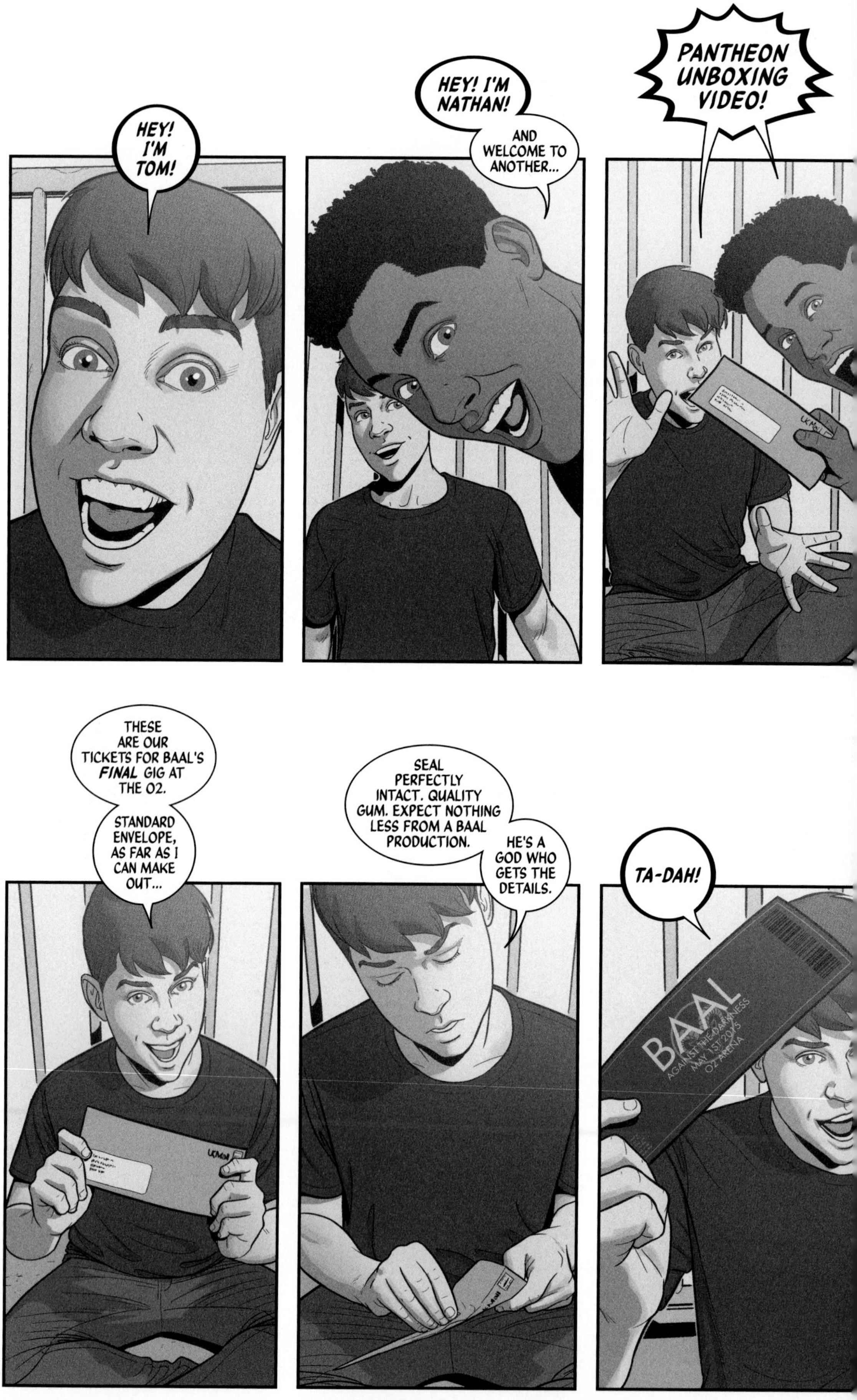
HEY! I'M TOM!
HEY! I'M NATHAN!
AND WELCOME TO ANOTHER...
PANTHEON UNBOXING VIDEO!
THESE ARE OUR TICKETS FOR BAAL'S *FINAL* GIG AT THE O2.
STANDARD ENVELOPE, AS FAR AS I CAN MAKE OUT...
SEAL PERFECTLY INTACT. QUALITY GUM. EXPECT NOTHING LESS FROM A BAAL PRODUCTION.
HE'S A GOD WHO GETS THE DETAILS.
TA-DAH!
BAAL
AGAINST THE DARKNESS
MAY 1ST 2015
O2 ARENA

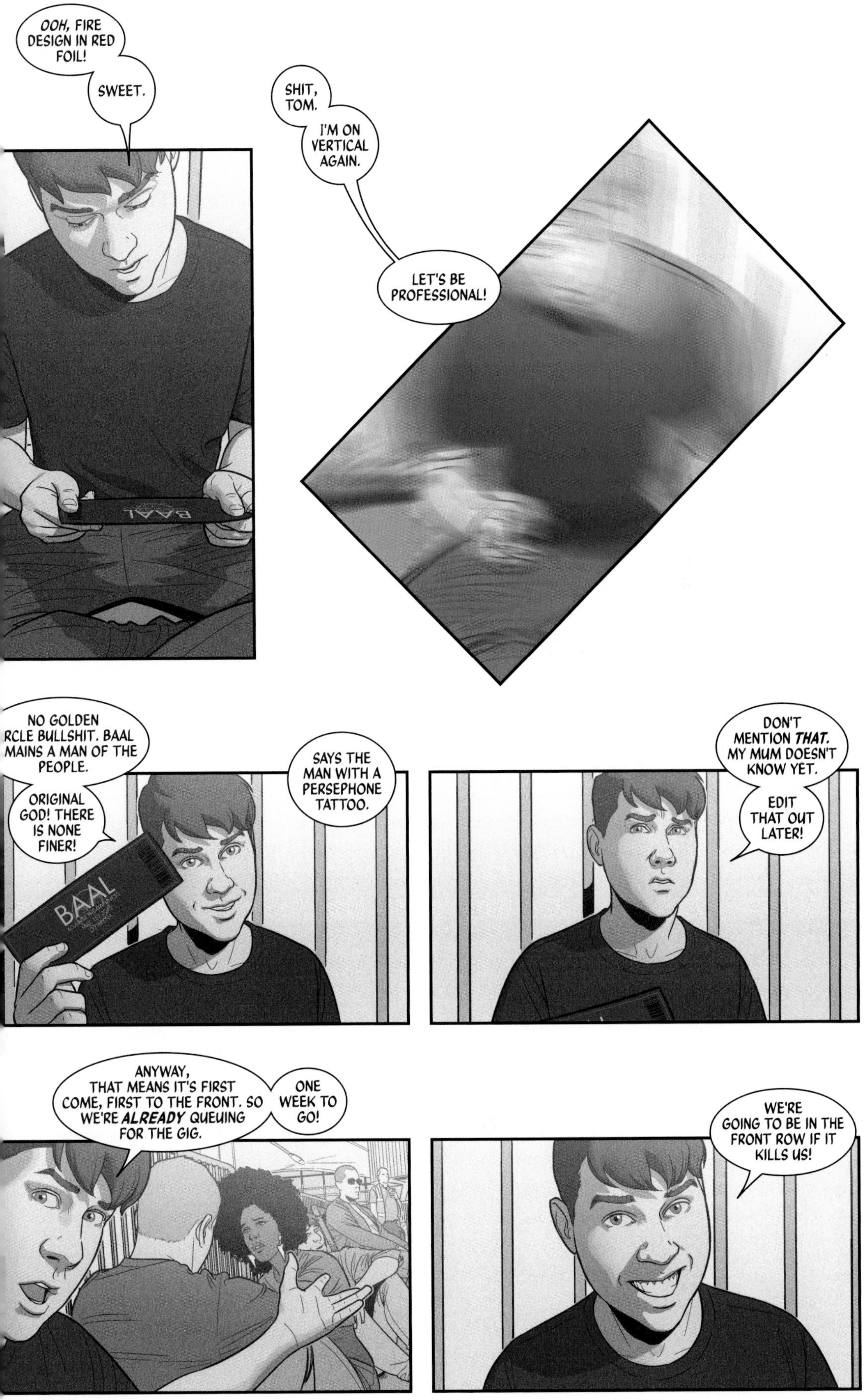
OOH, FIRE DESIGN IN RED FOIL!
SWEET.
SHIT, TOM.
I'M ON VERTICAL AGAIN.
LET'S BE PROFESSIONAL!
NO GOLDEN RCLE BULLSHIT. BAAL MAINS A MAN OF THE PEOPLE.
ORIGINAL GOD! THERE IS NONE FINER!
BAAL
SAYS THE MAN WITH A PERSEPHONE TATTOO.
DON'T MENTION ***THAT.*** MY MUM DOESN'T KNOW YET.
EDIT THAT OUT LATER!
ANYWAY, THAT MEANS IT'S FIRST COME, FIRST TO THE FRONT. SO WE'RE ***ALREADY*** QUEUING FOR THE GIG.
ONE WEEK TO GO!
WE'RE GOING TO BE IN THE FRONT ROW IF IT KILLS US!

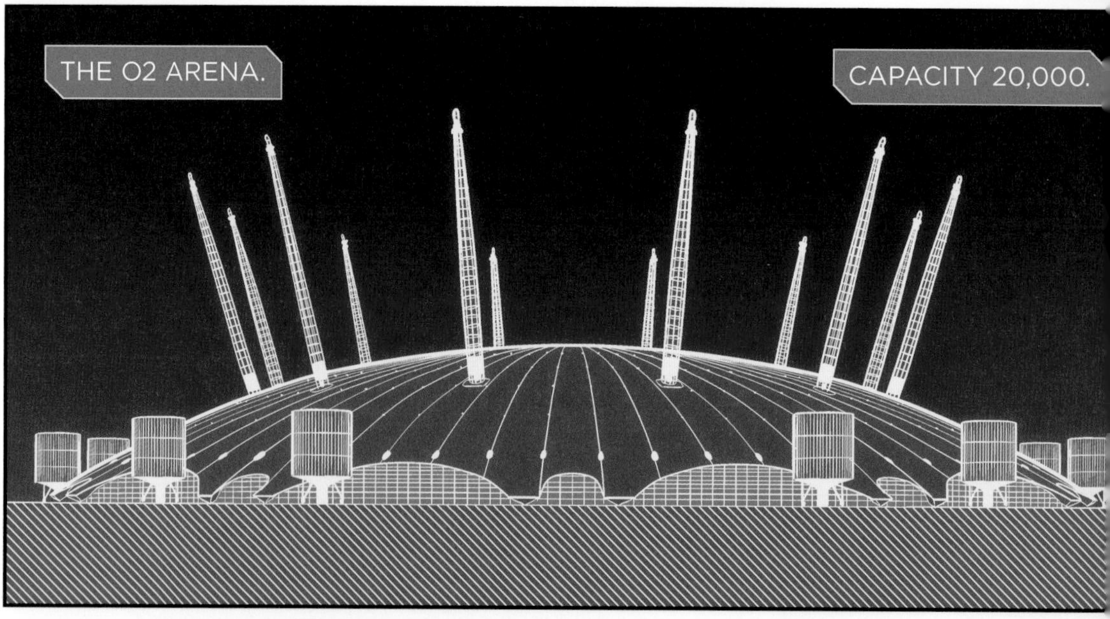
THE O2 ARENA.
CAPACITY 20,000.

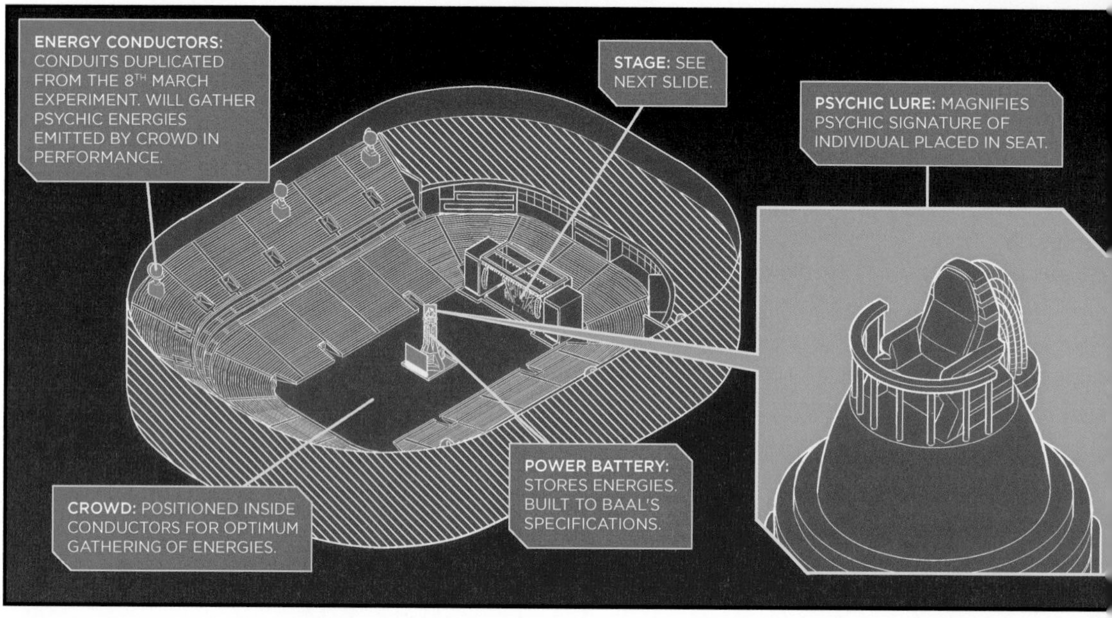
ENERGY CONDUCTORS: CONDUITS DUPLICATED FROM THE 8TH MARCH EXPERIMENT. WILL GATHER PSYCHIC ENERGIES EMITTED BY CROWD IN PERFORMANCE.
STAGE: SEE NEXT SLIDE.
PSYCHIC LURE: MAGNIFIES PSYCHIC SIGNATURE OF INDIVIDUAL PLACED IN SEAT.
CROWD: POSITIONED INSIDE CONDUCTORS FOR OPTIMUM GATHERING OF ENERGIES.
POWER BATTERY: STORES ENERGIES. BUILT TO BAAL'S SPECIFICATIONS.

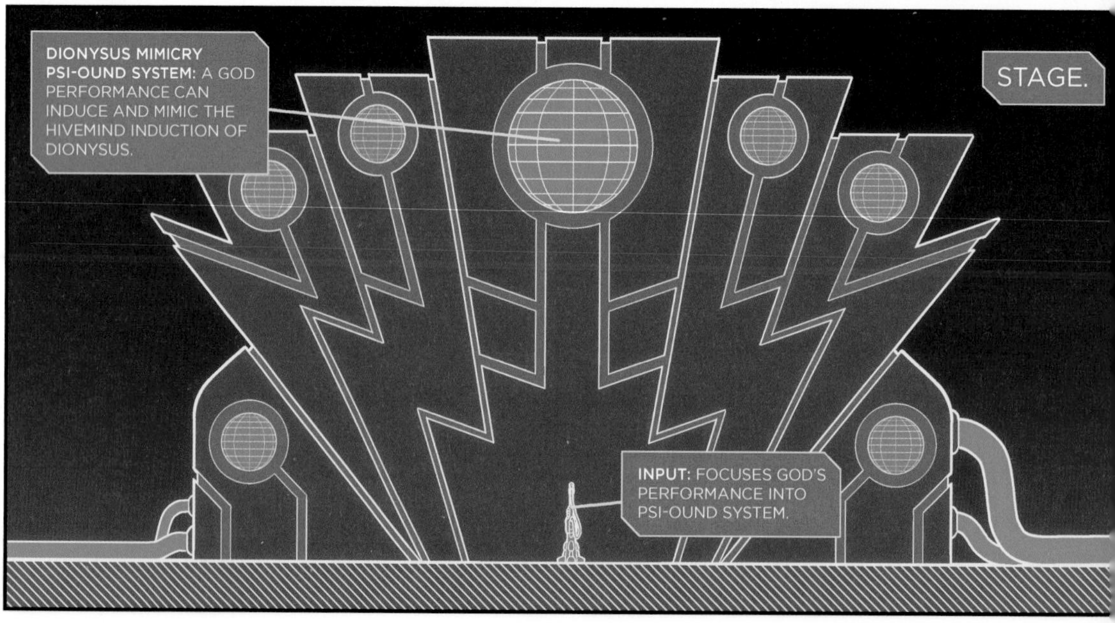
DIONYSUS MIMICRY PSI-OUND SYSTEM: A GOD PERFORMANCE CAN INDUCE AND MIMIC THE HIVEMIND INDUCTION OF DIONYSUS.
STAGE.
INPUT: FOCUSES GOD'S PERFORMANCE INTO PSI-OUND SYSTEM.

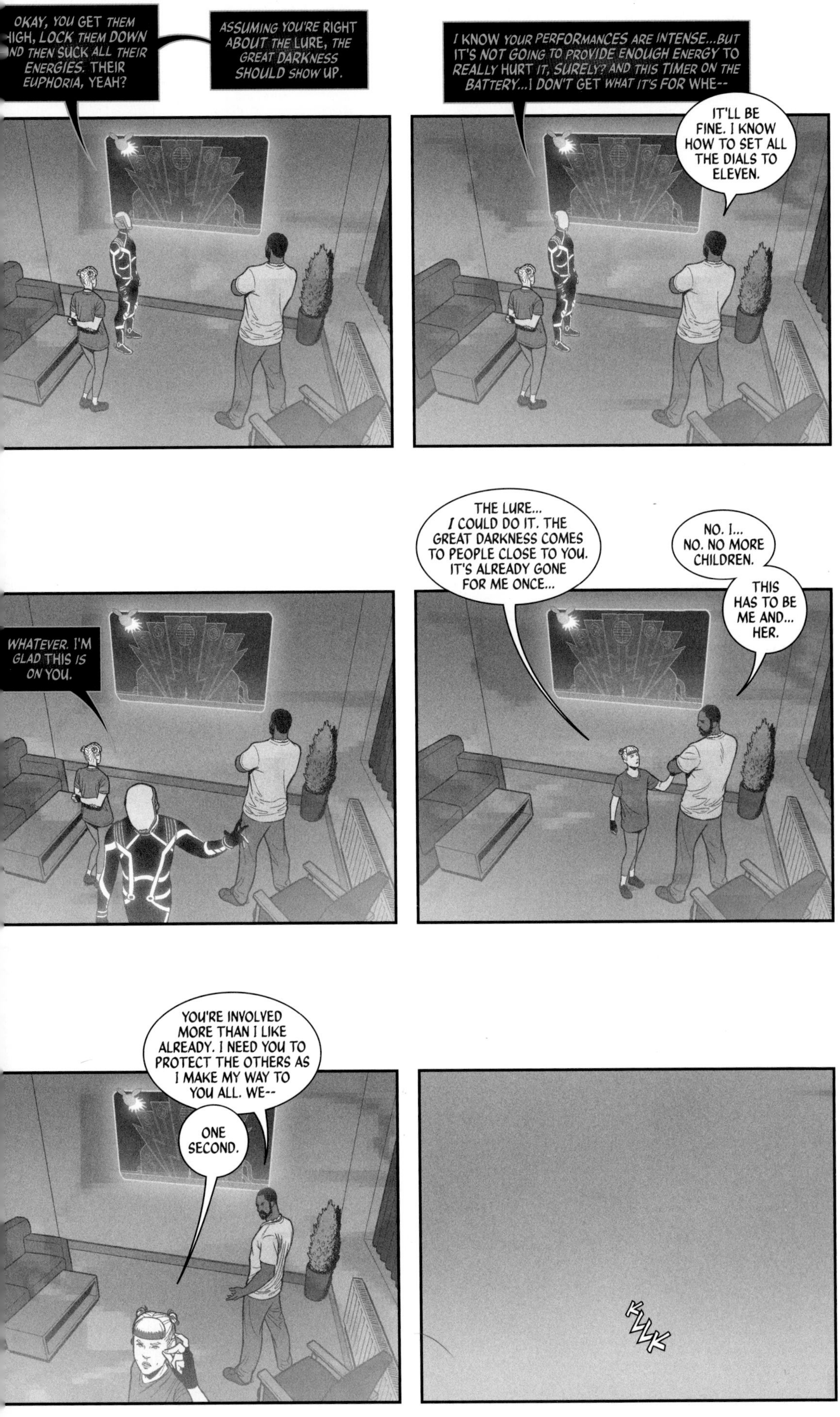

OKAY, YOU GET THEM HIGH, LOCK THEM DOWN AND THEN SUCK ALL THEIR ENERGIES. THEIR EUPHORIA, YEAH?
ASSUMING YOU'RE RIGHT ABOUT THE LURE, THE GREAT DARKNESS SHOULD SHOW UP.
I KNOW YOUR PERFORMANCES ARE INTENSE...BUT IT'S NOT GOING TO PROVIDE ENOUGH ENERGY TO REALLY HURT IT, SURELY? AND THIS TIMER ON THE BATTERY...I DON'T GET WHAT IT'S FOR WHE--
IT'LL BE FINE. I KNOW HOW TO SET ALL THE DIALS TO ELEVEN.
WHATEVER. I'M GLAD THIS IS ON YOU.
THE LURE... I COULD DO IT. THE GREAT DARKNESS COMES TO PEOPLE CLOSE TO YOU. IT'S ALREADY GONE FOR ME ONCE...
NO. I... NO. NO MORE CHILDREN.
THIS HAS TO BE ME AND... HER.
YOU'RE INVOLVED MORE THAN I LIKE ALREADY. I NEED YOU TO PROTECT THE OTHERS AS I MAKE MY WAY TO YOU ALL. WE--
ONE SECOND.
KLLK

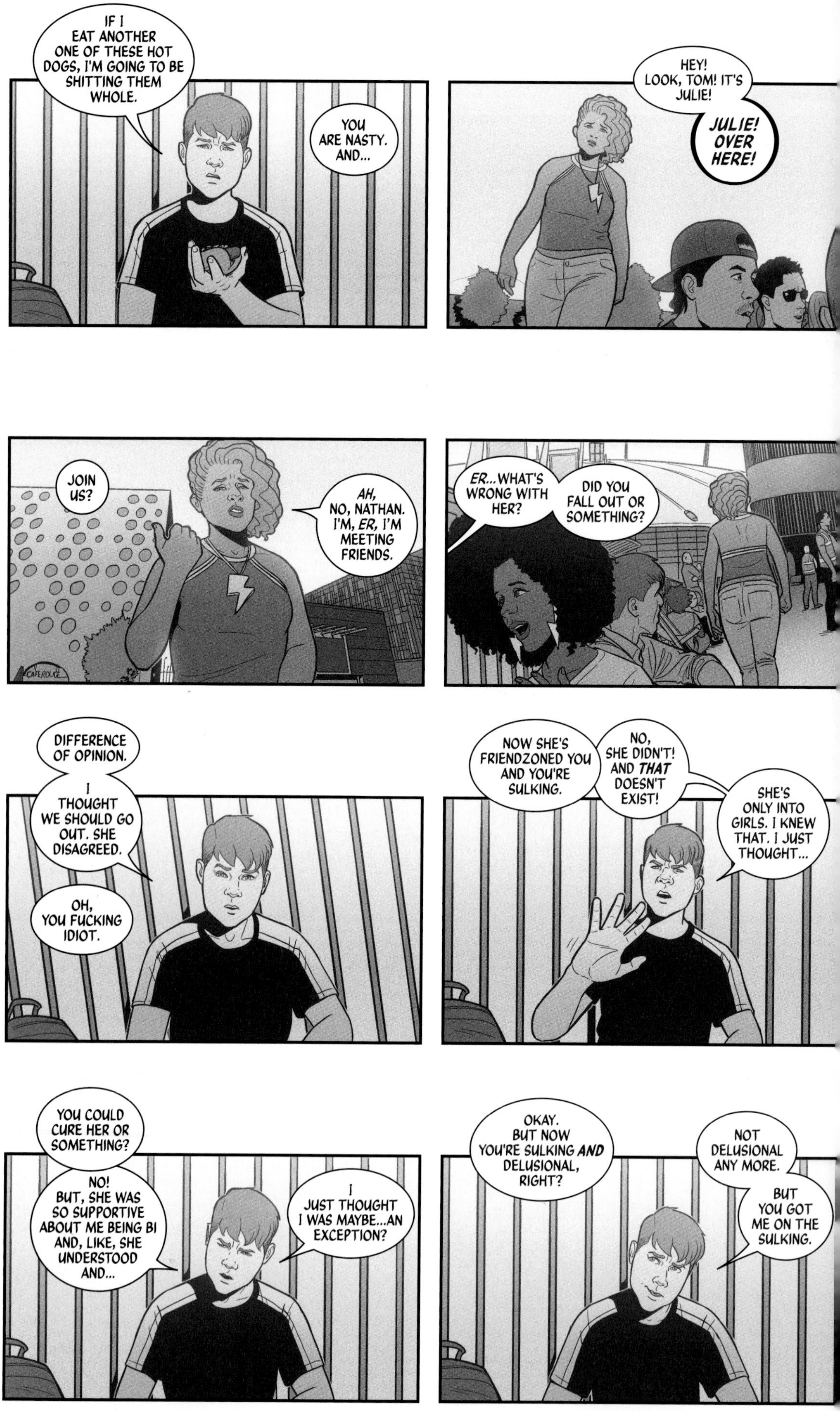
IF I EAT ANOTHER ONE OF THESE HOT DOGS, I'M GOING TO BE SHITTING THEM WHOLE.
YOU ARE NASTY. AND...
HEY! LOOK, TOM! IT'S JULIE!
JULIE! OVER HERE!
JOIN US?
AH, NO, NATHAN. I'M, ER, I'M MEETING FRIENDS.
ER... WHAT'S WRONG WITH HER?
DID YOU FALL OUT OR SOMETHING?
DIFFERENCE OF OPINION.
I THOUGHT WE SHOULD GO OUT. SHE DISAGREED.
OH, YOU FUCKING IDIOT.
NOW SHE'S FRIENDZONED YOU AND YOU'RE SULKING.
NO, SHE DIDN'T! AND THAT DOESN'T EXIST!
SHE'S ONLY INTO GIRLS. I KNEW THAT. I JUST THOUGHT...
YOU COULD CURE HER OR SOMETHING?
NO! BUT, SHE WAS SO SUPPORTIVE ABOUT ME BEING BI AND, LIKE, SHE UNDERSTOOD AND...
I JUST THOUGHT I WAS MAYBE...AN EXCEPTION?
OKAY. BUT NOW YOU'RE SULKING AND DELUSIONAL, RIGHT?
NOT DELUSIONAL ANY MORE.
BUT YOU GOT ME ON THE SULKING.

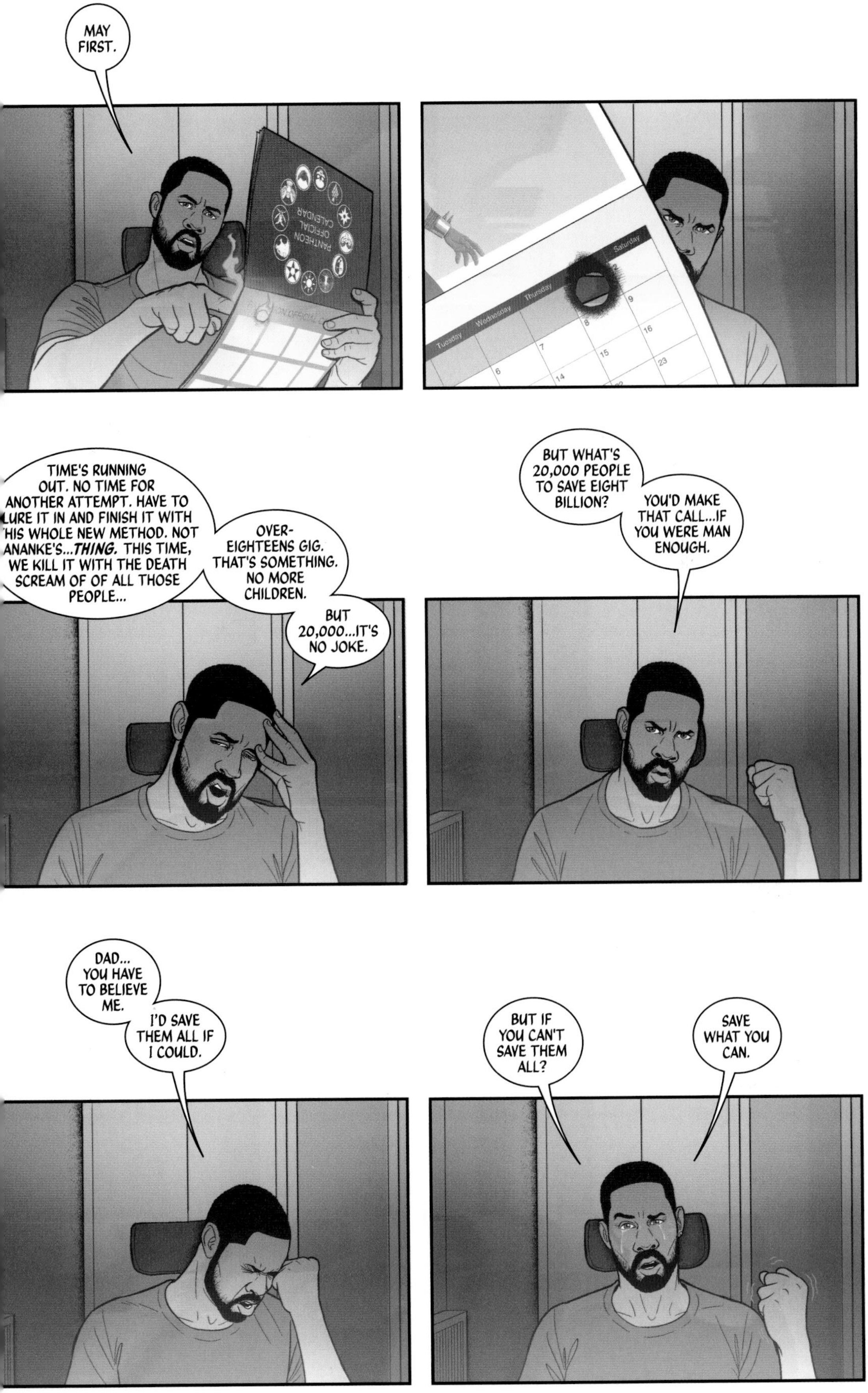
MAY FIRST.
TIME'S RUNNING OUT. NO TIME FOR ANOTHER ATTEMPT. HAVE TO LURE IT IN AND FINISH IT WITH THIS WHOLE NEW METHOD. NOT ANANKE'S...THING. THIS TIME, WE KILL IT WITH THE DEATH SCREAM OF OF ALL THOSE PEOPLE...
OVER-EIGHTEENS GIG. THAT'S SOMETHING. NO MORE CHILDREN.
BUT 20,000...IT'S NO JOKE.
BUT WHAT'S 20,000 PEOPLE TO SAVE EIGHT BILLION?
YOU'D MAKE THAT CALL...IF YOU WERE MAN ENOUGH.
DAD... YOU HAVE TO BELIEVE ME.
I'D SAVE THEM ALL IF I COULD.
BUT IF YOU CAN'T SAVE THEM ALL?
SAVE WHAT YOU CAN.

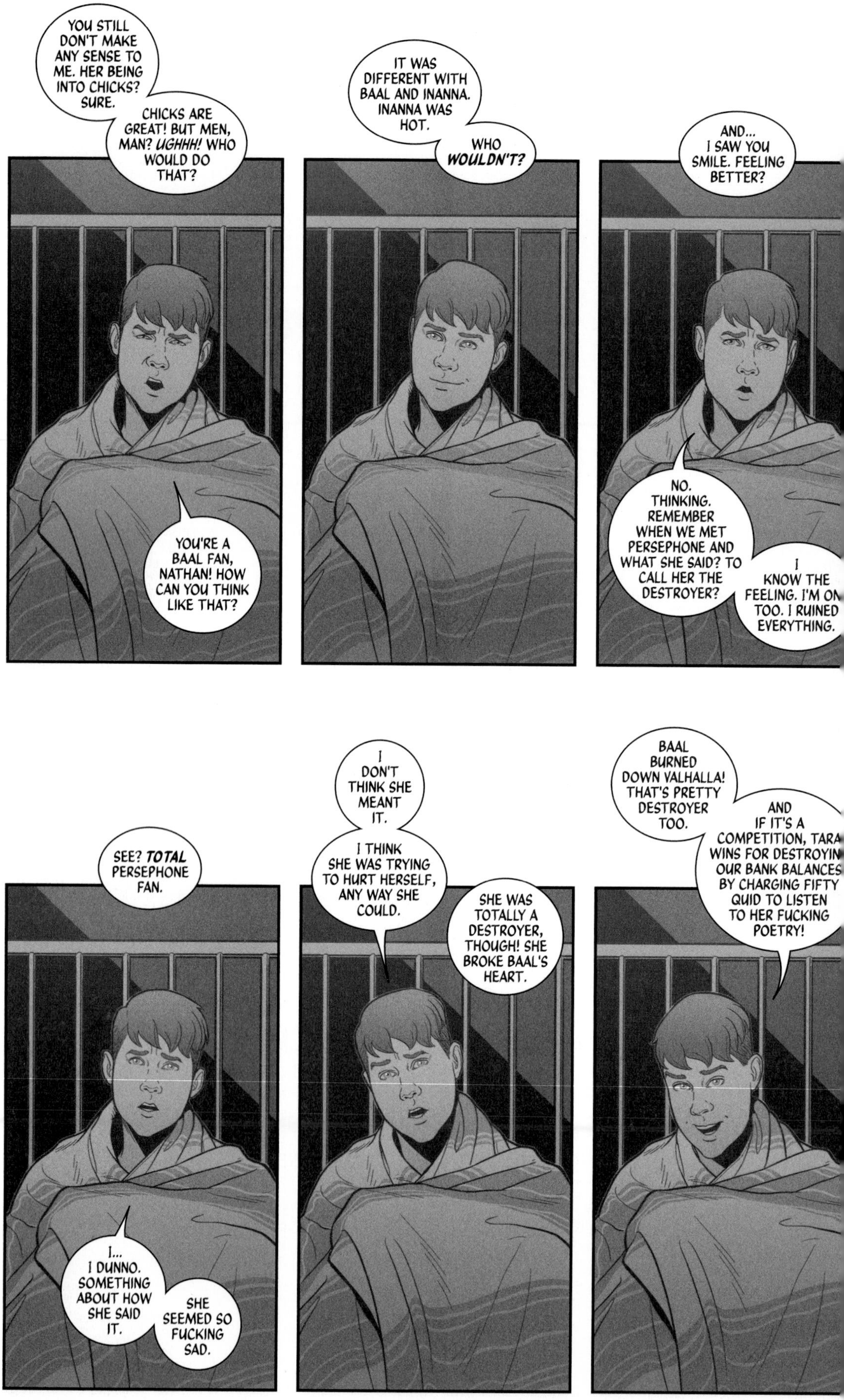
YOU STILL DON'T MAKE ANY SENSE TO ME. HER BEING INTO CHICKS? SURE.
CHICKS ARE GREAT! BUT MEN, MAN? *UGHHH!* WHO WOULD DO THAT?
YOU'RE A BAAL FAN, NATHAN! HOW CAN YOU THINK LIKE THAT?
IT WAS DIFFERENT WITH BAAL AND INANNA. INANNA WAS HOT.
WHO ***WOULDN'T?***
AND... I SAW YOU SMILE. FEELING BETTER?
NO. THINKING. REMEMBER WHEN WE MET PERSEPHONE AND WHAT SHE SAID? TO CALL HER THE DESTROYER?
I KNOW THE FEELING. I'M ON TOO. I RUINED EVERYTHING.
SEE? ***TOTAL*** PERSEPHONE FAN.
I... I DUNNO. SOMETHING ABOUT HOW SHE SAID IT.
SHE SEEMED SO FUCKING SAD.
I DON'T THINK SHE MEANT IT.
I THINK SHE WAS TRYING TO HURT HERSELF, ANY WAY SHE COULD.
SHE WAS TOTALLY A DESTROYER, THOUGH! SHE BROKE BAAL'S HEART.
BAAL BURNED DOWN VALHALLA! THAT'S PRETTY DESTROYER TOO.
AND IF IT'S A COMPETITION, TARA WINS FOR DESTROYIN OUR BANK BALANCES BY CHARGING FIFTY QUID TO LISTEN TO HER FUCKING POETRY!

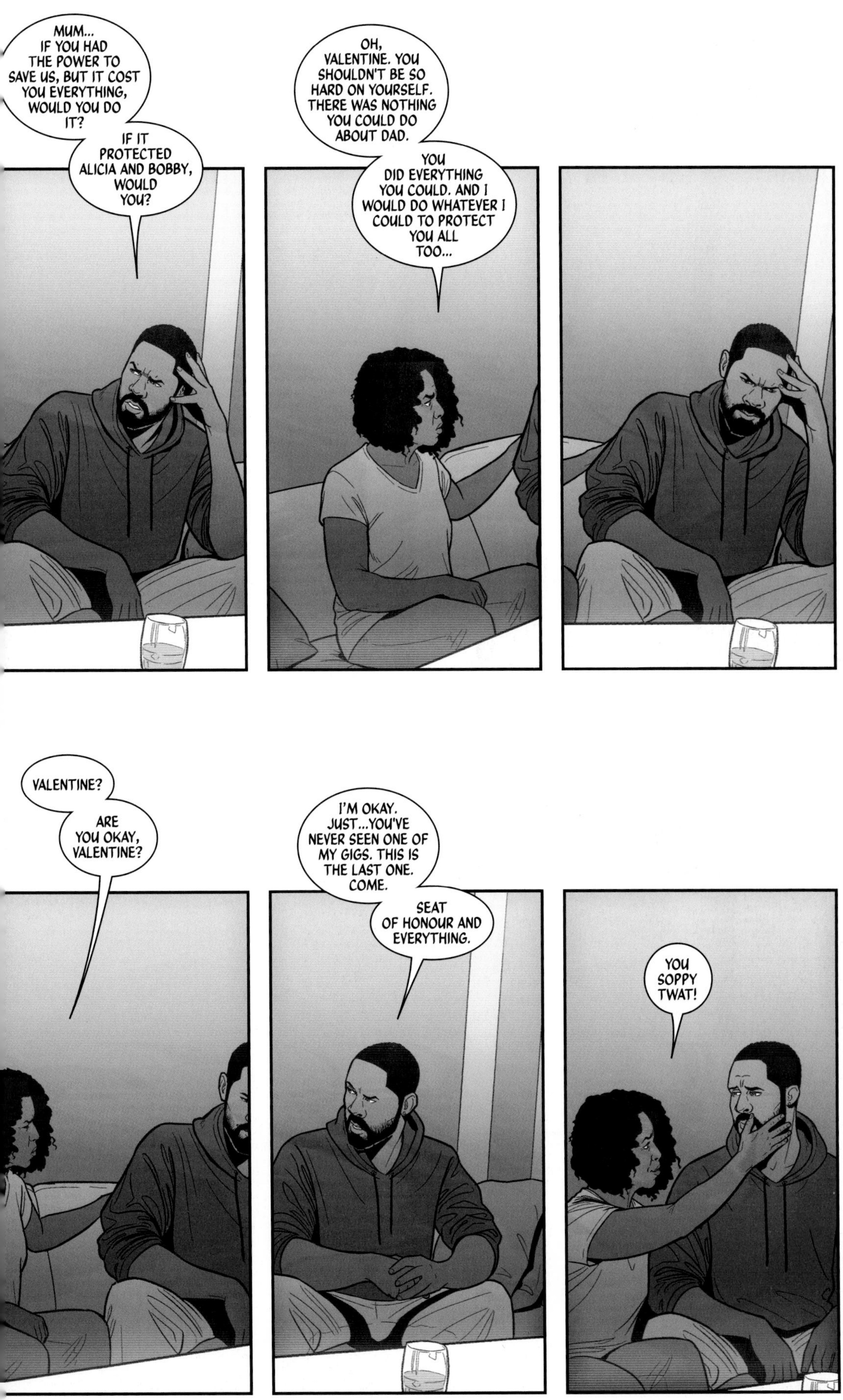
MUM... IF YOU HAD THE POWER TO SAVE US, BUT IT COST YOU EVERYTHING, WOULD YOU DO IT?
IF IT PROTECTED ALICIA AND BOBBY, WOULD YOU?
OH, VALENTINE. YOU SHOULDN'T BE SO HARD ON YOURSELF. THERE WAS NOTHING YOU COULD DO ABOUT DAD.
YOU DID EVERYTHING YOU COULD. AND I WOULD DO WHATEVER I COULD TO PROTECT YOU ALL TOO...
VALENTINE?
ARE YOU OKAY, VALENTINE?
I'M OKAY. JUST...YOU'VE NEVER SEEN ONE OF MY GIGS. THIS IS THE LAST ONE. COME.
SEAT OF HONOUR AND EVERYTHING.
YOU SOPPY TWAT!

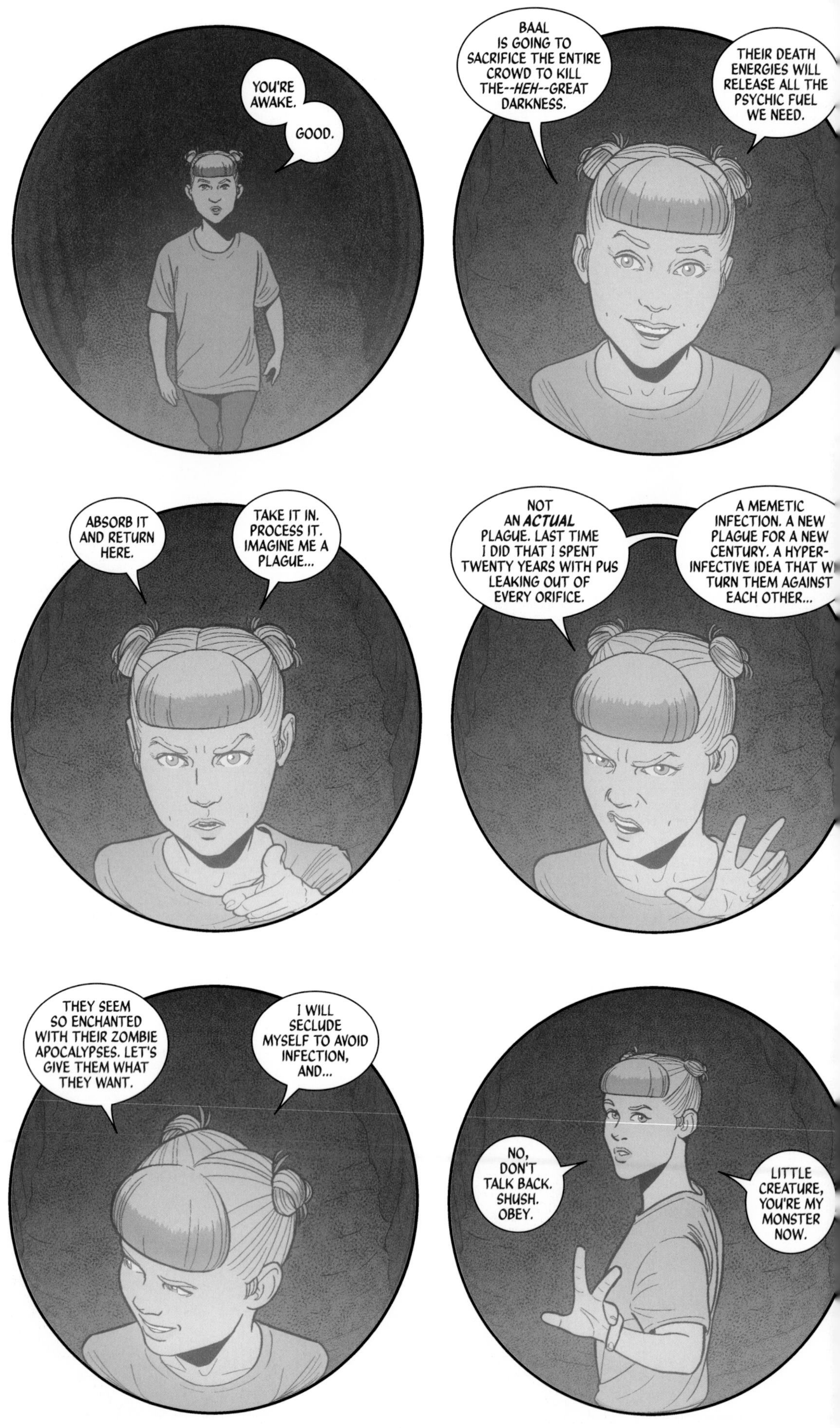
YOU'RE AWAKE.
GOOD.
BAAL IS GOING TO SACRIFICE THE ENTIRE CROWD TO KILL THE--*HEH*--GREAT DARKNESS.
THEIR DEATH ENERGIES WILL RELEASE ALL THE PSYCHIC FUEL WE NEED.
ABSORB IT AND RETURN HERE.
TAKE IT IN. PROCESS IT. IMAGINE ME A PLAGUE...
NOT AN ***ACTUAL*** PLAGUE. LAST TIME I DID THAT I SPENT TWENTY YEARS WITH PUS LEAKING OUT OF EVERY ORIFICE.
A MEMETIC INFECTION. A NEW PLAGUE FOR A NEW CENTURY. A HYPER-INFECTIVE IDEA THAT W TURN THEM AGAINST EACH OTHER...
THEY SEEM SO ENCHANTED WITH THEIR ZOMBIE APOCALYPSES. LET'S GIVE THEM WHAT THEY WANT.
I WILL SECLUDE MYSELF TO AVOID INFECTION, AND...
NO, DON'T TALK BACK. SHUSH. OBEY.
LITTLE CREATURE, YOU'RE MY MONSTER NOW.

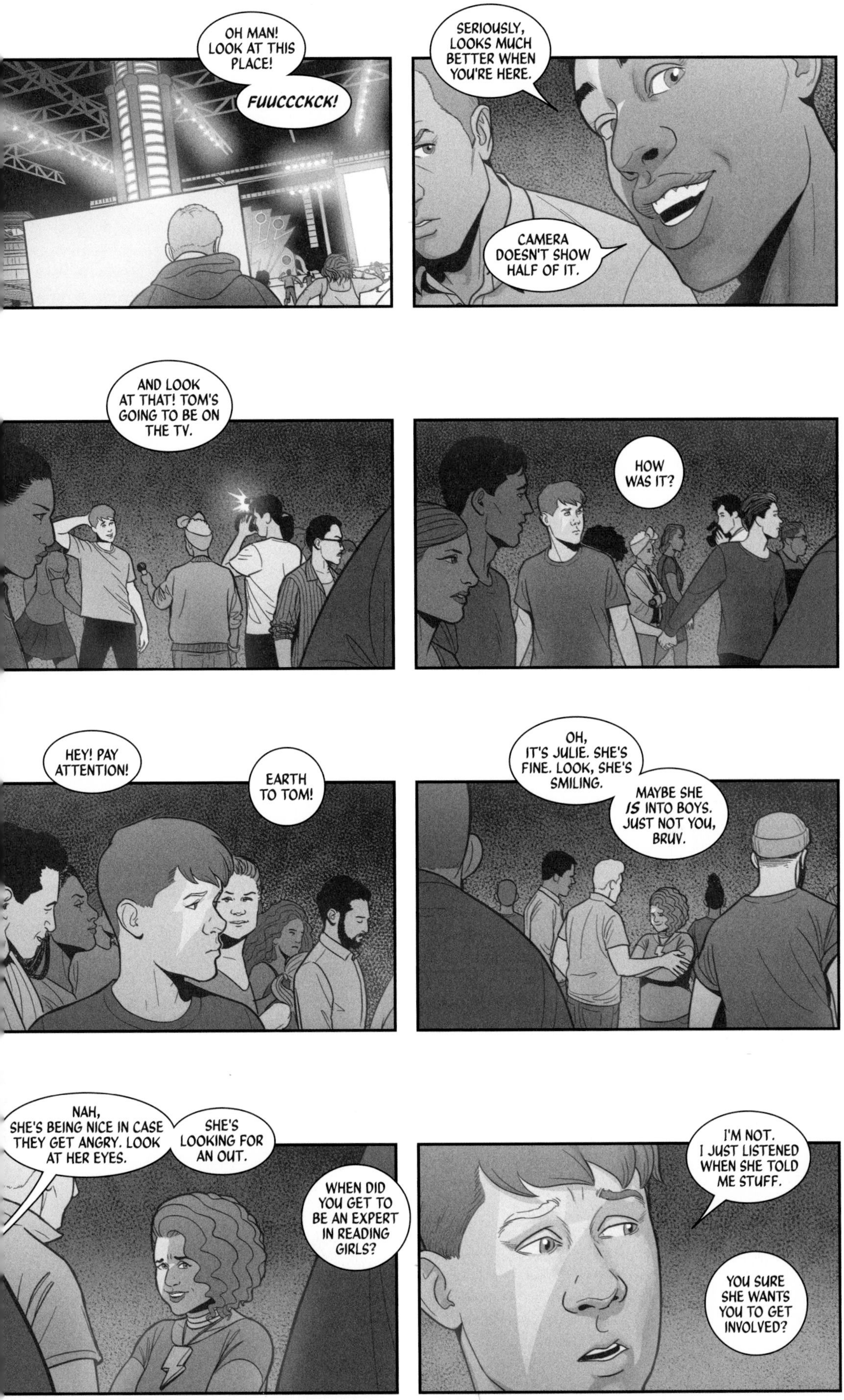
OH MAN! LOOK AT THIS PLACE!
FUUCCCKCK!
SERIOUSLY, LOOKS MUCH BETTER WHEN YOU'RE HERE.
CAMERA DOESN'T SHOW HALF OF IT.
AND LOOK AT THAT! TOM'S GOING TO BE ON THE TV.
HOW WAS IT?
HEY! PAY ATTENTION!
EARTH TO TOM!
OH, IT'S JULIE. SHE'S FINE. LOOK, SHE'S SMILING.
MAYBE SHE *IS* INTO BOYS. JUST NOT YOU, BRUV.
NAH, SHE'S BEING NICE IN CASE THEY GET ANGRY. LOOK AT HER EYES.
SHE'S LOOKING FOR AN OUT.
WHEN DID YOU GET TO BE AN EXPERT IN READING GIRLS?
I'M NOT. I JUST LISTENED WHEN SHE TOLD ME STUFF.
YOU SURE SHE WANTS YOU TO GET INVOLVED?

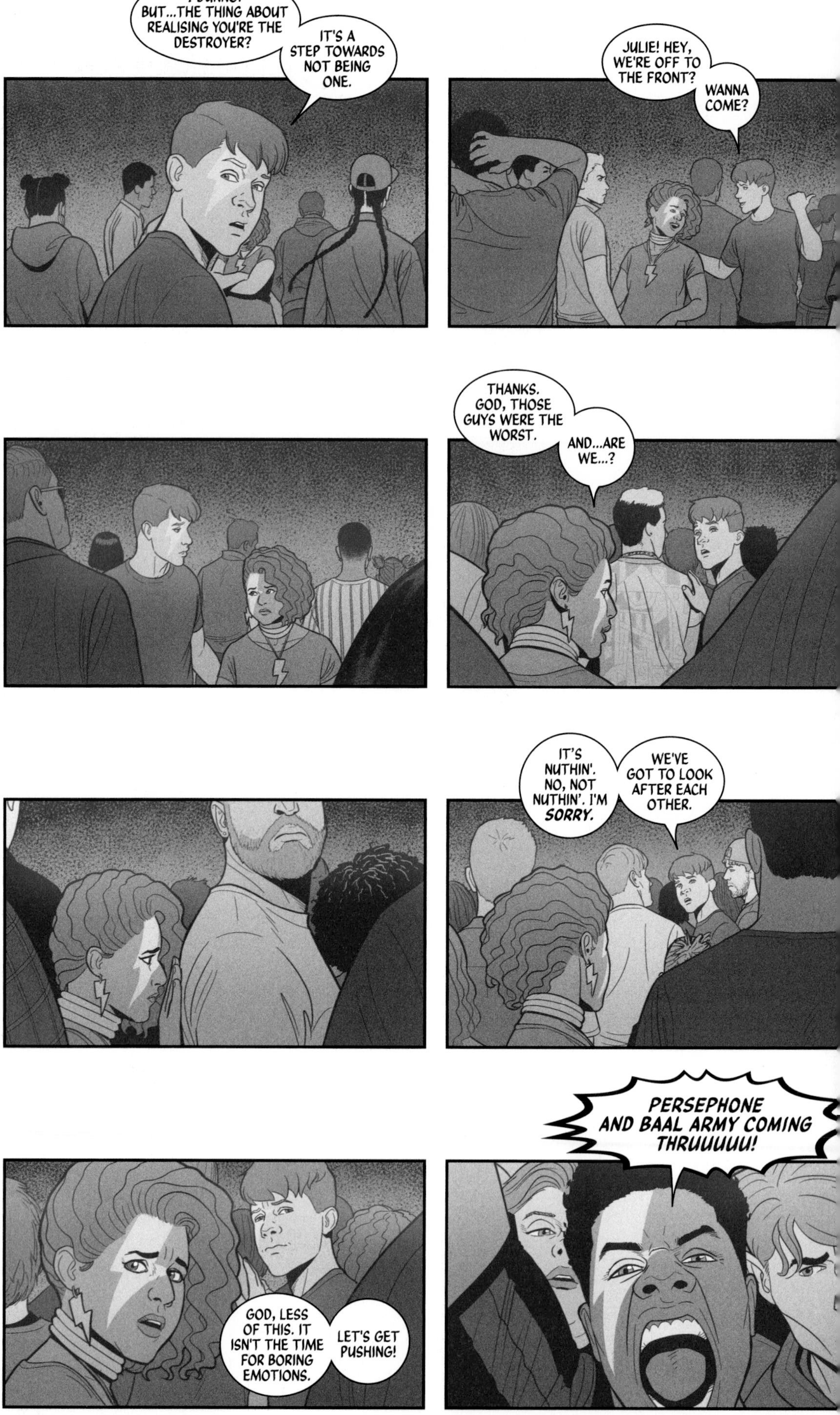
I DUNNO. BUT...THE THING ABOUT REALISING YOU'RE THE DESTROYER?
IT'S A STEP TOWARDS NOT BEING ONE.
JULIE! HEY, WE'RE OFF TO THE FRONT?
WANNA COME?
THANKS. GOD, THOSE GUYS WERE THE WORST.
AND...ARE WE...?
IT'S NUTHIN'. NO, NOT NUTHIN'. I'M *SORRY.*
WE'VE GOT TO LOOK AFTER EACH OTHER.
GOD, LESS OF THIS. IT ISN'T THE TIME FOR BORING EMOTIONS.
LET'S GET PUSHING!
PERSEPHONE AND BAAL ARMY COMING THRUUUUU!

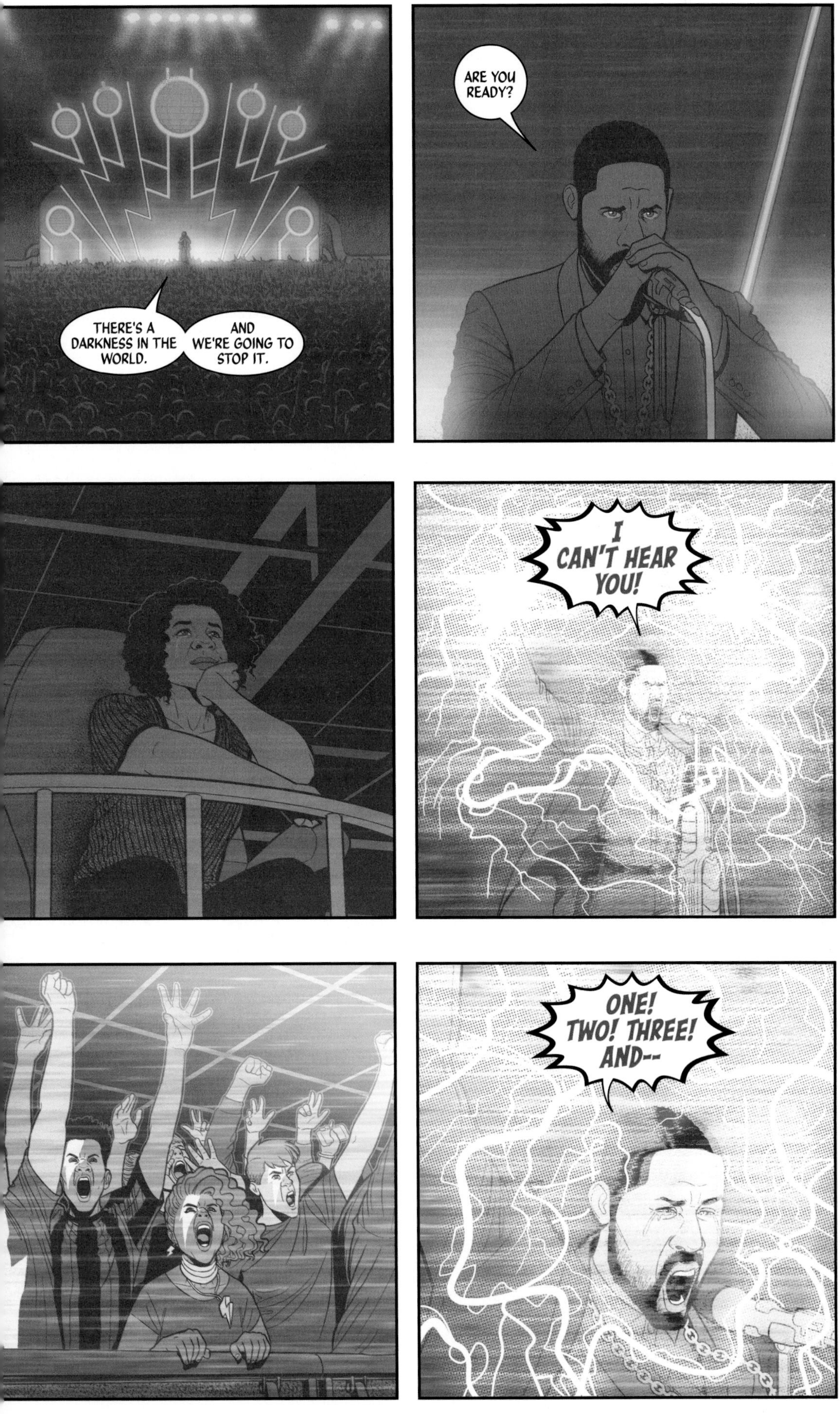
THERE'S A DARKNESS IN THE WORLD.
AND WE'RE GOING TO STOP IT.
ARE YOU READY?
I CAN'T HEAR YOU!
ONE! TWO! THREE! AND--

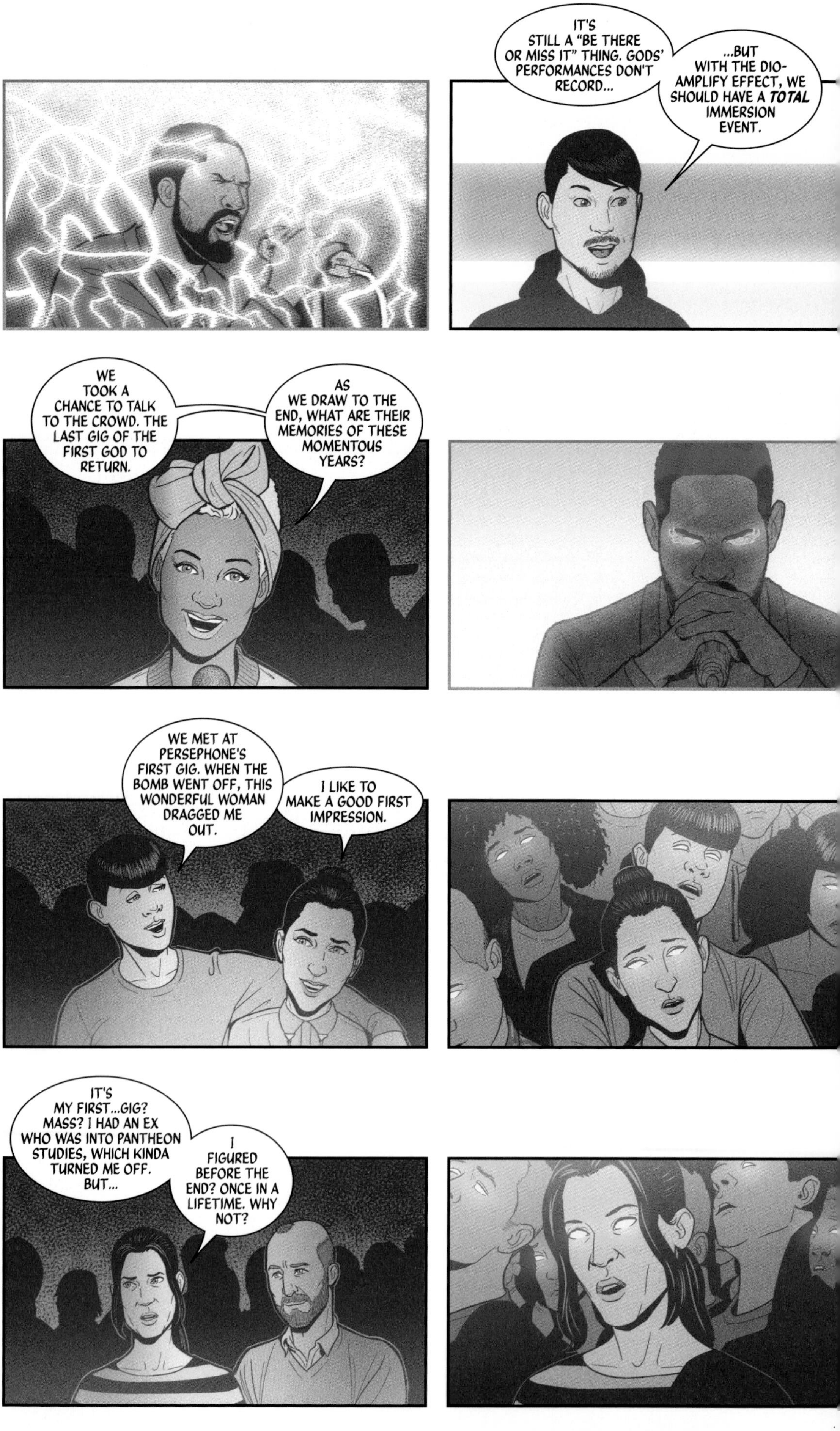
IT'S STILL A "BE THERE OR MISS IT" THING. GODS' PERFORMANCES DON'T RECORD...
...BUT WITH THE DIO-AMPLIFY EFFECT, WE SHOULD HAVE A *TOTAL* IMMERSION EVENT.
WE TOOK A CHANCE TO TALK TO THE CROWD. THE LAST GIG OF THE FIRST GOD TO RETURN.
AS WE DRAW TO THE END, WHAT ARE THEIR MEMORIES OF THESE MOMENTOUS YEARS?
WE MET AT PERSEPHONE'S FIRST GIG. WHEN THE BOMB WENT OFF, THIS WONDERFUL WOMAN DRAGGED ME OUT.
I LIKE TO MAKE A GOOD FIRST IMPRESSION.
IT'S MY FIRST...GIG? MASS? I HAD AN EX WHO WAS INTO PANTHEON STUDIES, WHICH KINDA TURNED ME OFF. BUT...
I FIGURED BEFORE THE END? ONCE IN A LIFETIME. WHY NOT?

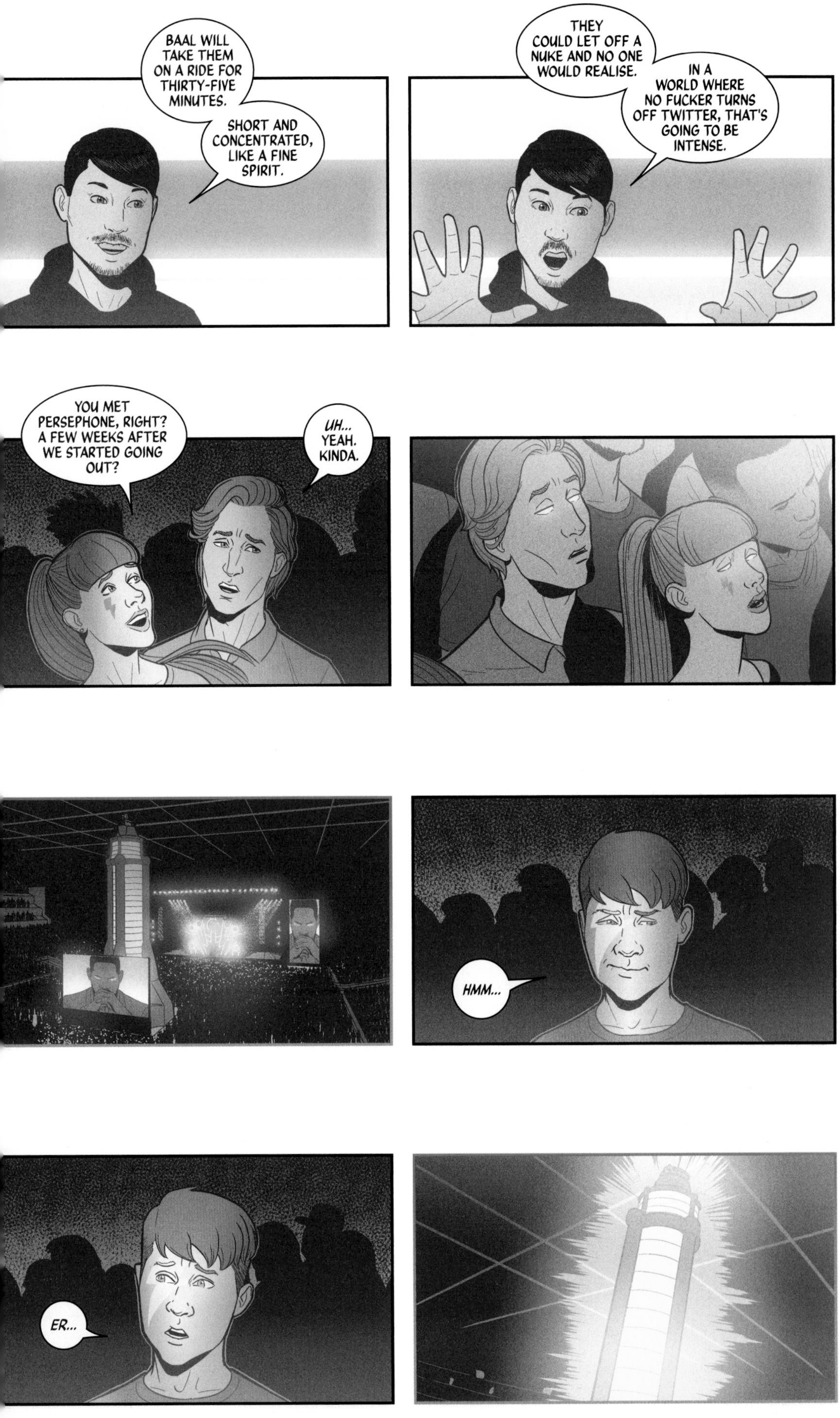
BAAL WILL TAKE THEM ON A RIDE FOR THIRTY-FIVE MINUTES.
SHORT AND CONCENTRATED, LIKE A FINE SPIRIT.
THEY COULD LET OFF A NUKE AND NO ONE WOULD REALISE.
IN A WORLD WHERE NO FUCKER TURNS OFF TWITTER, THAT'S GOING TO BE INTENSE.
YOU MET PERSEPHONE, RIGHT? A FEW WEEKS AFTER WE STARTED GOING OUT?
UH... YEAH. KINDA.
HMM...
ER...

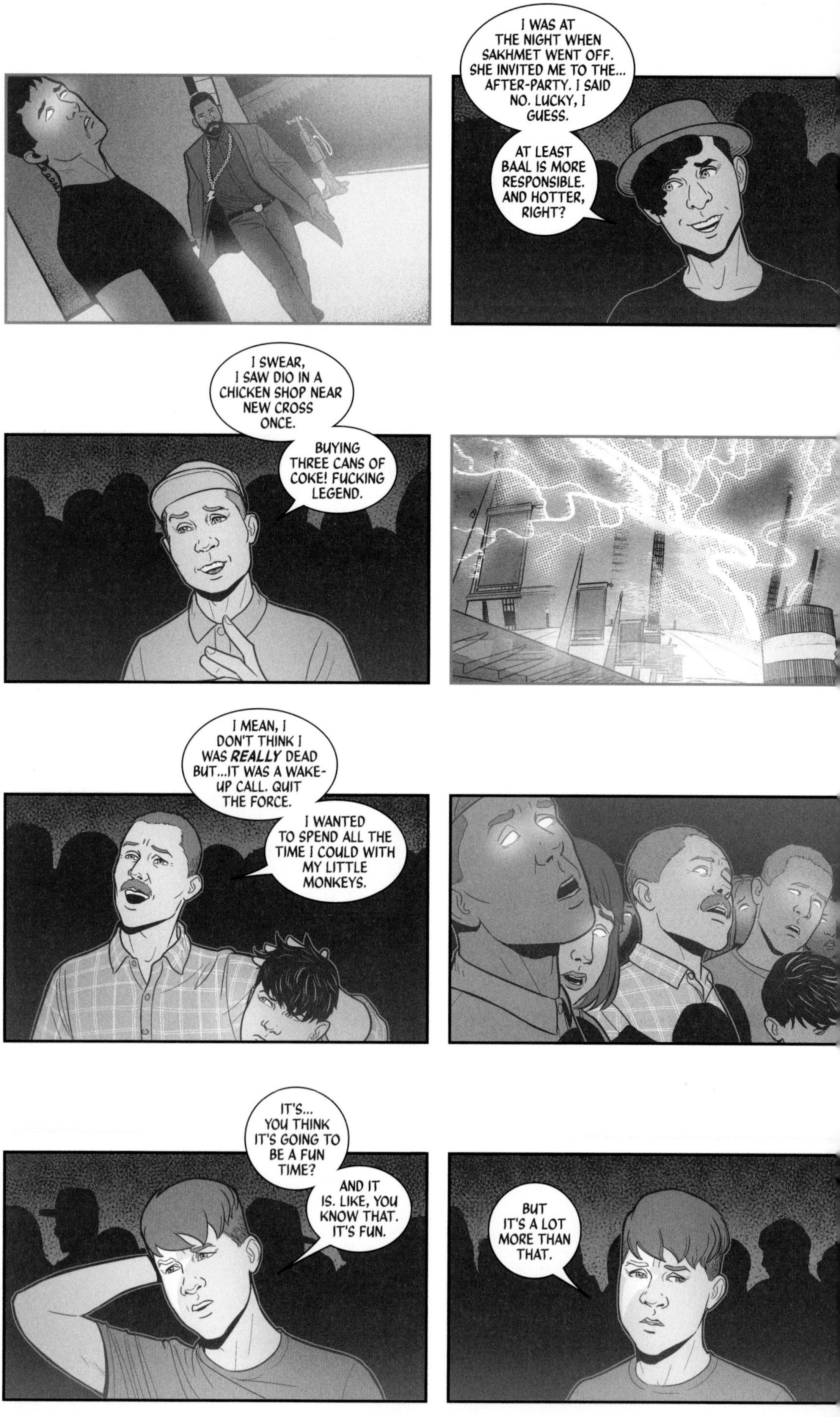
I WAS AT THE NIGHT WHEN SAKHMET WENT OFF. SHE INVITED ME TO THE... AFTER-PARTY. I SAID NO. LUCKY, I GUESS.
AT LEAST BAAL IS MORE RESPONSIBLE. AND HOTTER, RIGHT?
I SWEAR, I SAW DIO IN A CHICKEN SHOP NEAR NEW CROSS ONCE.
BUYING THREE CANS OF COKE! FUCKING LEGEND.
I MEAN, I DON'T THINK I WAS *REALLY* DEAD BUT...IT WAS A WAKE-UP CALL. QUIT THE FORCE.
I WANTED TO SPEND ALL THE TIME I COULD WITH MY LITTLE MONKEYS.
IT'S... YOU THINK IT'S GOING TO BE A FUN TIME?
AND IT IS. LIKE, YOU KNOW THAT. IT'S FUN.
BUT IT'S A LOT MORE THAN THAT.

HER FLAT WAS A MESS BUT SHE LET ME TAKE A SELFIE WITH HER AND...

I'VE NEVER HAD SO MANY LIKES ON A PHOTO BEFORE!

MY COSPLAY WAS SO GOOD THEY THOUGHT I WAS SAKHMET! THEY SMASHED MY WALL!

THEY THREW ME MONEY TO FIX IT ALL UP. I USED THE LAST OF IT ON MY TICKET!

IT'S OKAY. I'M KEEPING YOU SAFE UNTIL BAAL GETS BACK...

ANY SIGN OF THE GREAT DARKNESS?

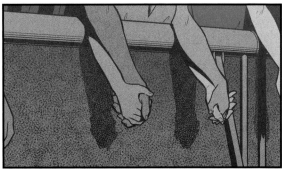

I'M JUST GRATEFUL WE GOT TO BE HERE. ALL OF US.

WE'RE HISTORY.

DON'T WORRY.

IT'LL ALL BE OVER SOON.

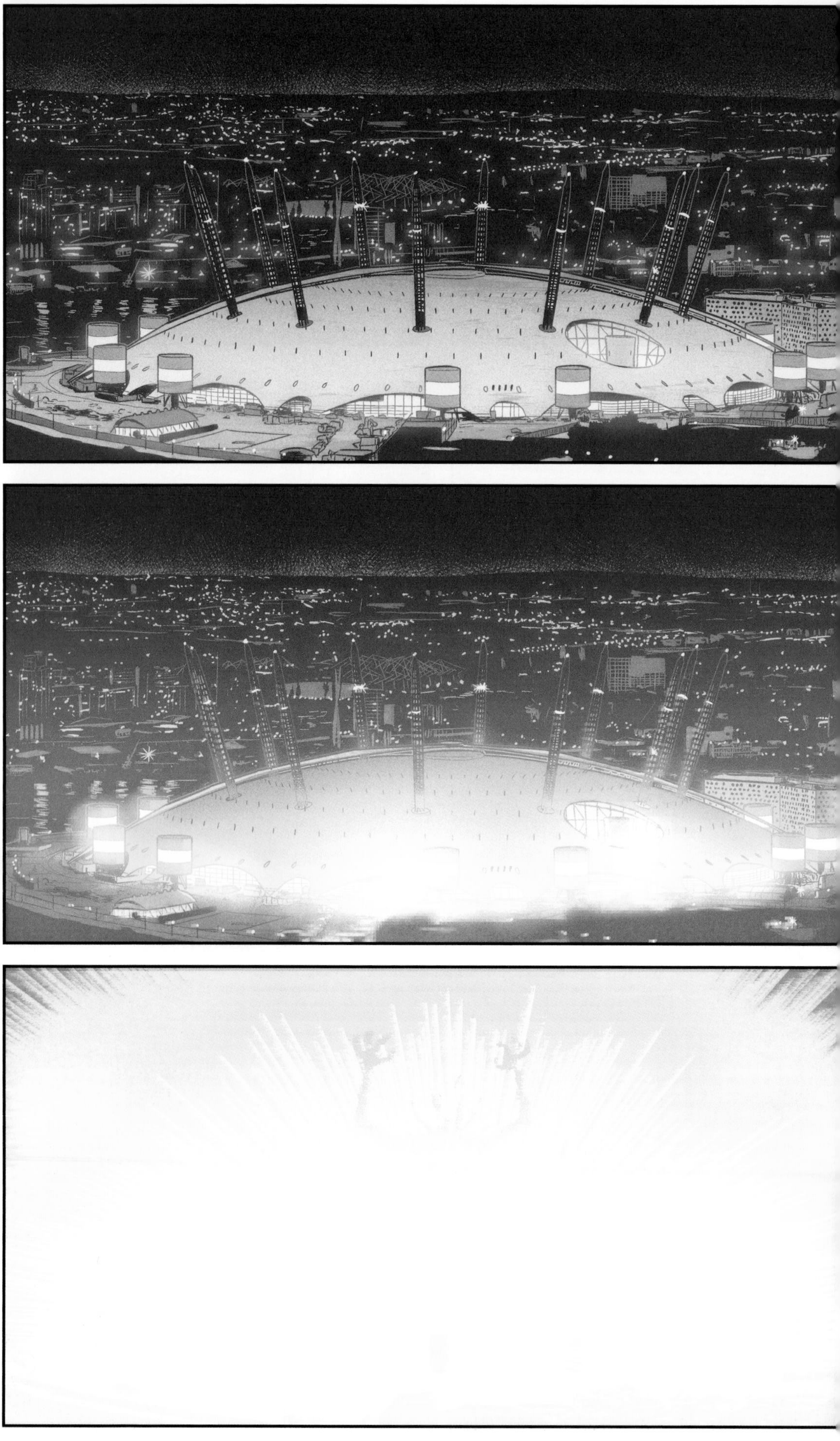

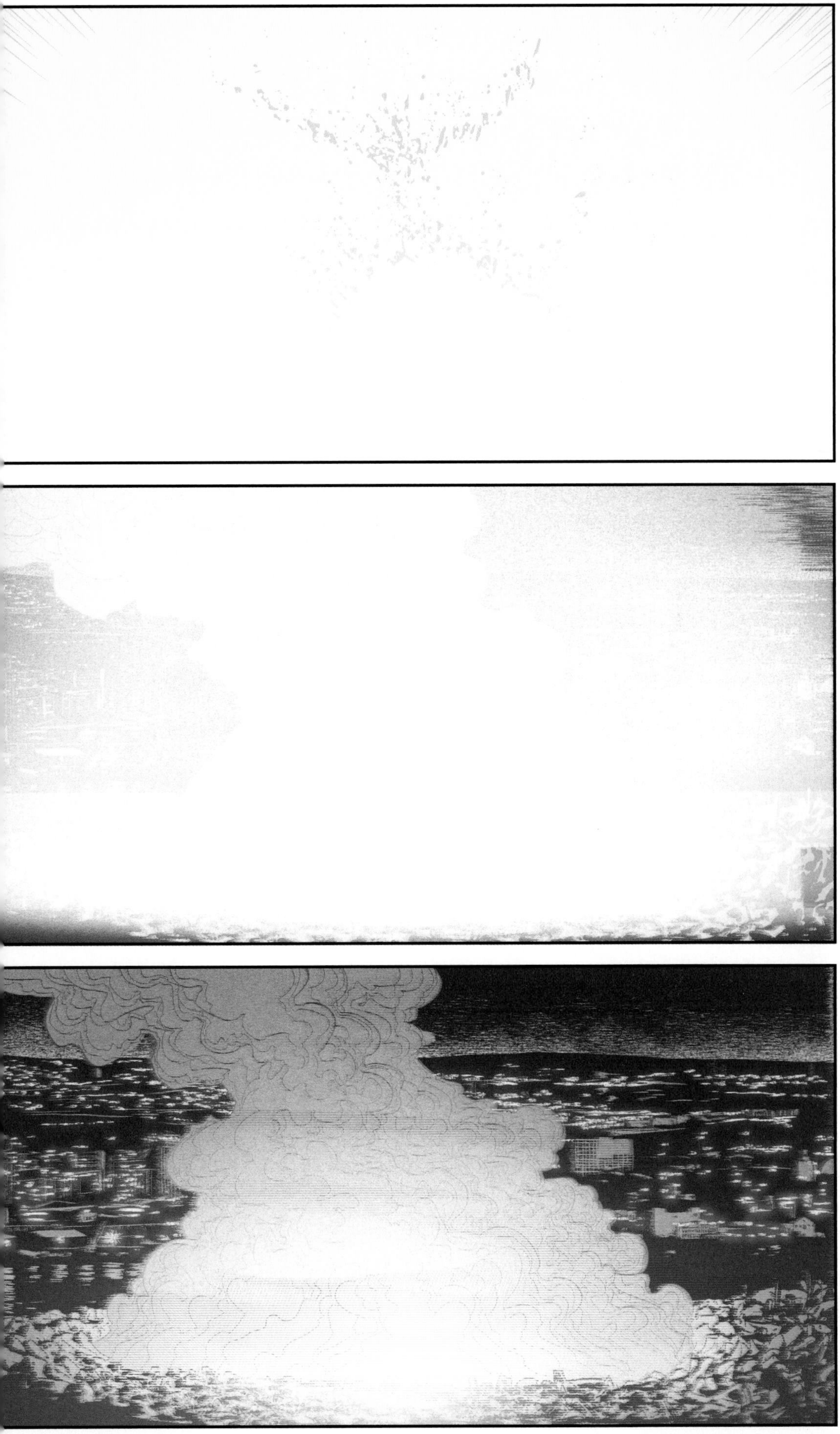

TOTAL ECLIPSE

1 MAY 2015

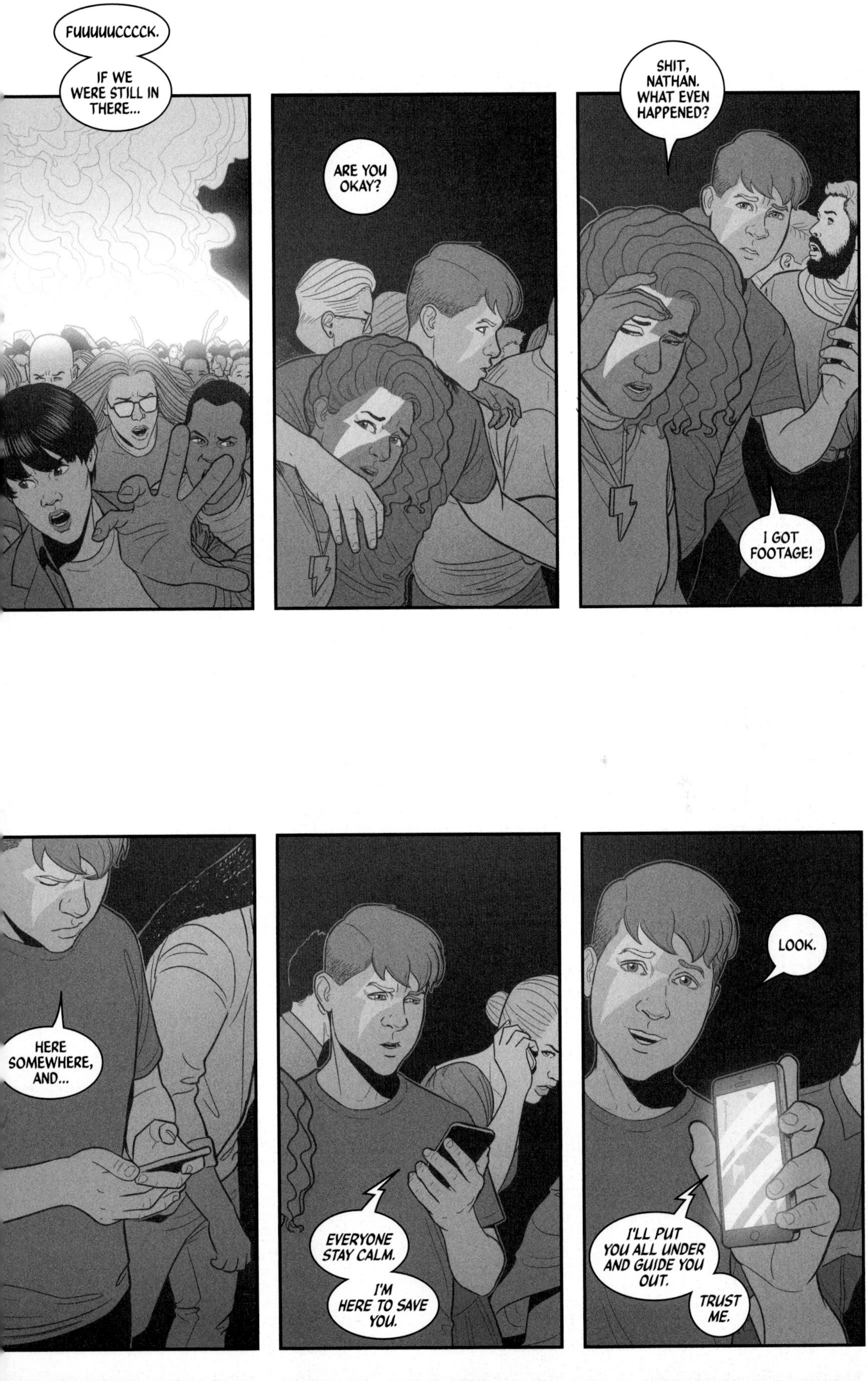
FUUUUUCCCCK.
IF WE WERE STILL IN THERE...
ARE YOU OKAY?
SHIT, NATHAN. WHAT EVEN HAPPENED?
I GOT FOOTAGE!
HERE SOMEWHERE, AND...
EVERYONE STAY CALM.
I'M HERE TO SAVE YOU.
LOOK.
I'LL PUT YOU ALL UNDER AND GUIDE YOU OUT.
TRUST ME.

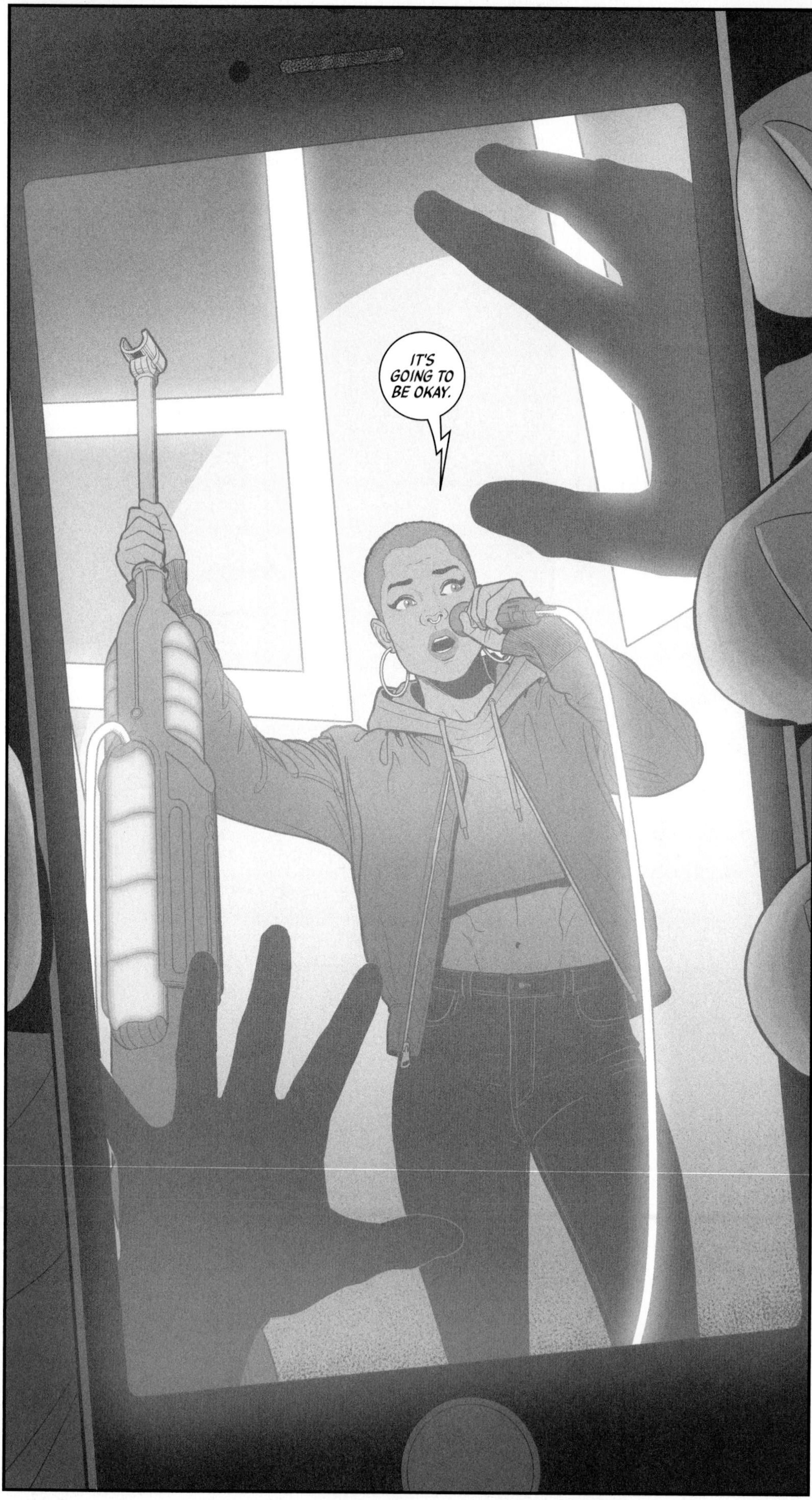
IT'S GOING TO BE OKAY.

FOR A CERTAIN
VALUE OF "OKAY"

1 MAY 2015

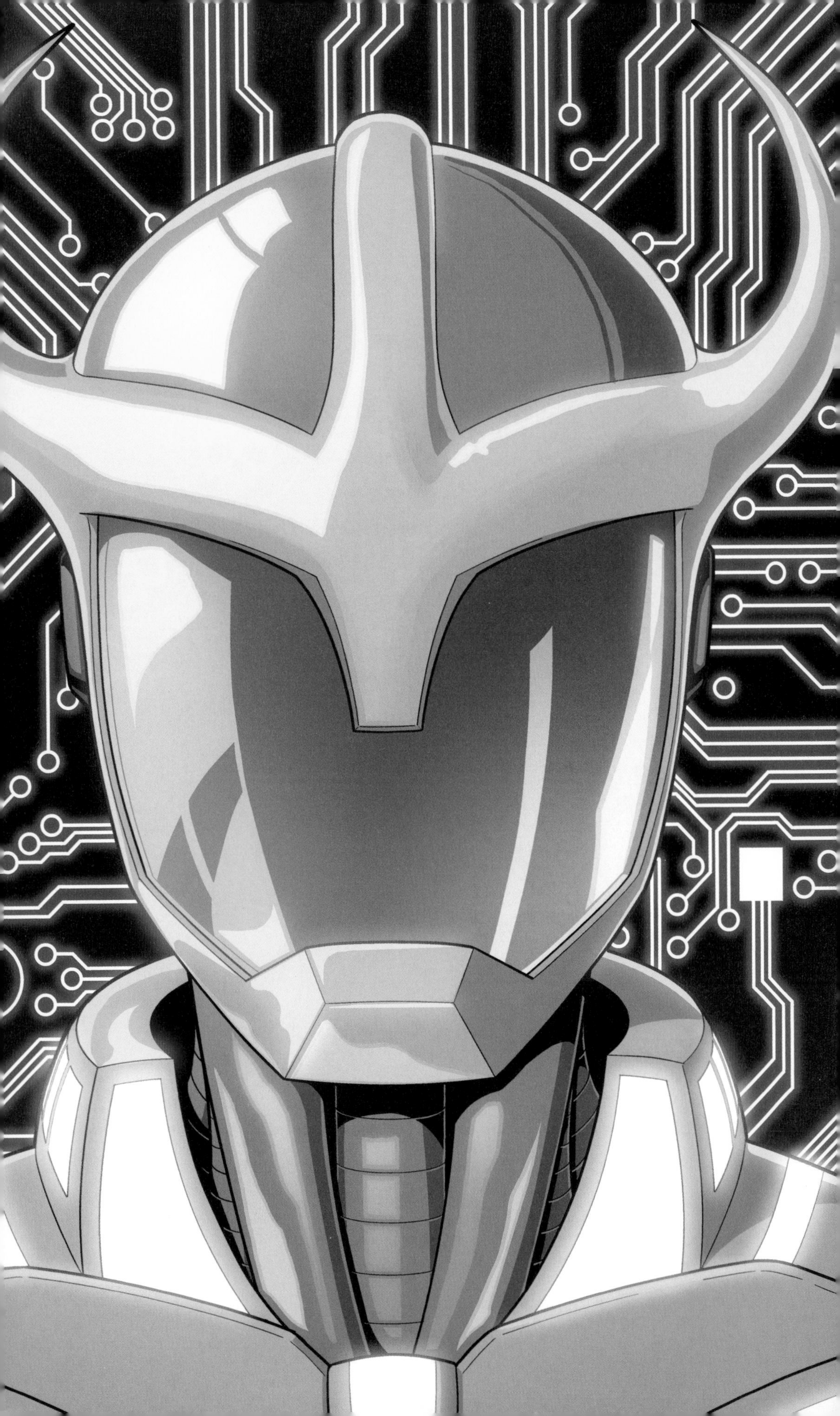

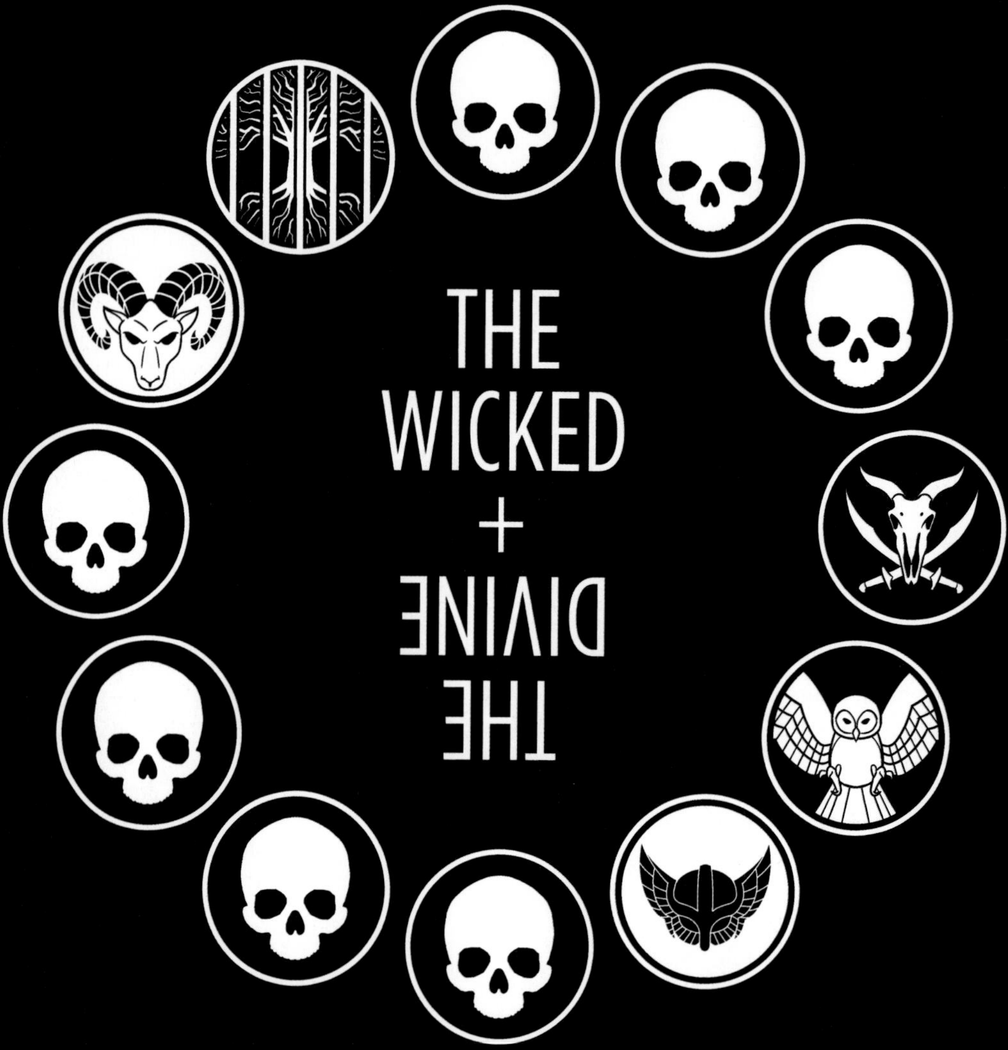
THE
WICKED
+
THE
DIVINE

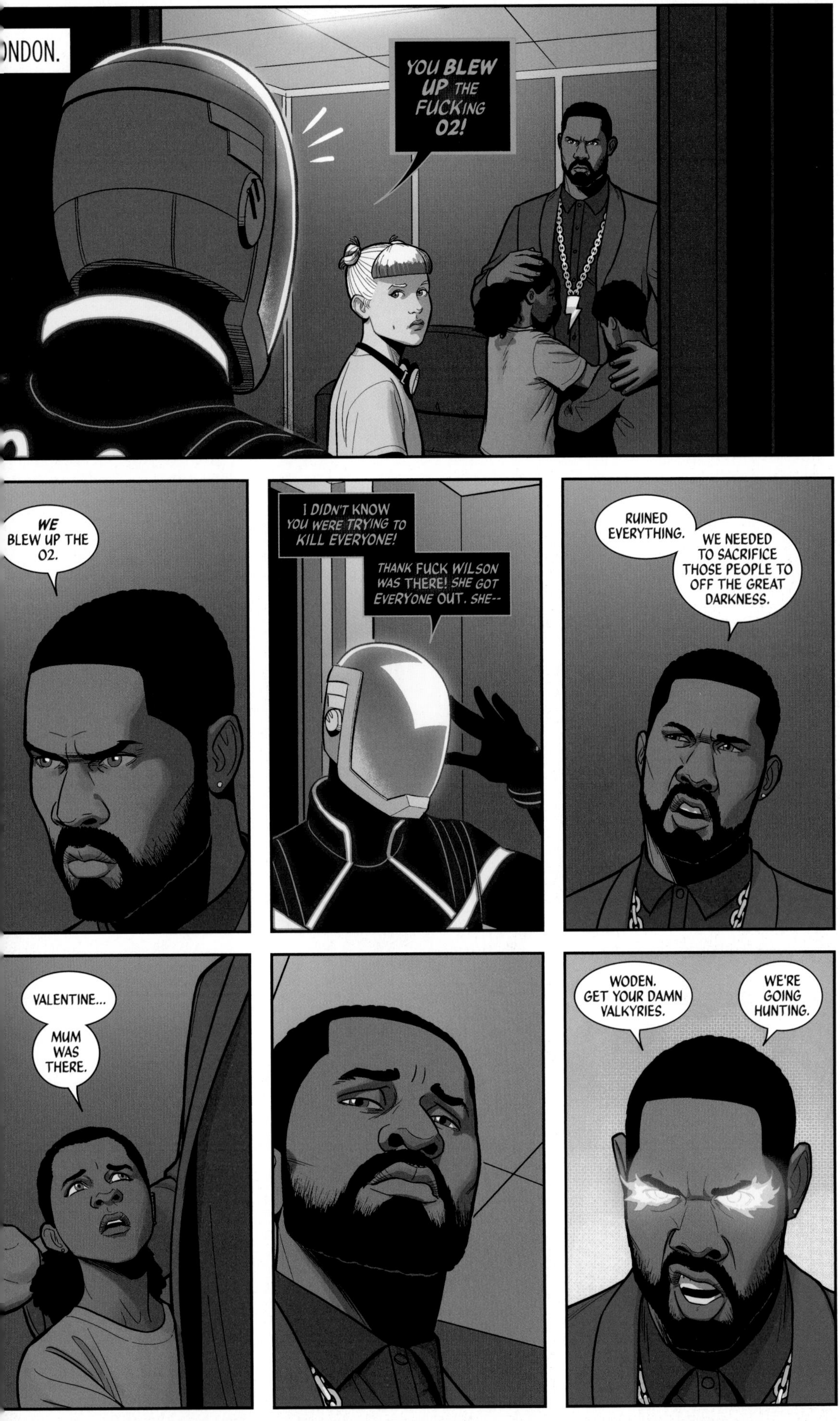

ONDON.
YOU BLEW UP THE FUCKING O2!
WE BLEW UP THE O2.
I DIDN'T KNOW YOU WERE TRYING TO KILL EVERYONE!
THANK FUCK WILSON WAS THERE! SHE GOT EVERYONE OUT. SHE--
RUINED EVERYTHING.
WE NEEDED TO SACRIFICE THOSE PEOPLE TO OFF THE GREAT DARKNESS.
VALENTINE...
MUM WAS THERE.
WODEN. GET YOUR DAMN VALKYRIES.
WE'RE GOING HUNTING.

THE DIFFICULT
SOPHOMORE
ALBUM

1 MAY 2015

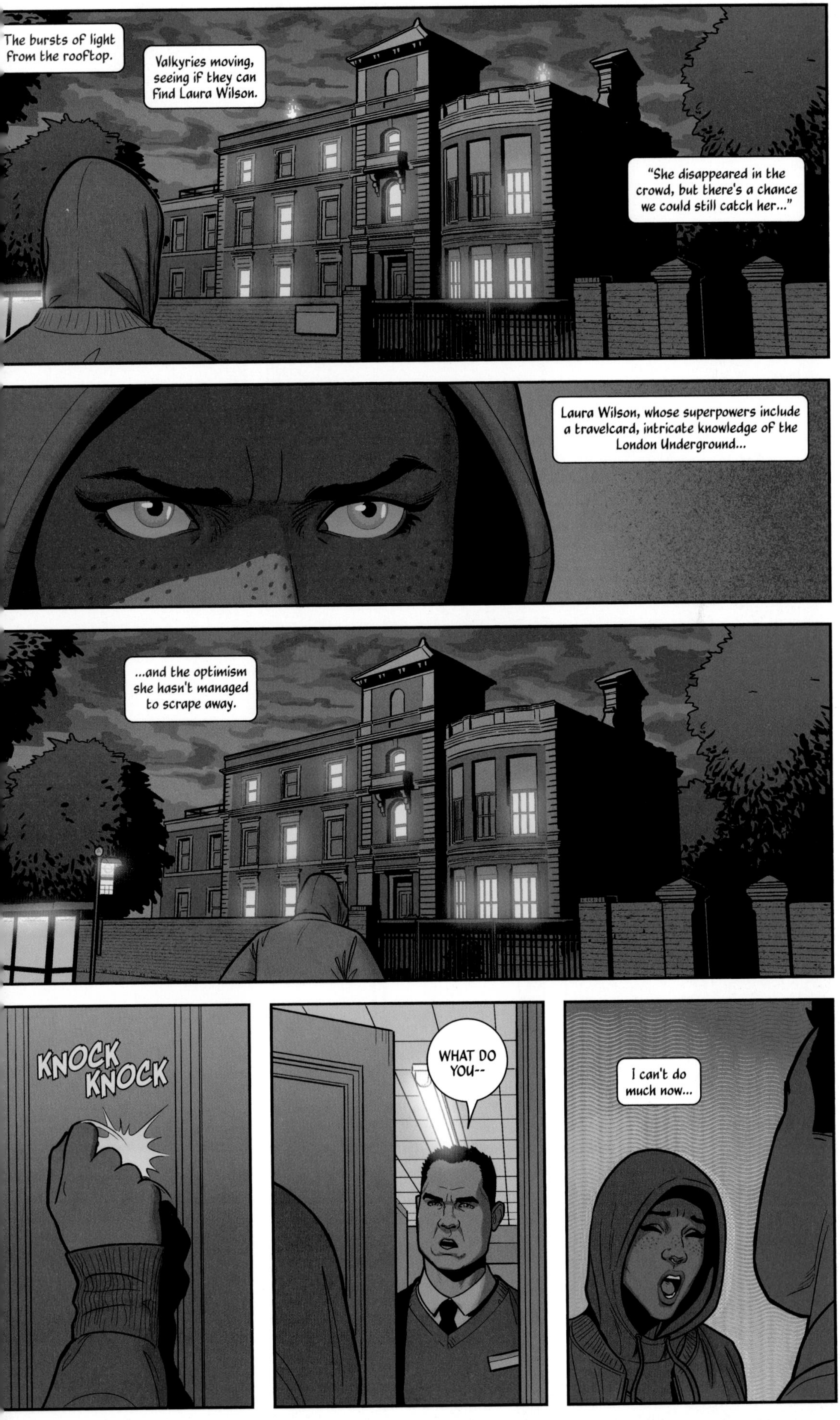
The bursts of light from the rooftop.
Valkyries moving, seeing if they can find Laura Wilson.
"She disappeared in the crowd, but there's a chance we could still catch her..."
Laura Wilson, whose superpowers include a travelcard, intricate knowledge of the London Underground...
...and the optimism she hasn't managed to scrape away.
KNOCK KNOCK
WHAT DO YOU--
I can't do much now...

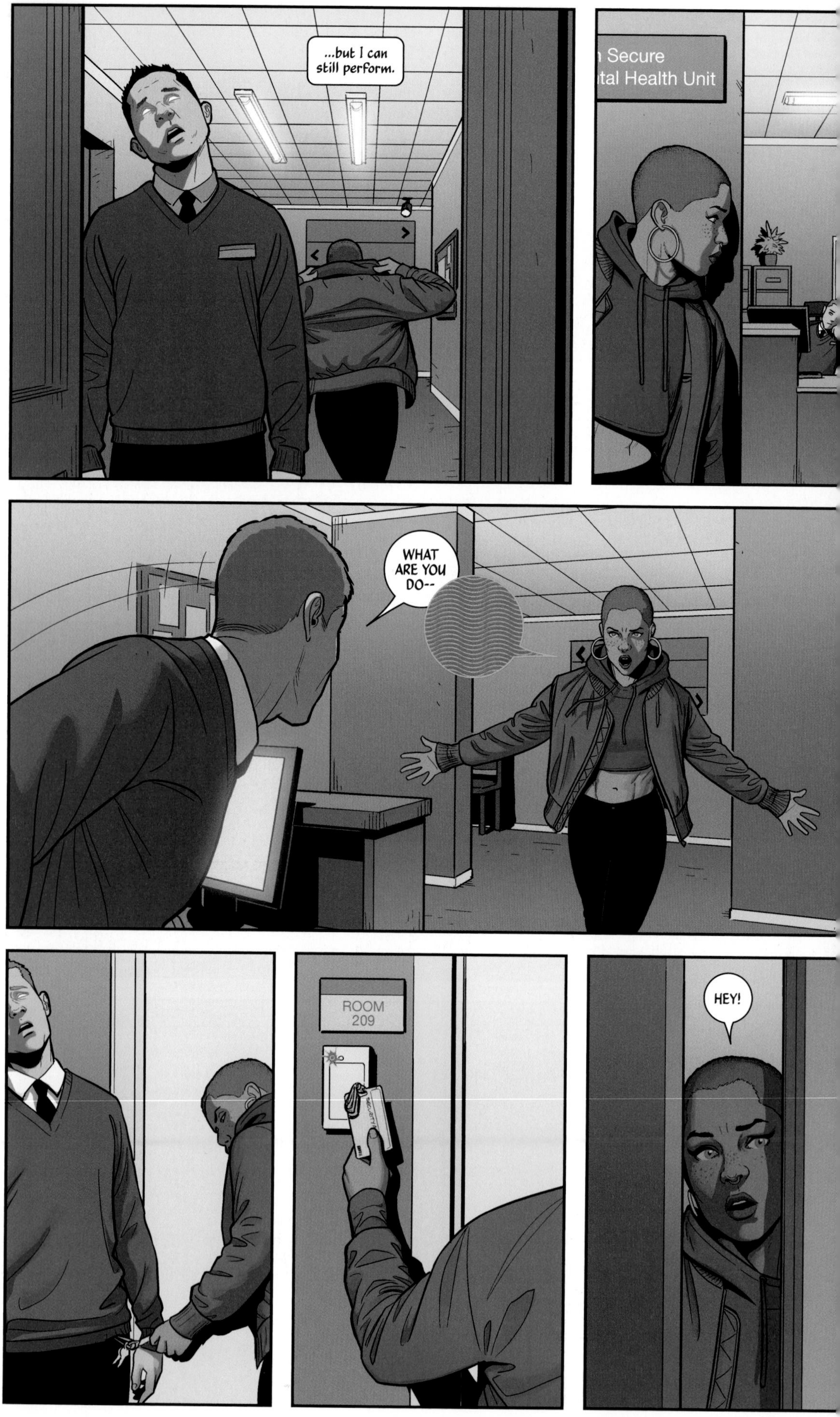
...but I can still perform.
Secure
tal Health Unit
WHAT ARE YOU DO--
ROOM 209
HEY!

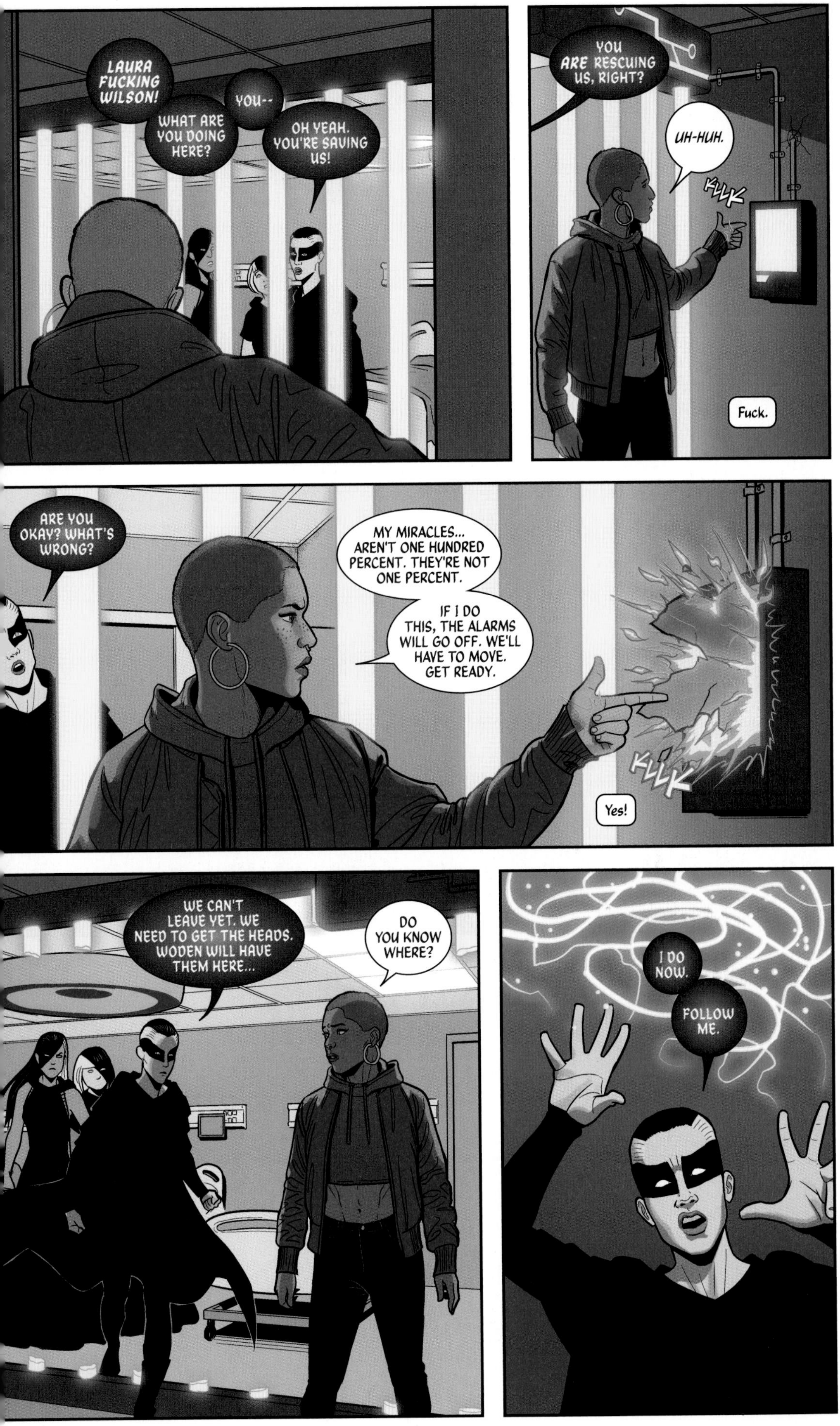

LAURA FUCKING WILSON!
WHAT ARE YOU DOING HERE?
YOU--
OH YEAH. YOU'RE SAVING US!
YOU ARE RESCUING US, RIGHT?
UH-HUH.
KLLK
Fuck.
ARE YOU OKAY? WHAT'S WRONG?
MY MIRACLES... AREN'T ONE HUNDRED PERCENT. THEY'RE NOT ONE PERCENT.
IF I DO THIS, THE ALARMS WILL GO OFF. WE'LL HAVE TO MOVE. GET READY.
KLLK
Yes!
WE CAN'T LEAVE YET. WE NEED TO GET THE HEADS. WODEN WILL HAVE THEM HERE...
DO YOU KNOW WHERE?
I DO NOW.
FOLLOW ME.

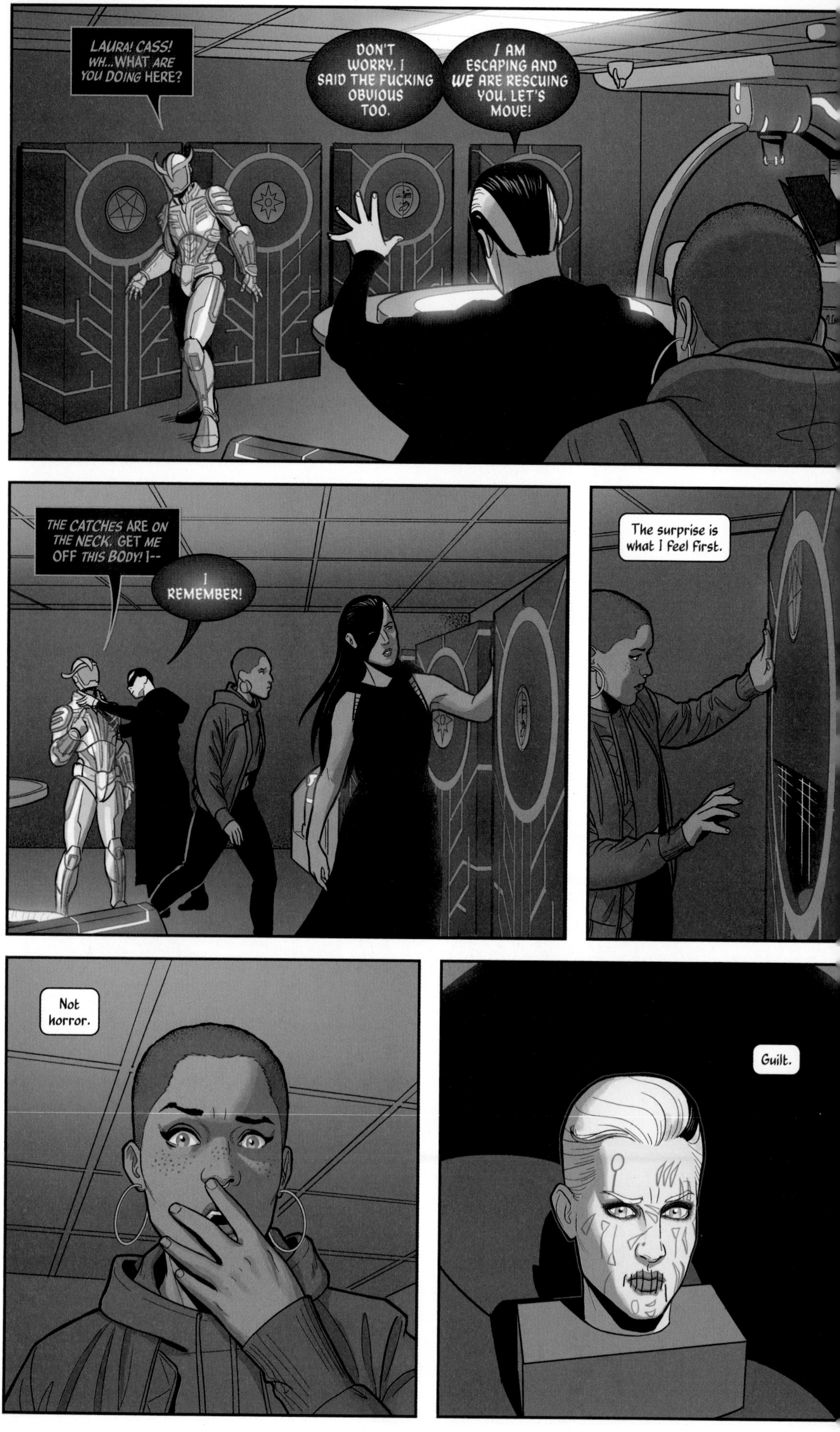
LAURA! CASS! WH...WHAT ARE YOU DOING HERE?
DON'T WORRY. I SAID THE FUCKING OBVIOUS TOO.
I AM ESCAPING AND WE ARE RESCUING YOU. LET'S MOVE!
THE CATCHES ARE ON THE NECK. GET ME OFF THIS BODY! I--
I REMEMBER!
The surprise is what I feel first.
Not horror.
Guilt.

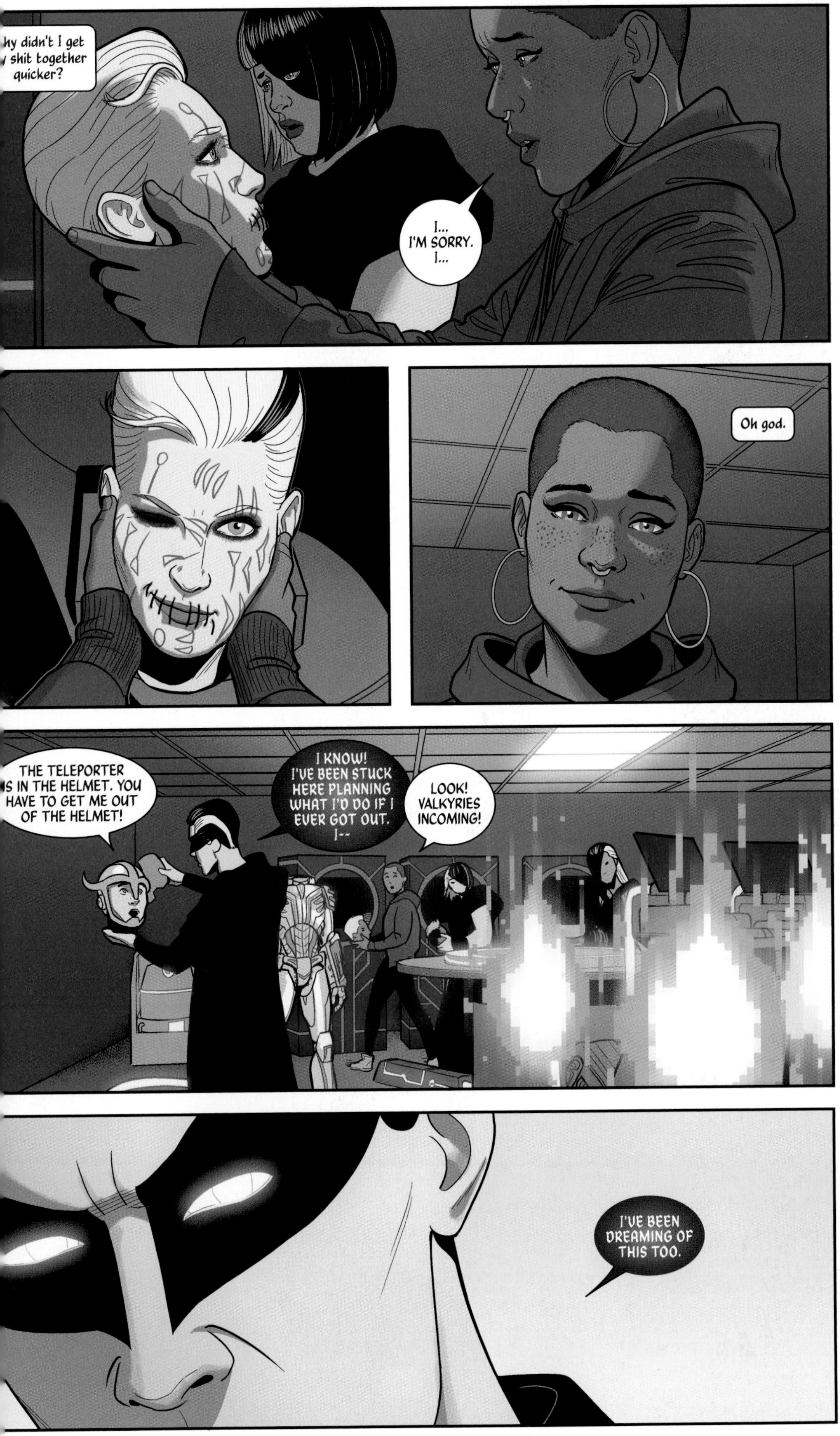
hy didn't I get
y shit together
quicker?
I...
I'M SORRY.
I...
Oh god.
THE TELEPORTER
S IN THE HELMET. YOU
HAVE TO GET ME OUT
OF THE HELMET!
I KNOW!
I'VE BEEN STUCK
HERE PLANNING
WHAT I'D DO IF I
EVER GOT OUT.
I--
LOOK!
VALKYRIES
INCOMING!
I'VE BEEN
DREAMING OF
THIS TOO.

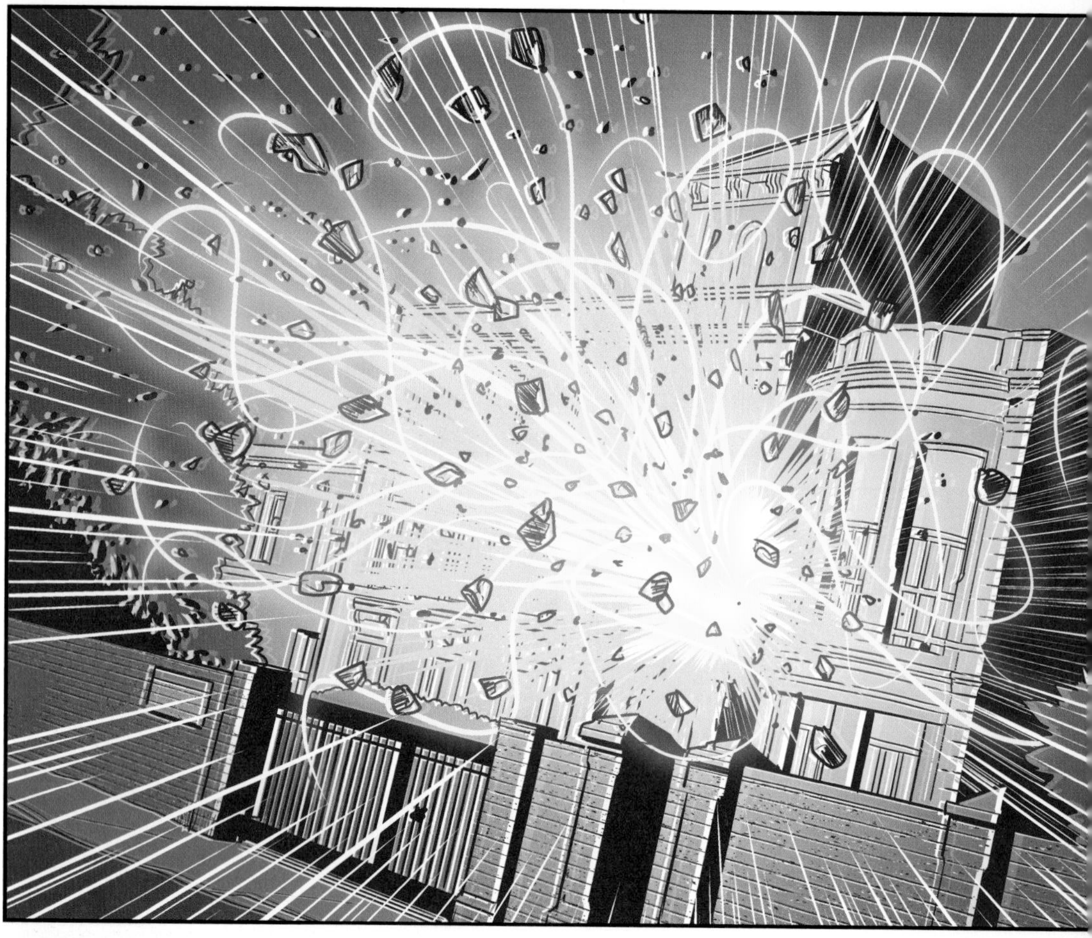

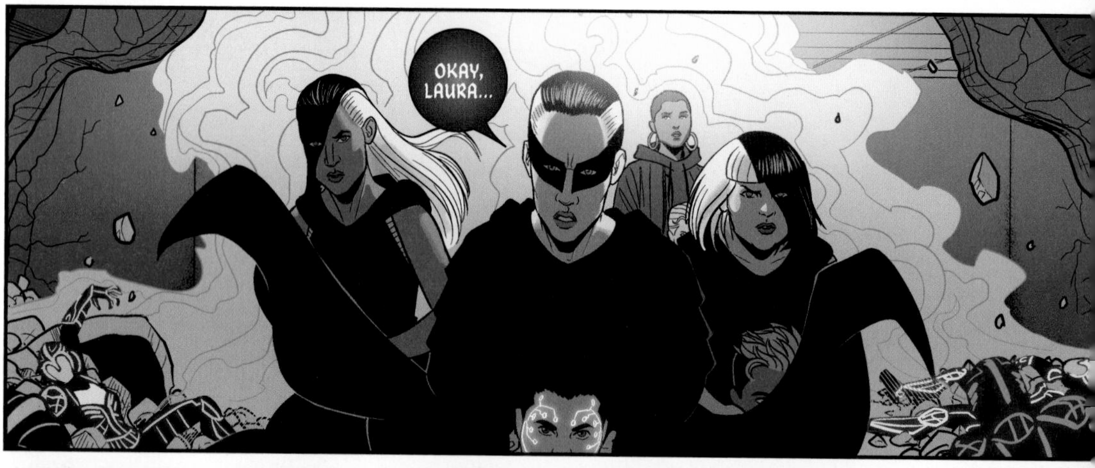
OKAY, LAURA...

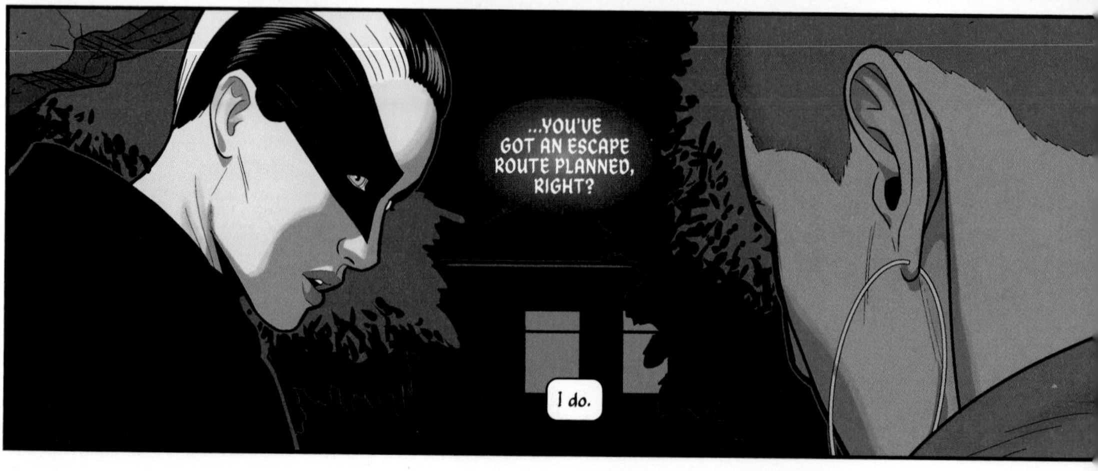
...YOU'VE GOT AN ESCAPE ROUTE PLANNED, RIGHT?
I do.

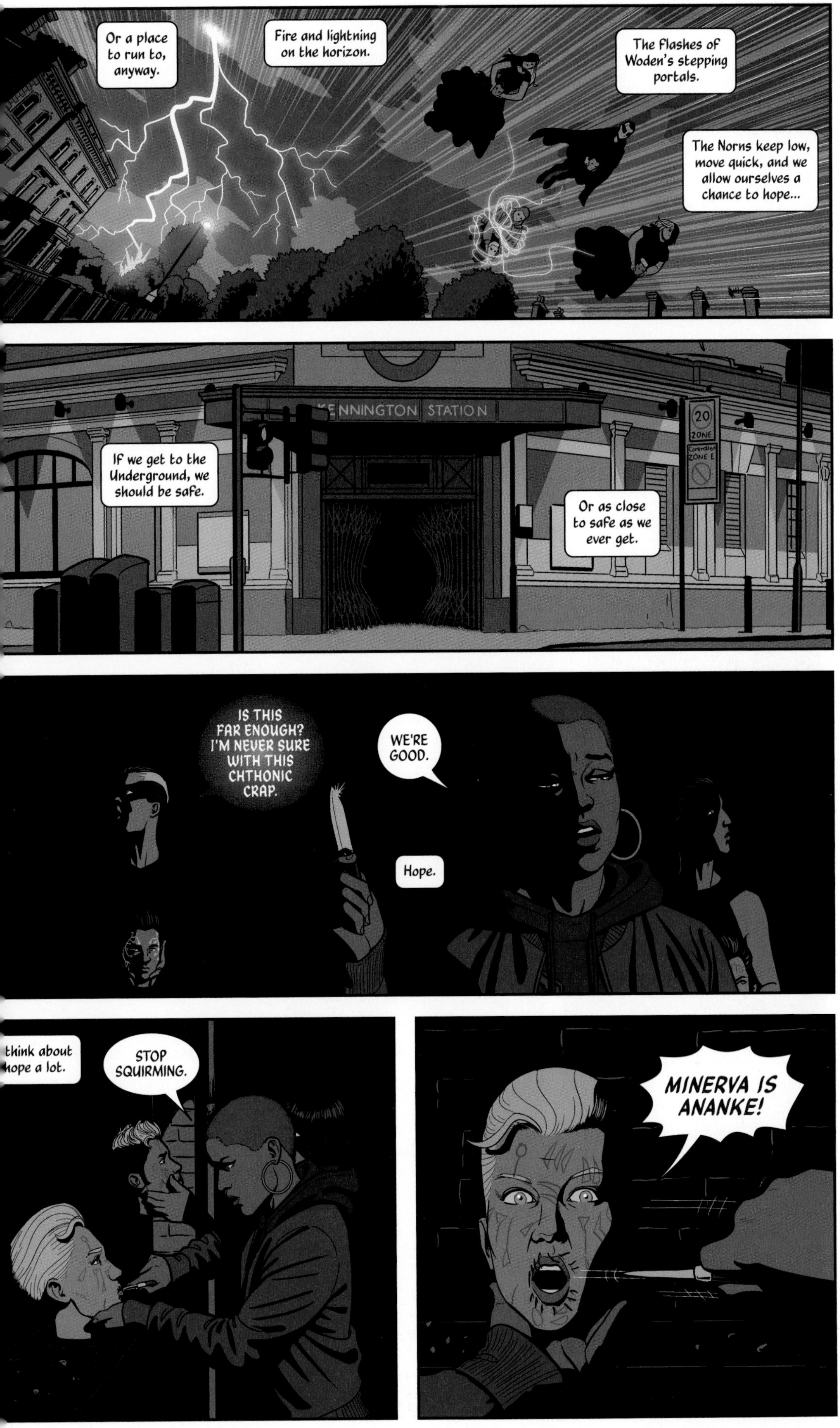

Or a place to run to, anyway.
Fire and lightning on the horizon.
The flashes of Woden's stepping portals.
The Norns keep low, move quick, and we allow ourselves a chance to hope...
KENNINGTON STATION
20 ZONE
Controlled ZONE E
If we get to the Underground, we should be safe.
Or as close to safe as we ever get.
IS THIS FAR ENOUGH? I'M NEVER SURE WITH THIS CHTHONIC CRAP.
WE'RE GOOD.
Hope.
think about hope a lot.
STOP SQUIRMING.
MINERVA IS ANANKE!

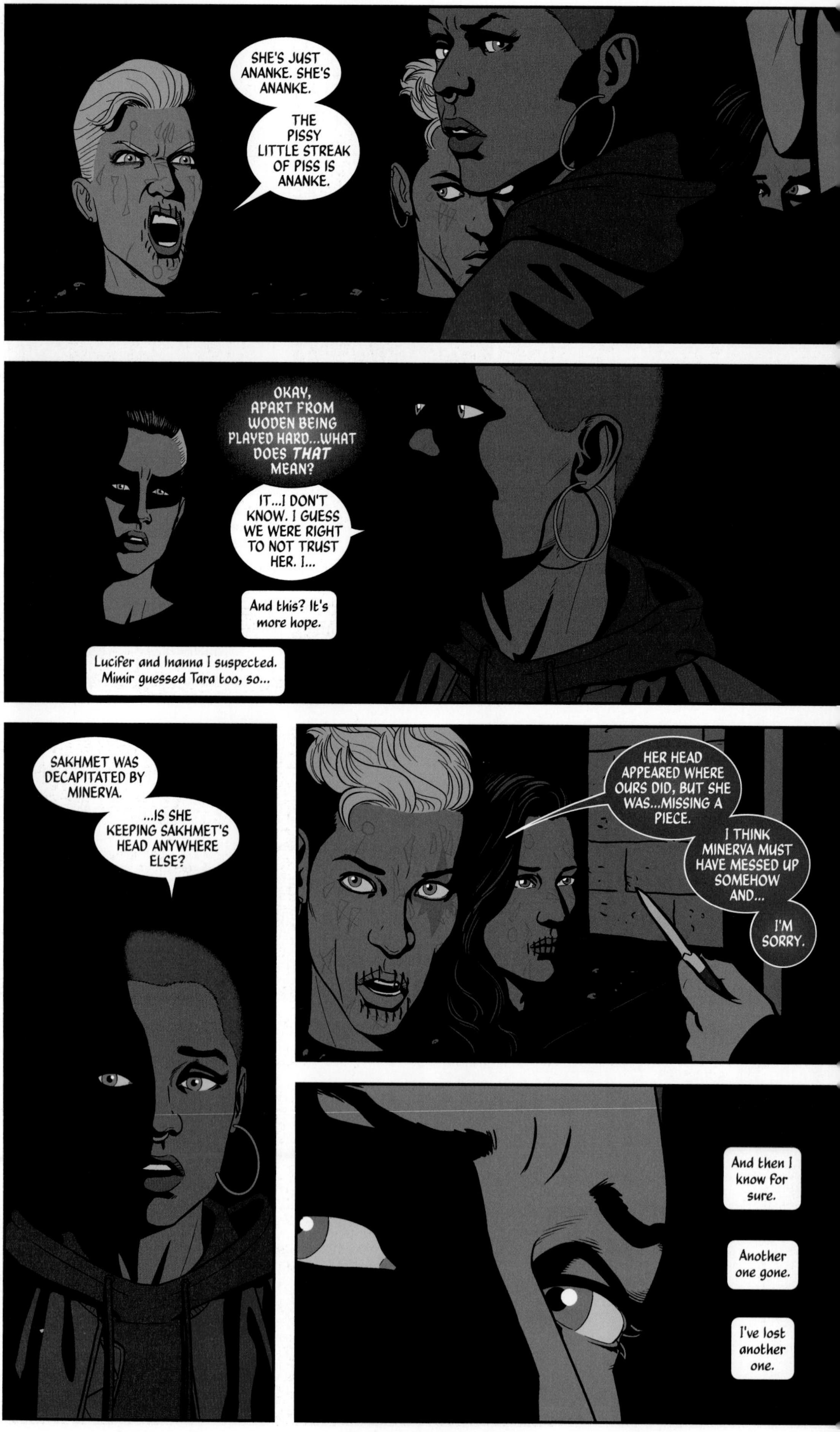

SHE'S JUST ANANKE. SHE'S ANANKE.
THE PISSY LITTLE STREAK OF PISS IS ANANKE.
OKAY, APART FROM WODEN BEING PLAYED HARD...WHAT DOES THAT MEAN?
IT...I DON'T KNOW. I GUESS WE WERE RIGHT TO NOT TRUST HER. I...
And this? It's more hope.
Lucifer and Inanna I suspected. Mimir guessed Tara too, so...
SAKHMET WAS DECAPITATED BY MINERVA.
...IS SHE KEEPING SAKHMET'S HEAD ANYWHERE ELSE?
HER HEAD APPEARED WHERE OURS DID, BUT SHE WAS...MISSING A PIECE.
I THINK MINERVA MUST HAVE MESSED UP SOMEHOW AND...
I'M SORRY.
And then I know for sure.
Another one gone.
I've lost another one.

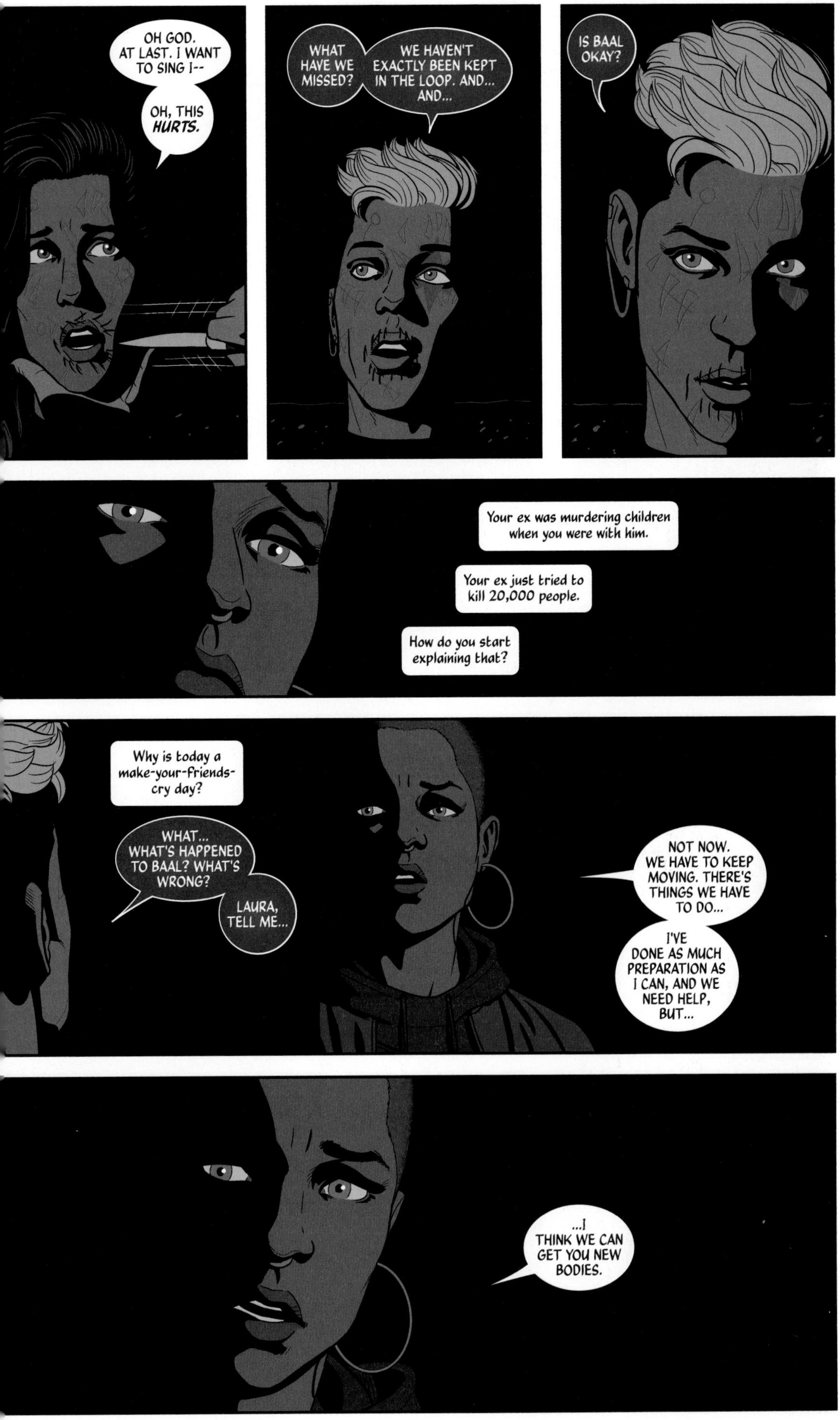
OH GOD. AT LAST. I WANT TO SING I--
OH, THIS *HURTS.*
WHAT HAVE WE MISSED?
WE HAVEN'T EXACTLY BEEN KEPT IN THE LOOP. AND... AND...
IS BAAL OKAY?
Your ex was murdering children when you were with him.
Your ex just tried to kill 20,000 people.
How do you start explaining that?
Why is today a make-your-friends-cry day?
WHAT... WHAT'S HAPPENED TO BAAL? WHAT'S WRONG?
LAURA, TELL ME...
NOT NOW. WE HAVE TO KEEP MOVING. THERE'S THINGS WE HAVE TO DO...
I'VE DONE AS MUCH PREPARATION AS I CAN, AND WE NEED HELP, BUT...
...I THINK WE CAN GET YOU NEW BODIES.

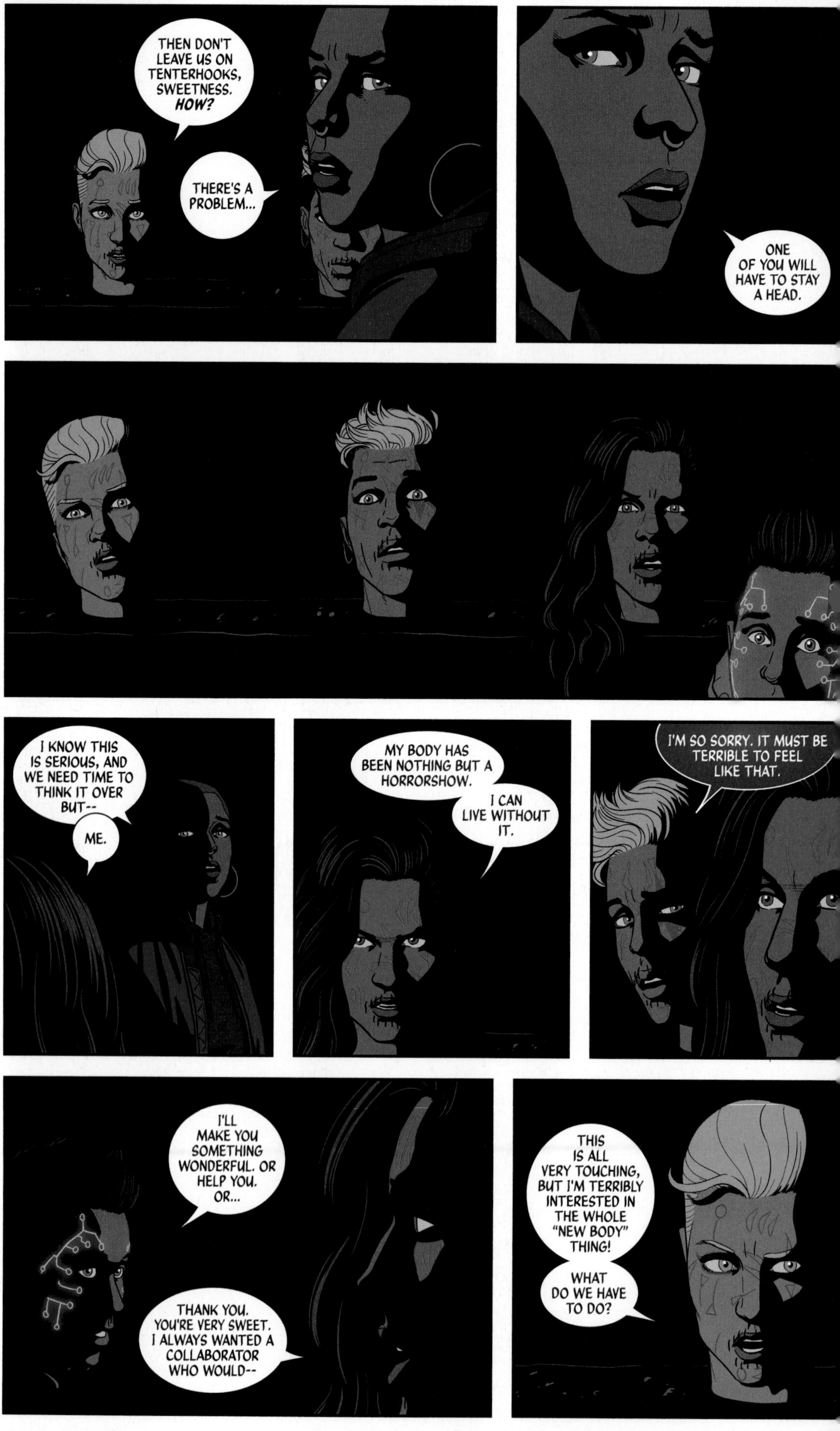
THEN DON'T LEAVE US ON TENTERHOOKS, SWEETNESS. *HOW?*
THERE'S A PROBLEM...
ONE OF YOU WILL HAVE TO STAY A HEAD.
I KNOW THIS IS SERIOUS, AND WE NEED TIME TO THINK IT OVER BUT--
ME.
MY BODY HAS BEEN NOTHING BUT A HORRORSHOW.
I CAN LIVE WITHOUT IT.
I'M SO SORRY. IT MUST BE TERRIBLE TO FEEL LIKE THAT.
I'LL MAKE YOU SOMETHING WONDERFUL. OR HELP YOU. OR...
THANK YOU. YOU'RE VERY SWEET. I ALWAYS WANTED A COLLABORATOR WHO WOULD--
THIS IS ALL VERY TOUCHING, BUT I'M TERRIBLY INTERESTED IN THE WHOLE "NEW BODY" THING!
WHAT DO WE HAVE TO DO?

I HEAR YOU
CALLING

2 MAY 2015

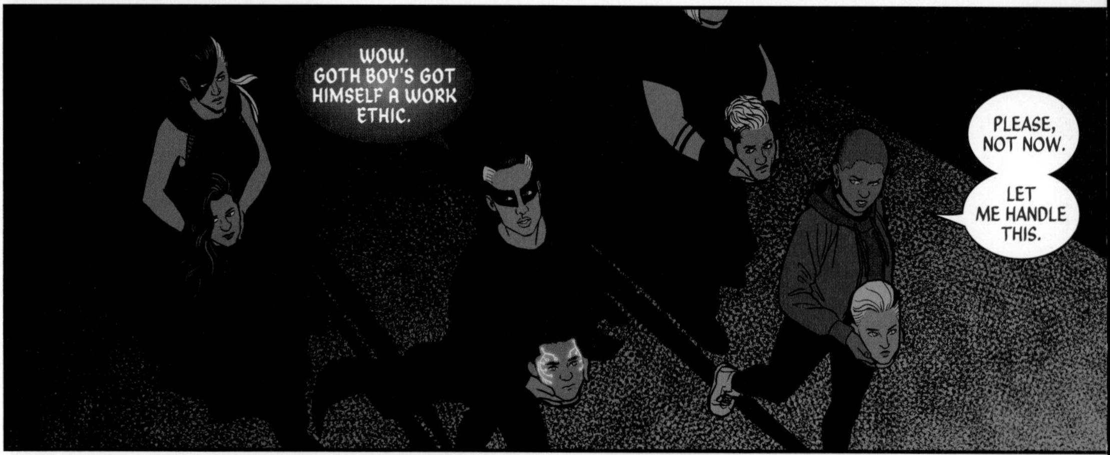
WOW. GOTH BOY'S GOT HIMSELF A WORK ETHIC.
PLEASE, NOT NOW.
LET ME HANDLE THIS.

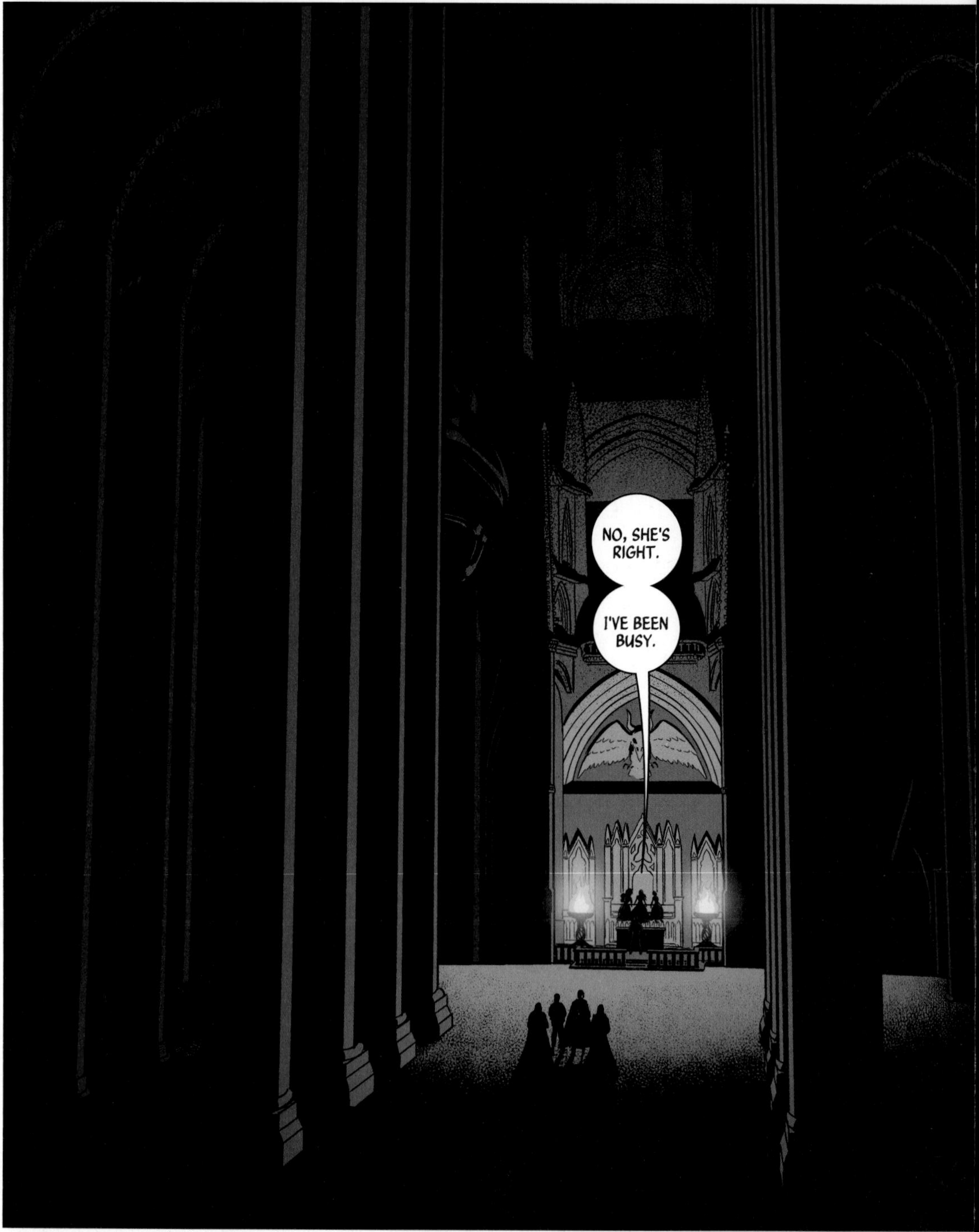
NO, SHE'S RIGHT.
I'VE BEEN BUSY.

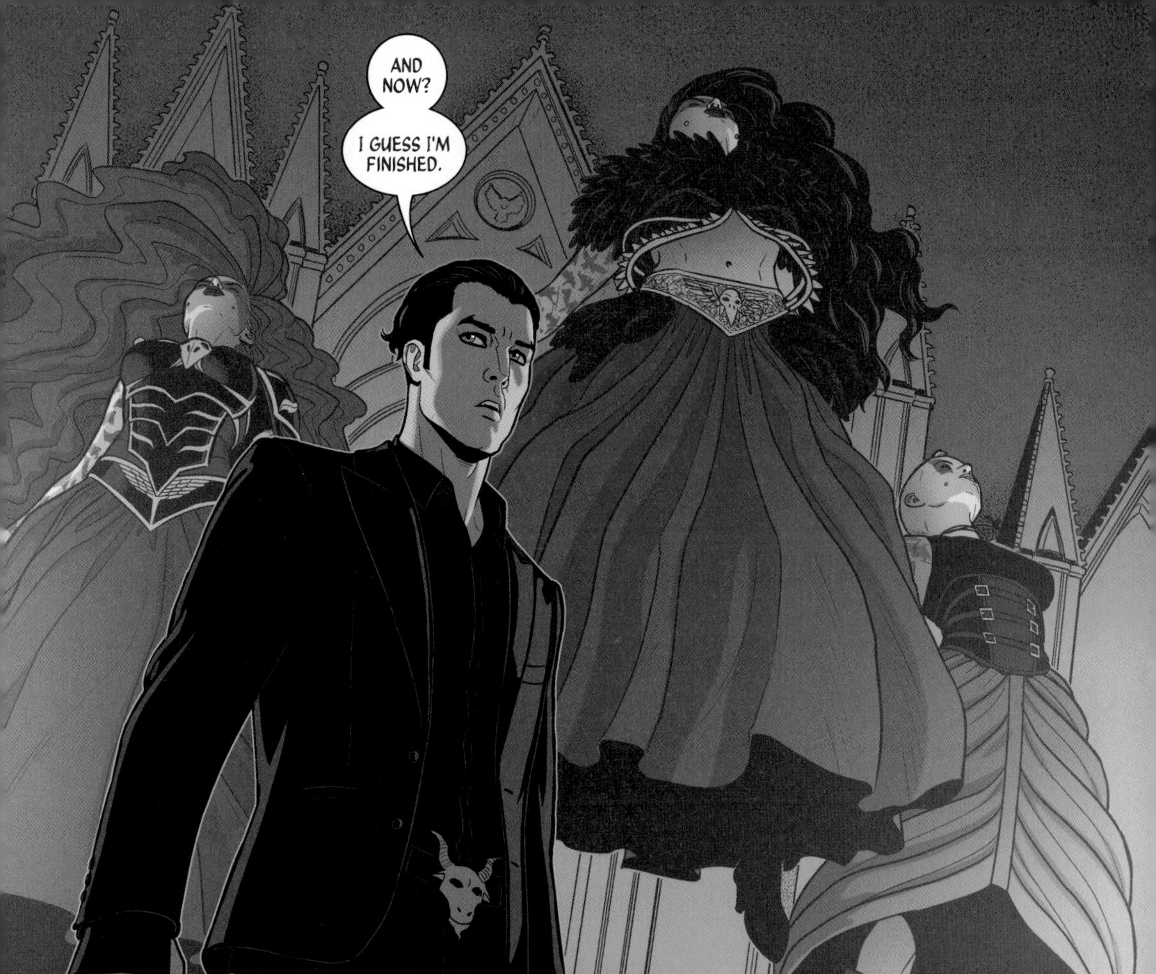
AND NOW?
I GUESS I'M FINISHED.

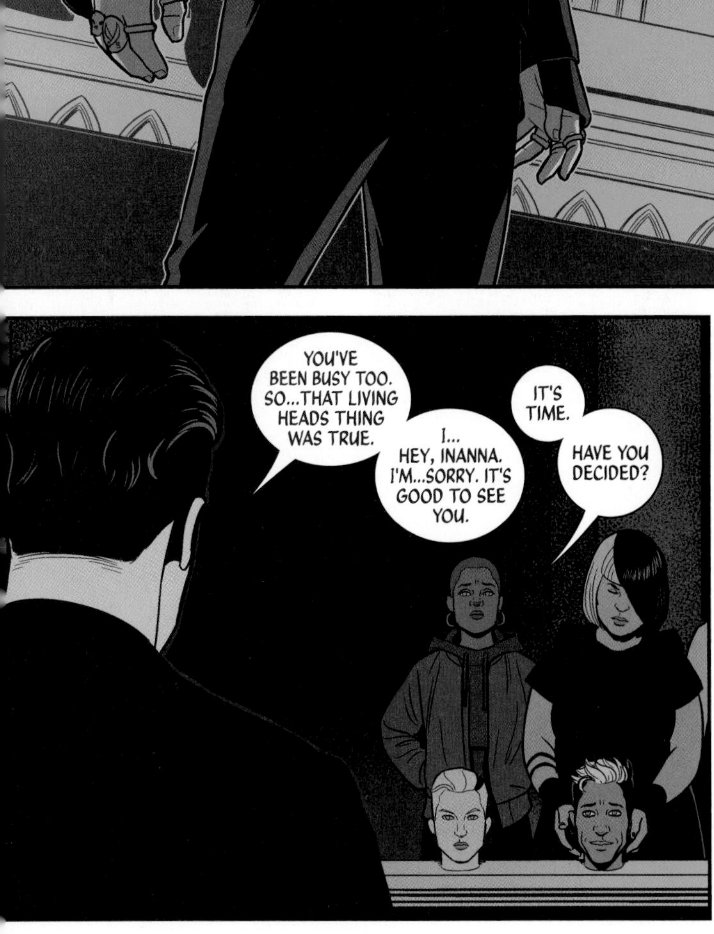
YOU'VE BEEN BUSY TOO. SO...THAT LIVING HEADS THING WAS TRUE.
I... HEY, INANNA. I'M...SORRY. IT'S GOOD TO SEE YOU.
IT'S TIME.
HAVE YOU DECIDED?

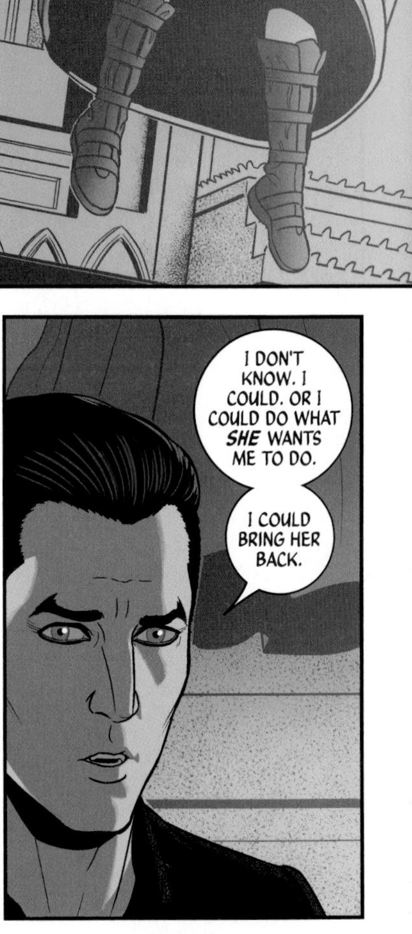
I DON'T KNOW. I COULD. OR I COULD DO WHAT *SHE* WANTS ME TO DO.
I COULD BRING HER BACK.

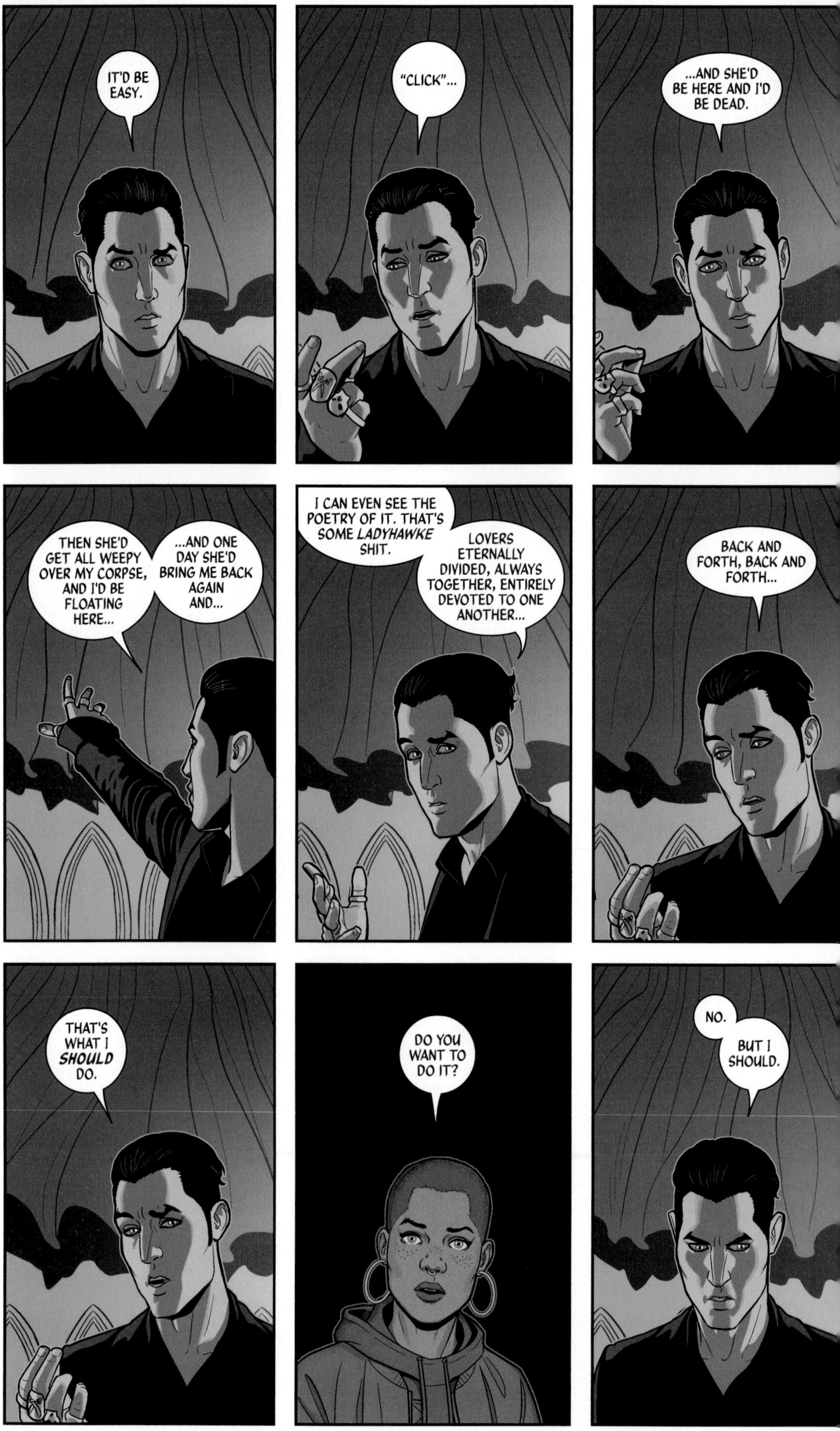
IT'D BE EASY.
"CLICK"...
...AND SHE'D BE HERE AND I'D BE DEAD.
THEN SHE'D GET ALL WEEPY OVER MY CORPSE, AND I'D BE FLOATING HERE...
...AND ONE DAY SHE'D BRING ME BACK AGAIN AND...
I CAN EVEN SEE THE POETRY OF IT. THAT'S SOME *LADYHAWKE* SHIT.
LOVERS ETERNALLY DIVIDED, ALWAYS TOGETHER, ENTIRELY DEVOTED TO ONE ANOTHER...
BACK AND FORTH, BACK AND FORTH...
THAT'S WHAT I ***SHOULD*** DO.
DO YOU WANT TO DO IT?
NO.
BUT I SHOULD.

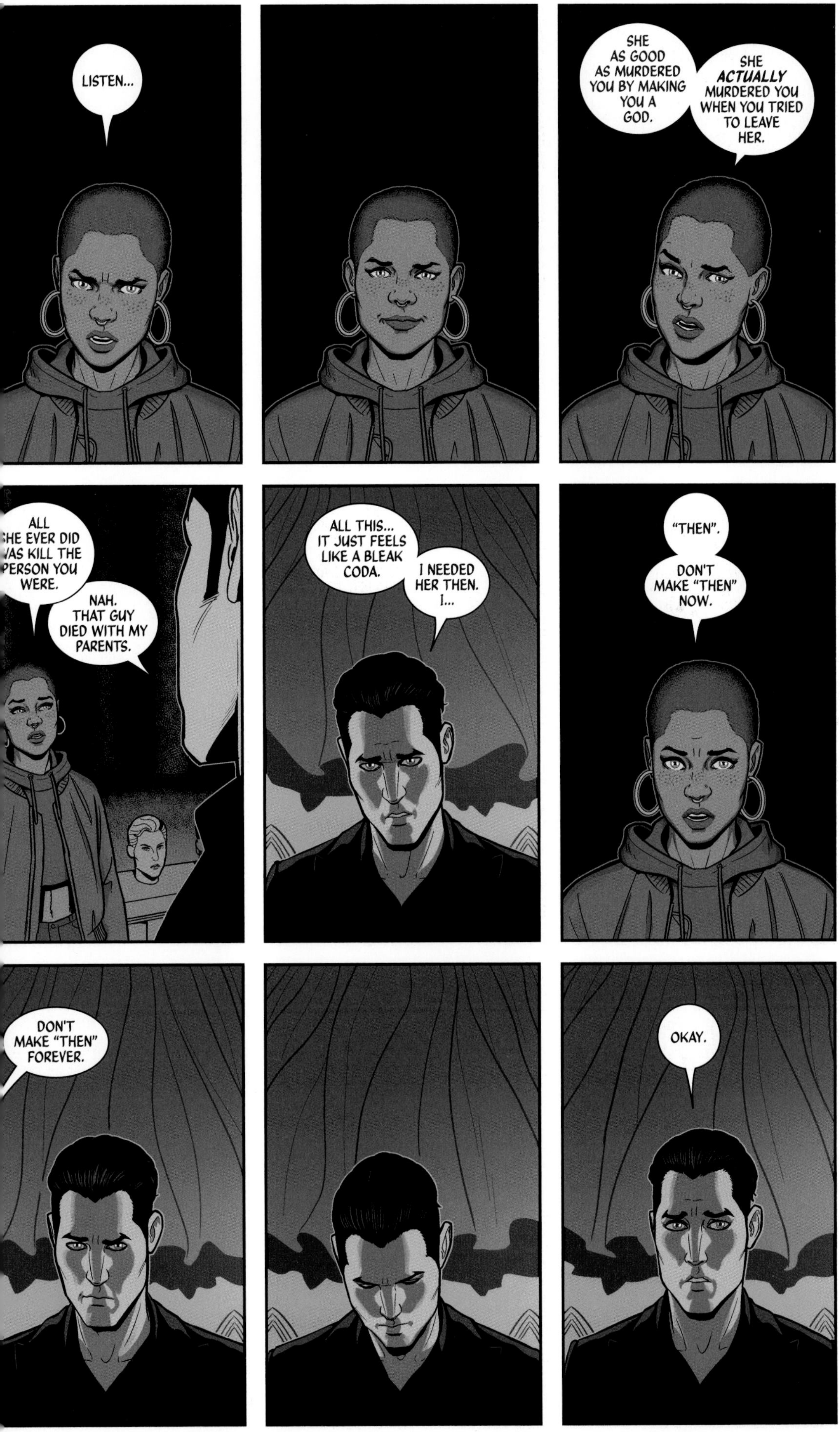
LISTEN...
SHE AS GOOD AS MURDERED YOU BY MAKING YOU A GOD.
SHE *ACTUALLY* MURDERED YOU WHEN YOU TRIED TO LEAVE HER.
ALL SHE EVER DID WAS KILL THE PERSON YOU WERE.
NAH. THAT GUY DIED WITH MY PARENTS.
ALL THIS... IT JUST FEELS LIKE A BLEAK CODA.
I NEEDED HER THEN. I...
"THEN".
DON'T MAKE "THEN" NOW.
DON'T MAKE "THEN" FOREVER.
OKAY.

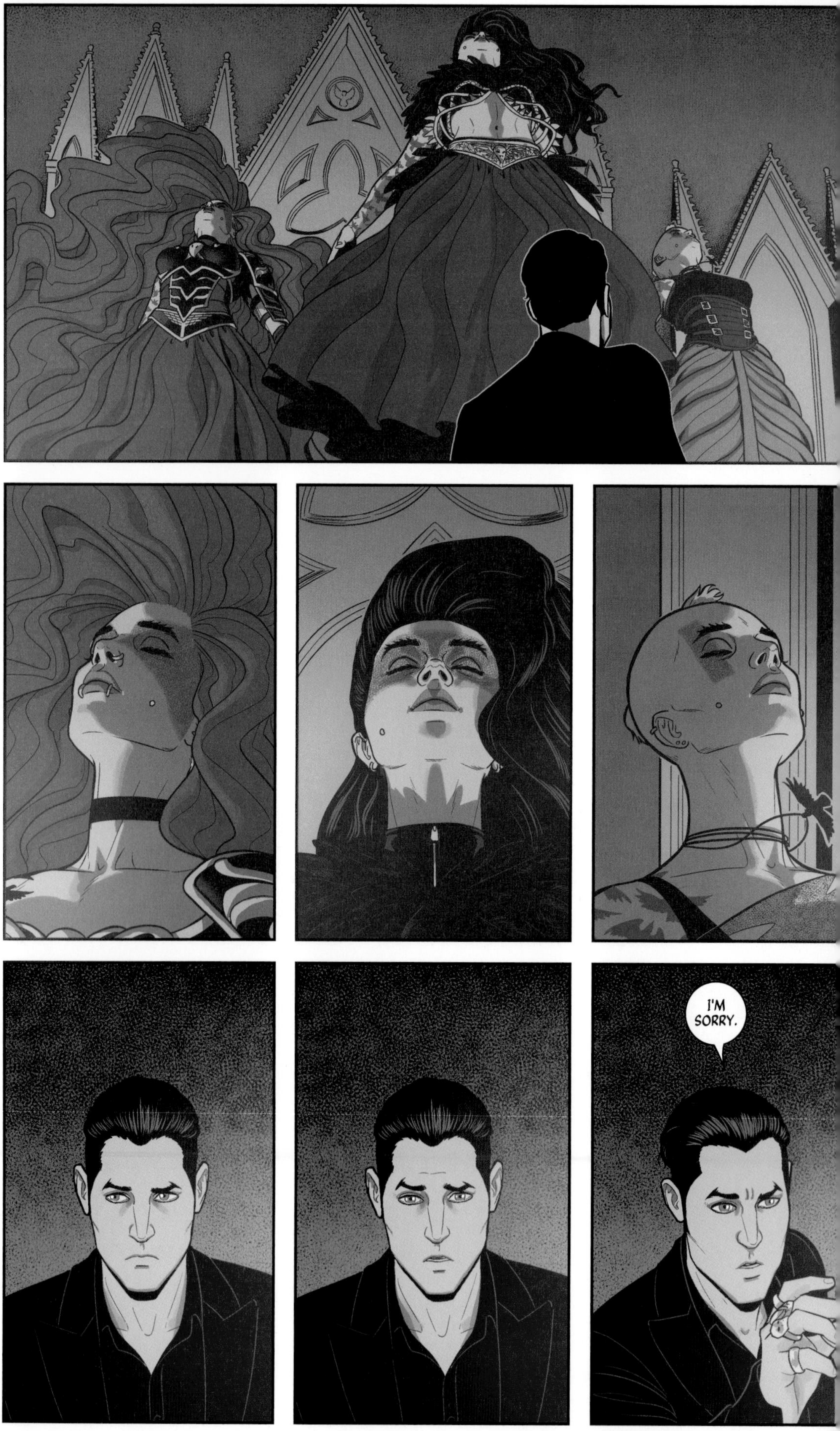
I'M SORRY.

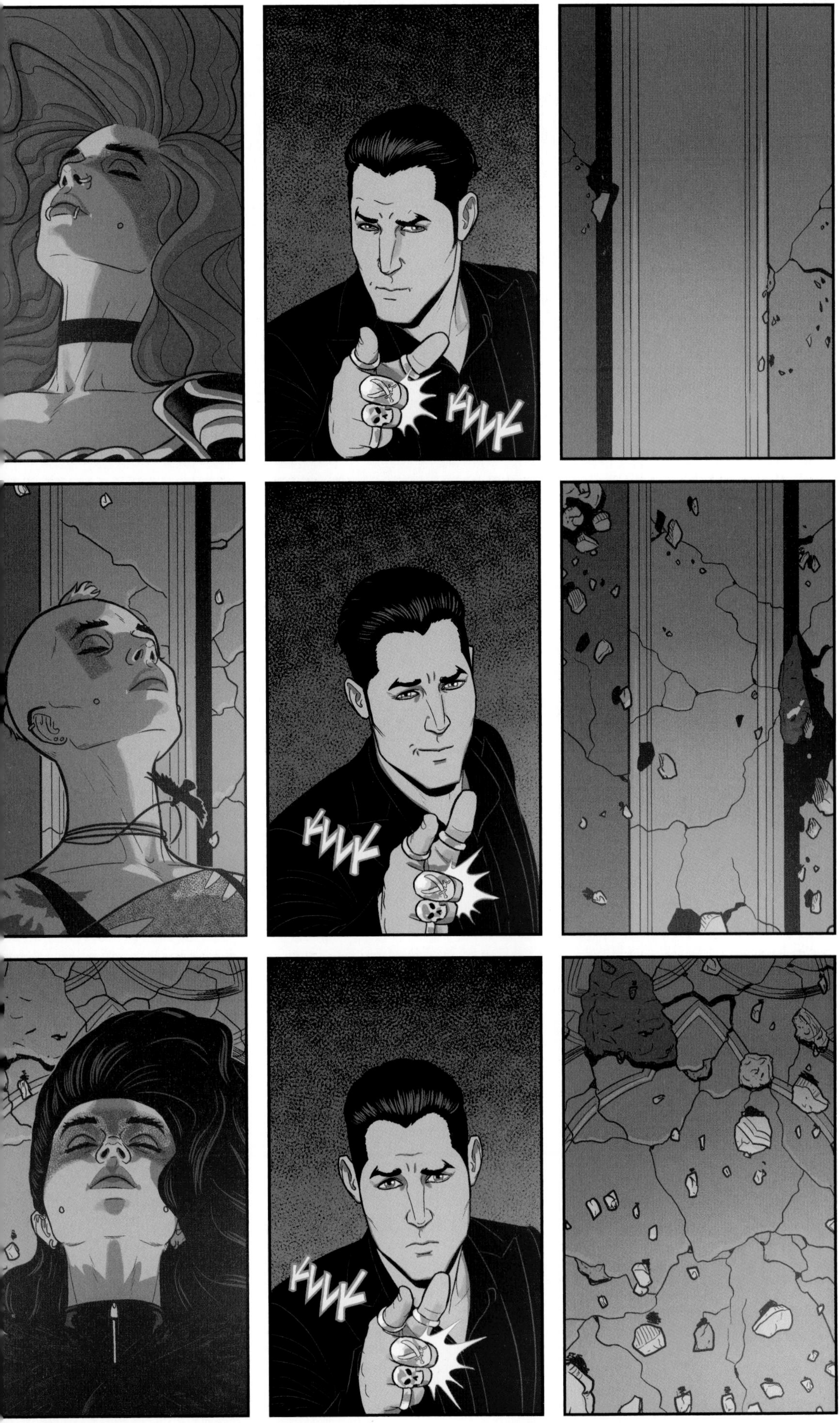
KLIK
KLIK
KLIK

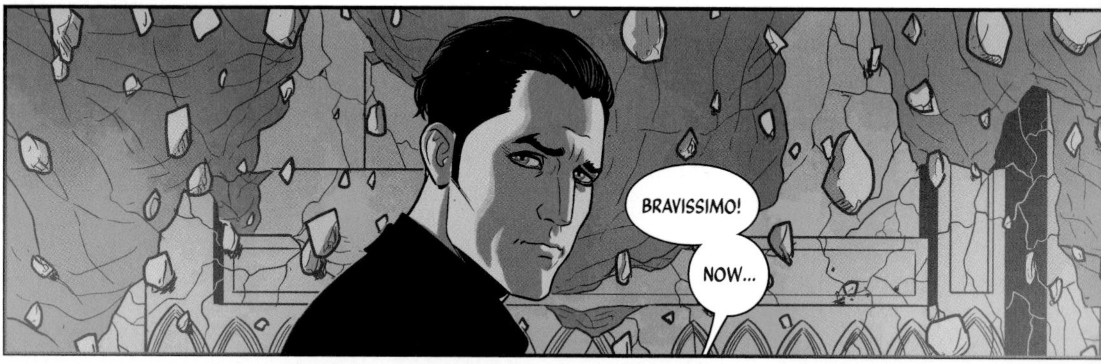
BRAVISSIMO!
NOW...

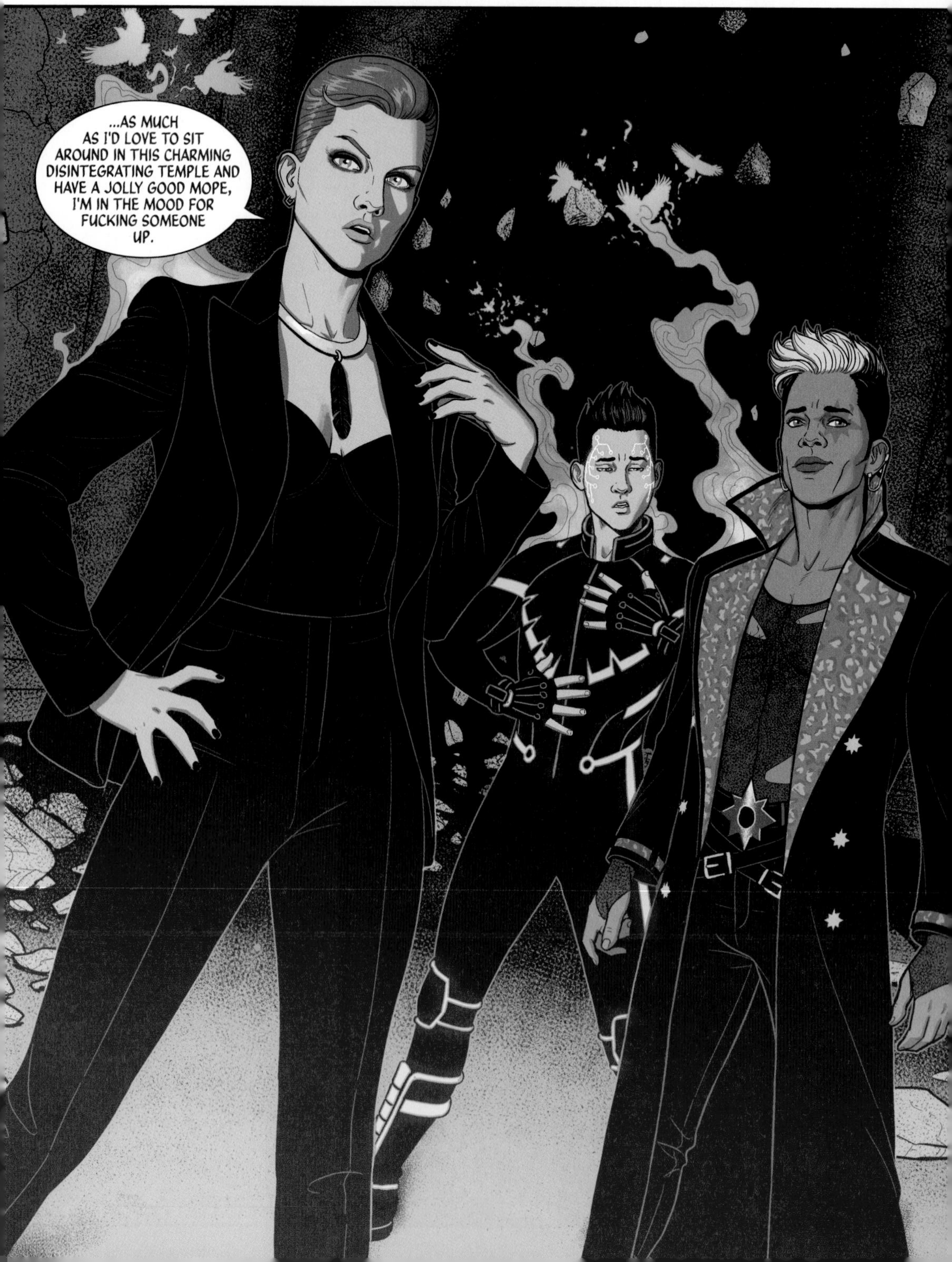
...AS MUCH AS I'D LOVE TO SIT AROUND IN THIS CHARMING DISINTEGRATING TEMPLE AND HAVE A JOLLY GOOD MOPE, I'M IN THE MOOD FOR FUCKING SOMEONE UP.

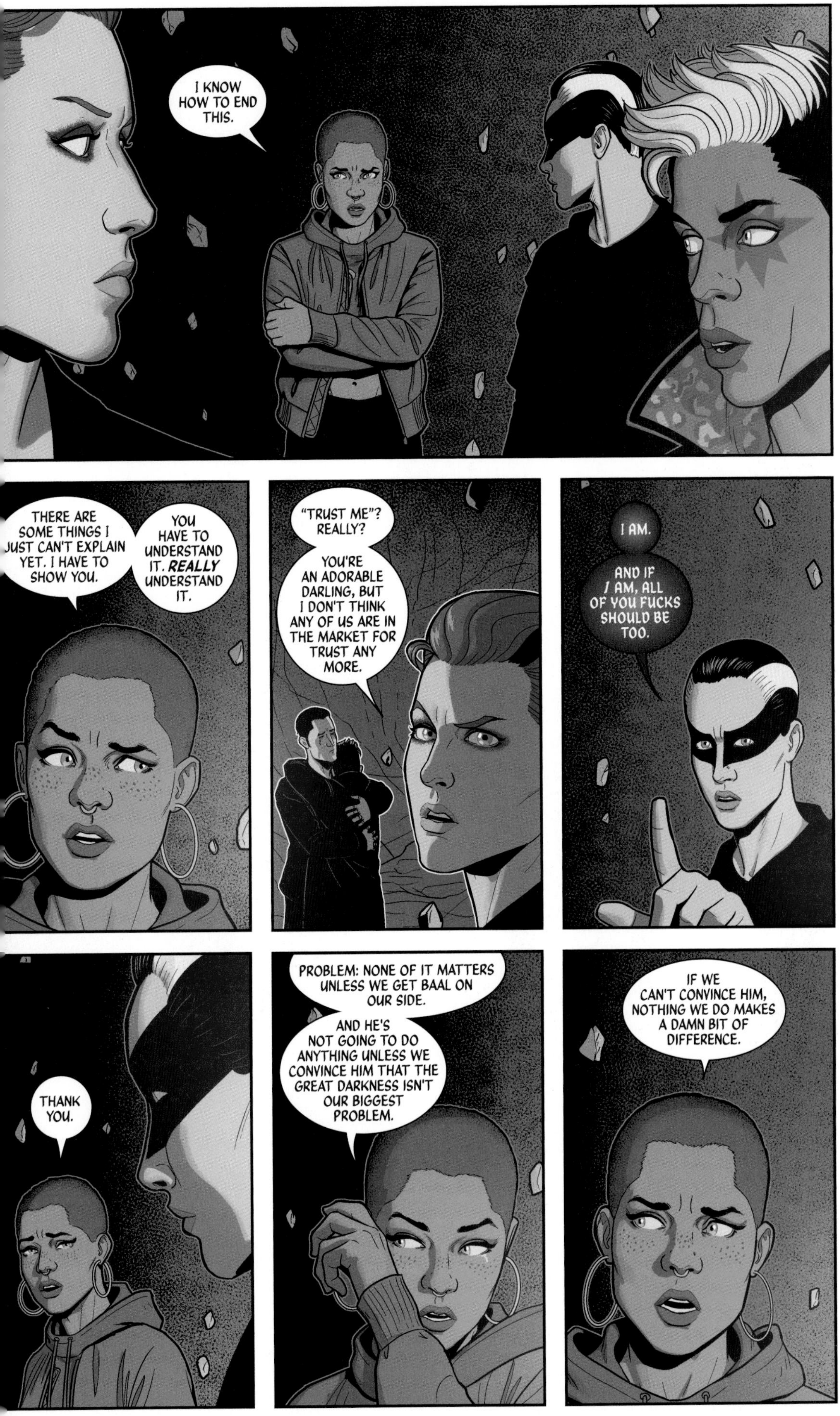
I KNOW HOW TO END THIS.
THERE ARE SOME THINGS I JUST CAN'T EXPLAIN YET. I HAVE TO SHOW YOU.
YOU HAVE TO UNDERSTAND IT. REALLY UNDERSTAND IT.
"TRUST ME"? REALLY?
YOU'RE AN ADORABLE DARLING, BUT I DON'T THINK ANY OF US ARE IN THE MARKET FOR TRUST ANY MORE.
I AM.
AND IF I AM, ALL OF YOU FUCKS SHOULD BE TOO.
THANK YOU.
PROBLEM: NONE OF IT MATTERS UNLESS WE GET BAAL ON OUR SIDE.
AND HE'S NOT GOING TO DO ANYTHING UNLESS WE CONVINCE HIM THAT THE GREAT DARKNESS ISN'T OUR BIGGEST PROBLEM.
IF WE CAN'T CONVINCE HIM, NOTHING WE DO MAKES A DAMN BIT OF DIFFERENCE.

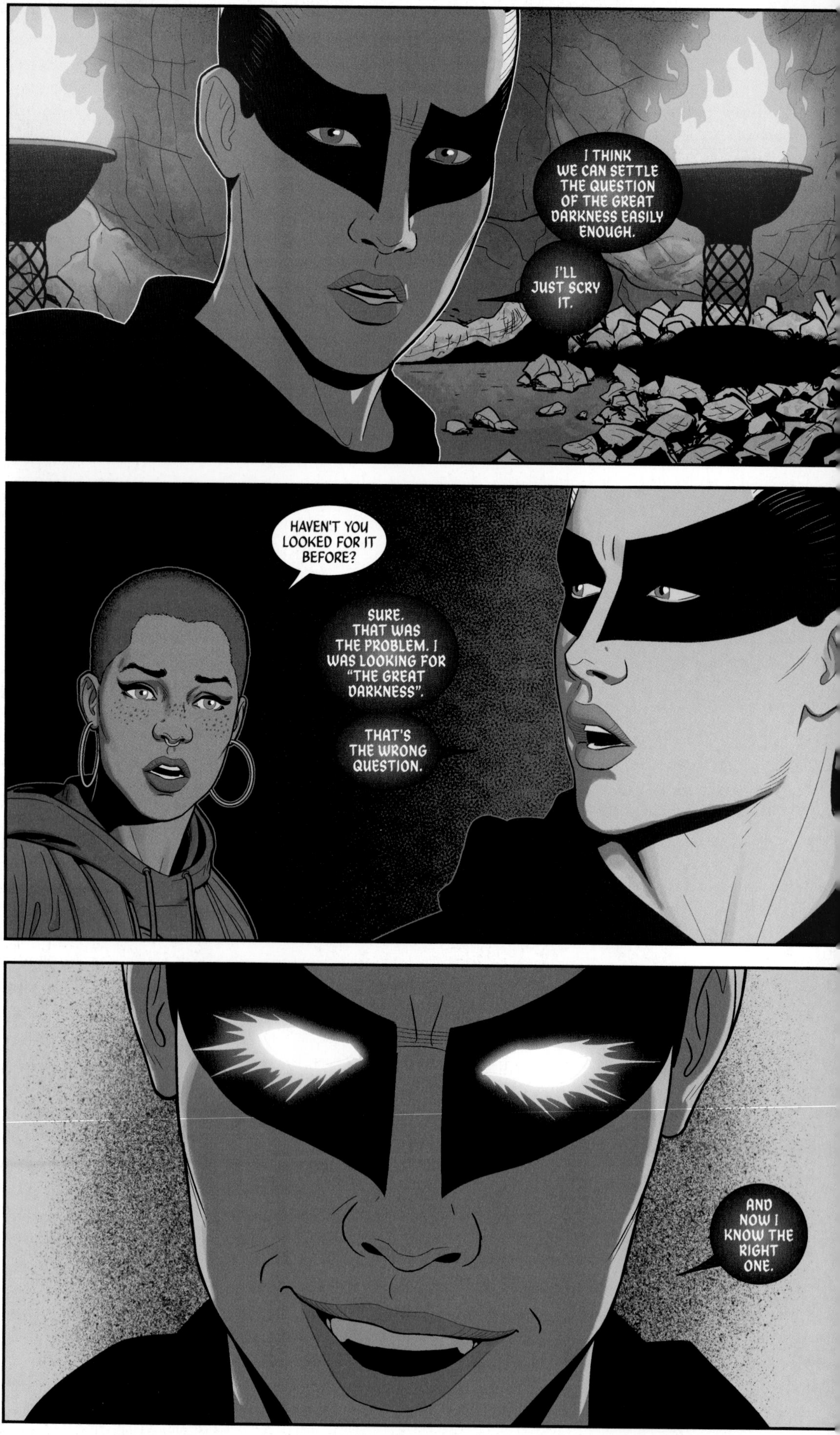
I THINK WE CAN SETTLE THE QUESTION OF THE GREAT DARKNESS EASILY ENOUGH.
I'LL JUST SCRY IT.
HAVEN'T YOU LOOKED FOR IT BEFORE?
SURE. THAT WAS THE PROBLEM. I WAS LOOKING FOR "THE GREAT DARKNESS".
THAT'S THE WRONG QUESTION.
AND NOW I KNOW THE RIGHT ONE.

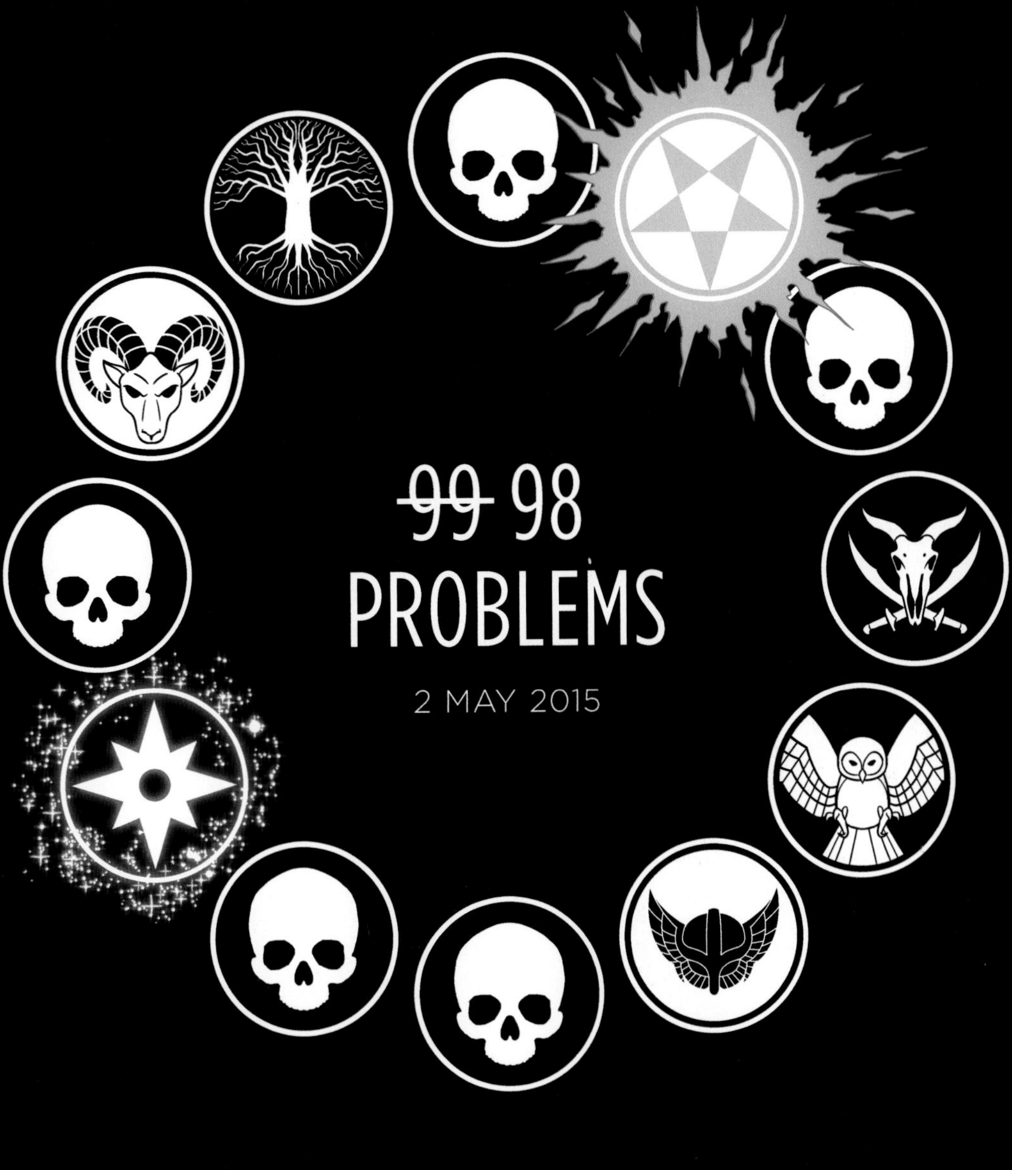

~~99~~ 98 PROBLEMS

2 MAY 2015

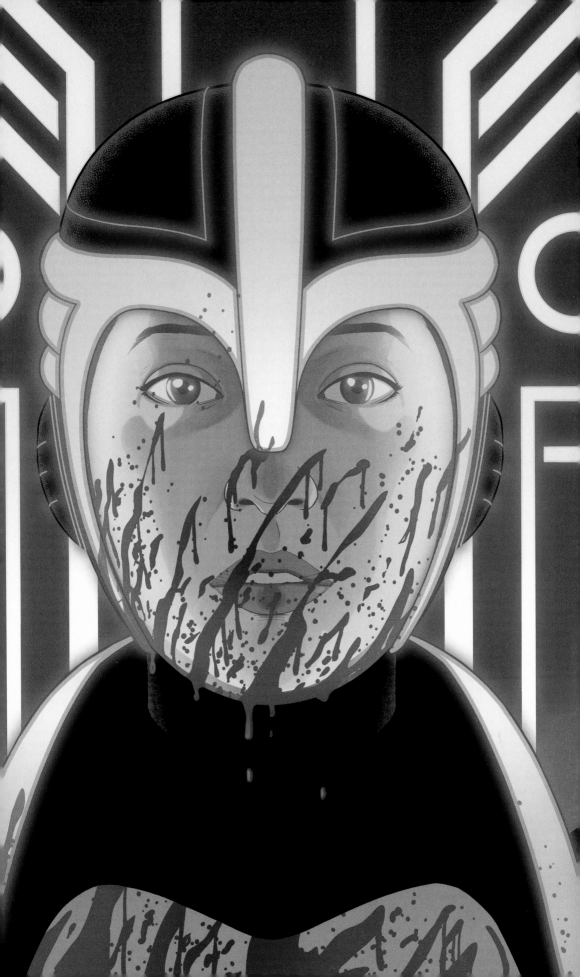

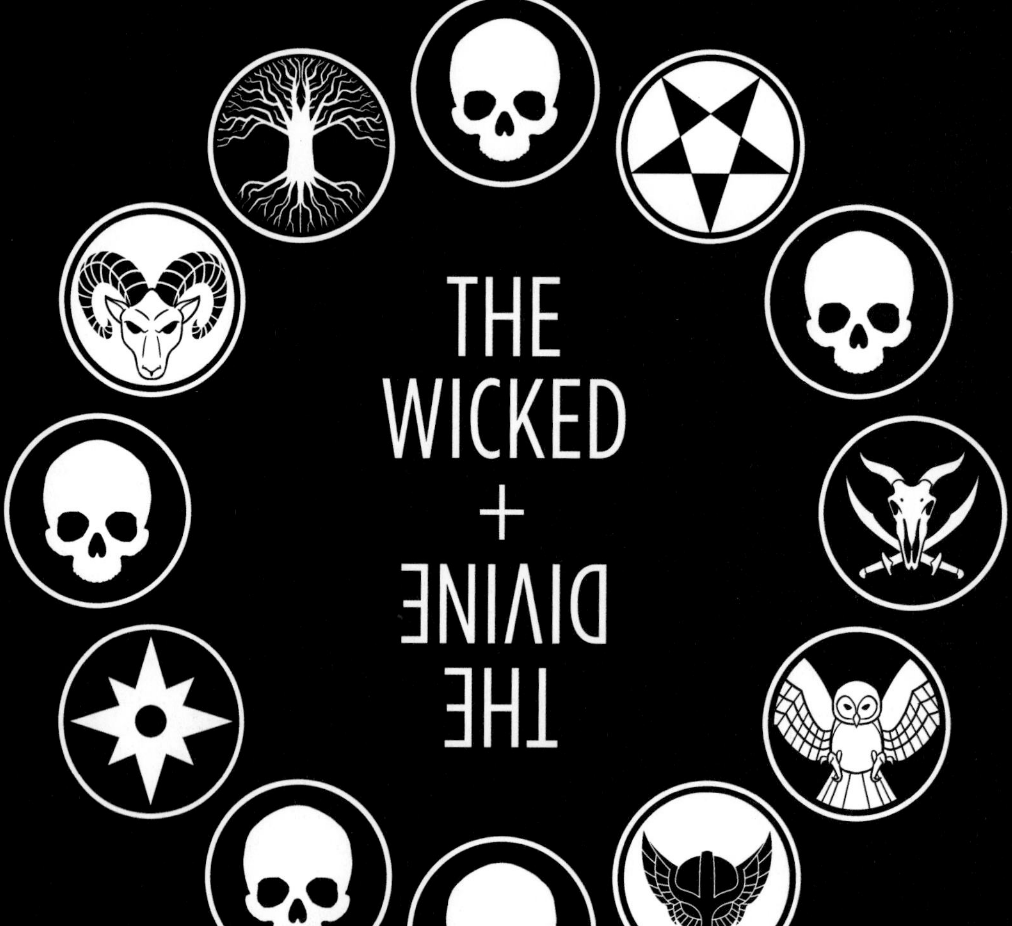
THE
WICKED
+
THE
DIVINE

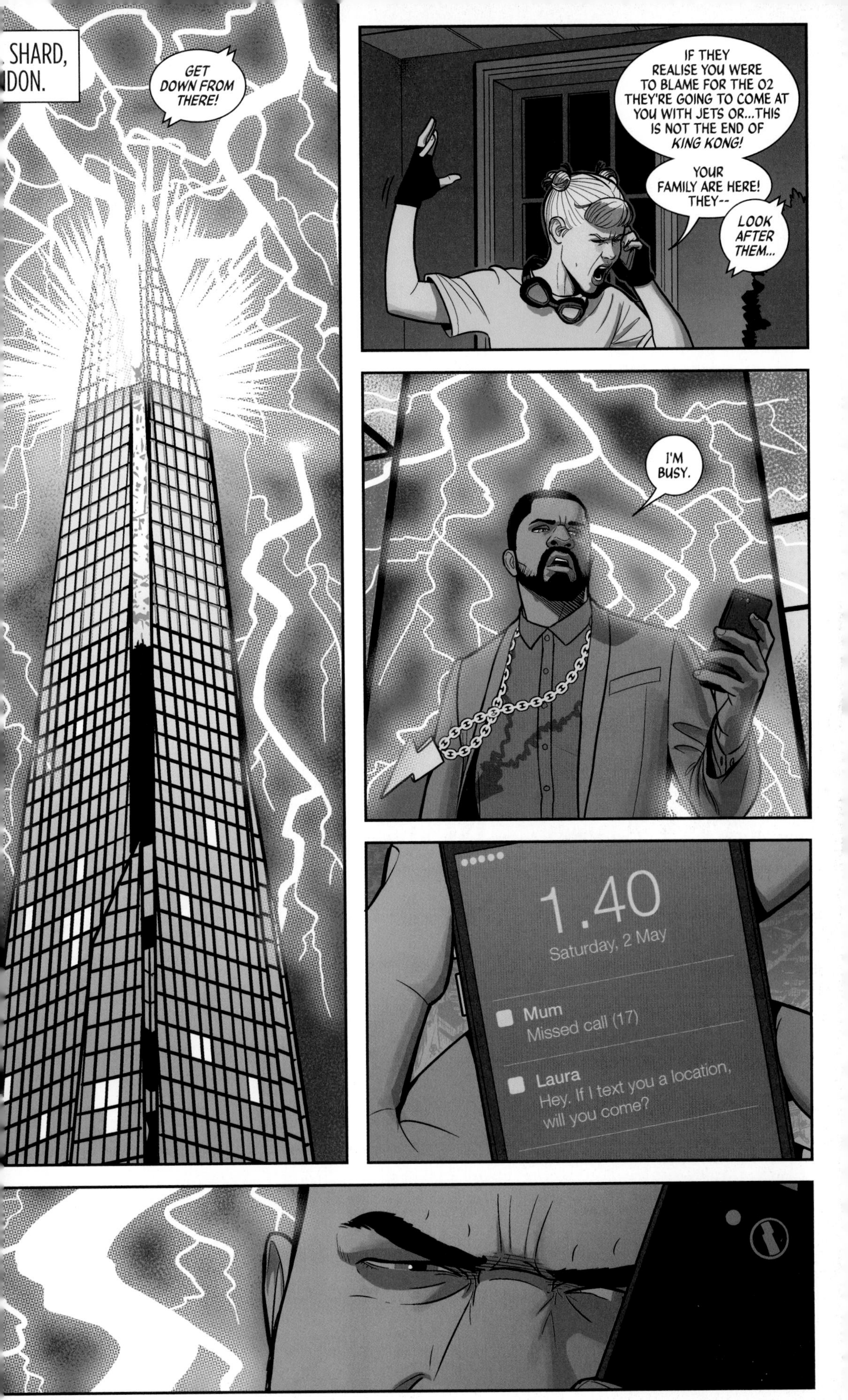

SHARD,
DON.
GET DOWN FROM THERE!
IF THEY REALISE YOU WERE TO BLAME FOR THE O2 THEY'RE GOING TO COME AT YOU WITH JETS OR...THIS IS NOT THE END OF KING KONG!
YOUR FAMILY ARE HERE! THEY--
LOOK AFTER THEM...
I'M BUSY.
1.40
Saturday, 2 May
Mum
Missed call (17)
Laura
Hey. If I text you a location, will you come?

THE TRUTH
WILL SET YOU
FREE AND/OR
KILL YOU

2 MAY 2015

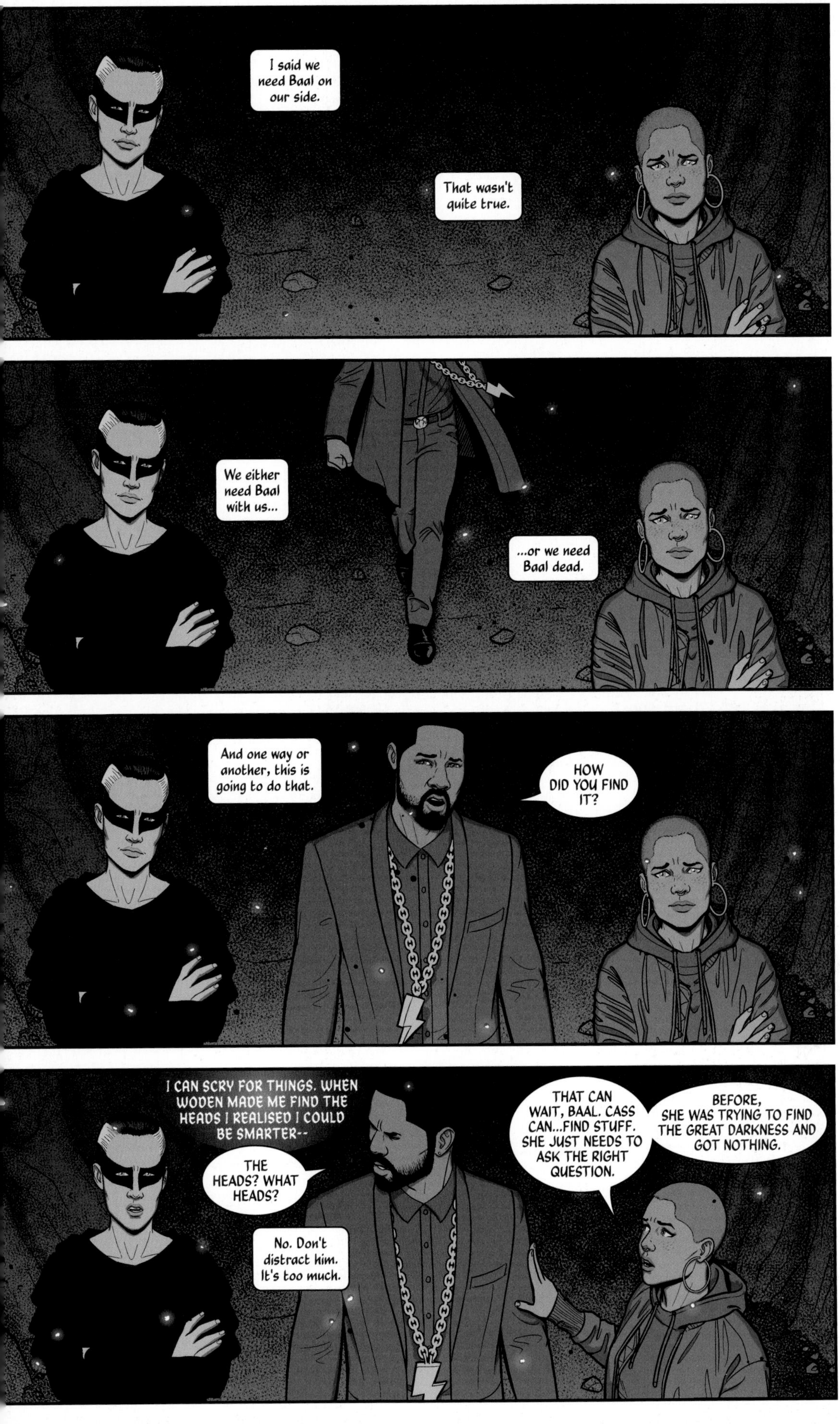

I said we need Baal on our side.
That wasn't quite true.
We either need Baal with us...
...or we need Baal dead.
And one way or another, this is going to do that.
HOW DID YOU FIND IT?
I CAN SCRY FOR THINGS. WHEN WODEN MADE ME FIND THE HEADS I REALISED I COULD BE SMARTER--
THE HEADS? WHAT HEADS?
No. Don't distract him. It's too much.
THAT CAN WAIT, BAAL. CASS CAN...FIND STUFF. SHE JUST NEEDS TO ASK THE RIGHT QUESTION.
BEFORE, SHE WAS TRYING TO FIND THE GREAT DARKNESS AND GOT NOTHING.

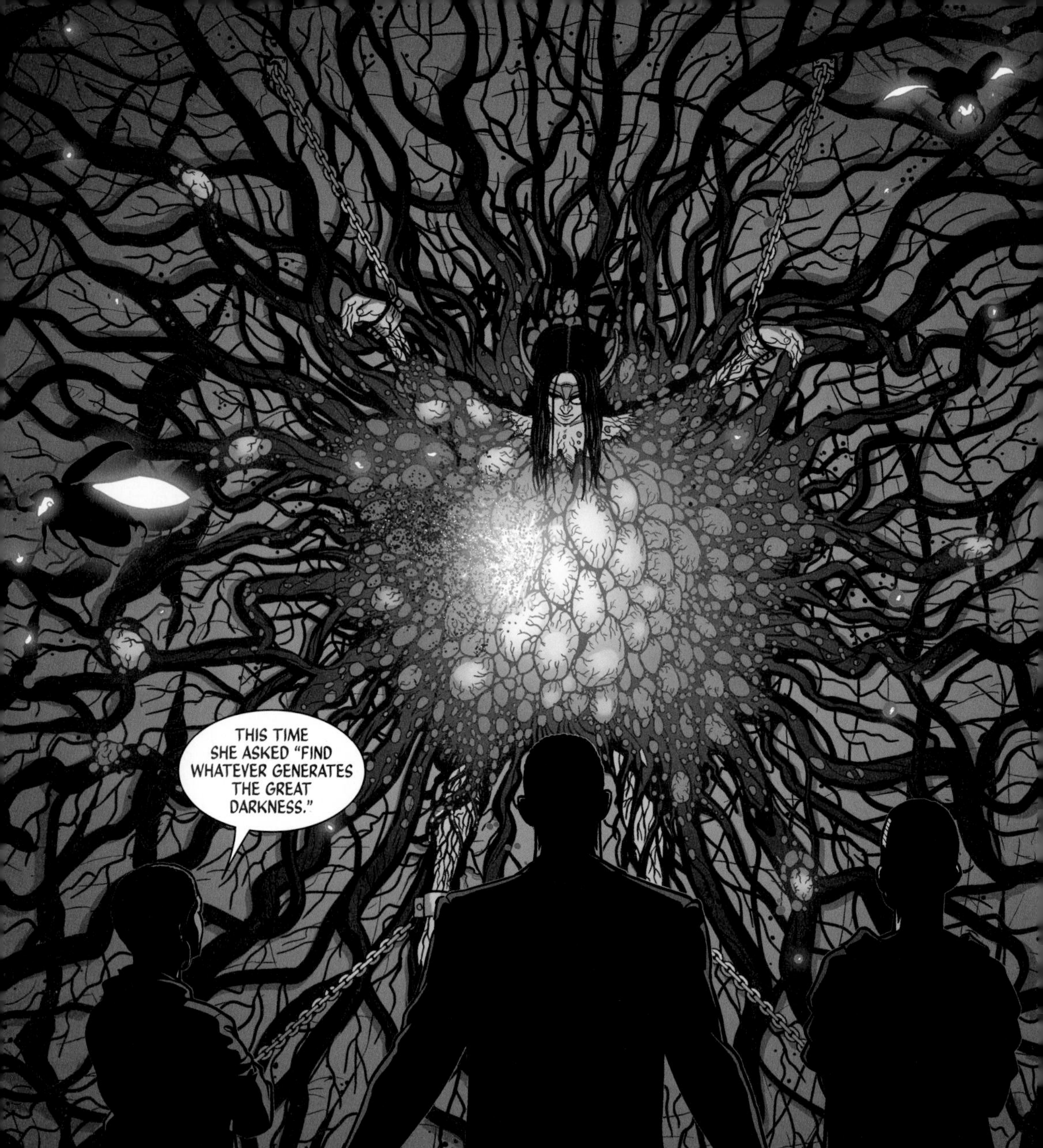
THIS TIME SHE ASKED "FIND WHATEVER GENERATES THE GREAT DARKNESS."

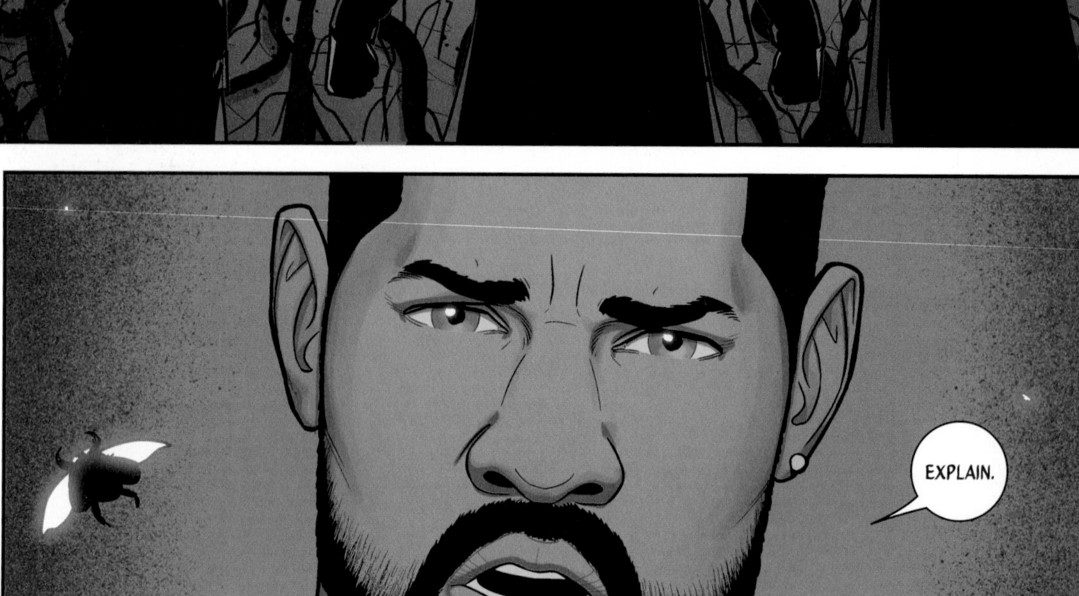
EXPLAIN.

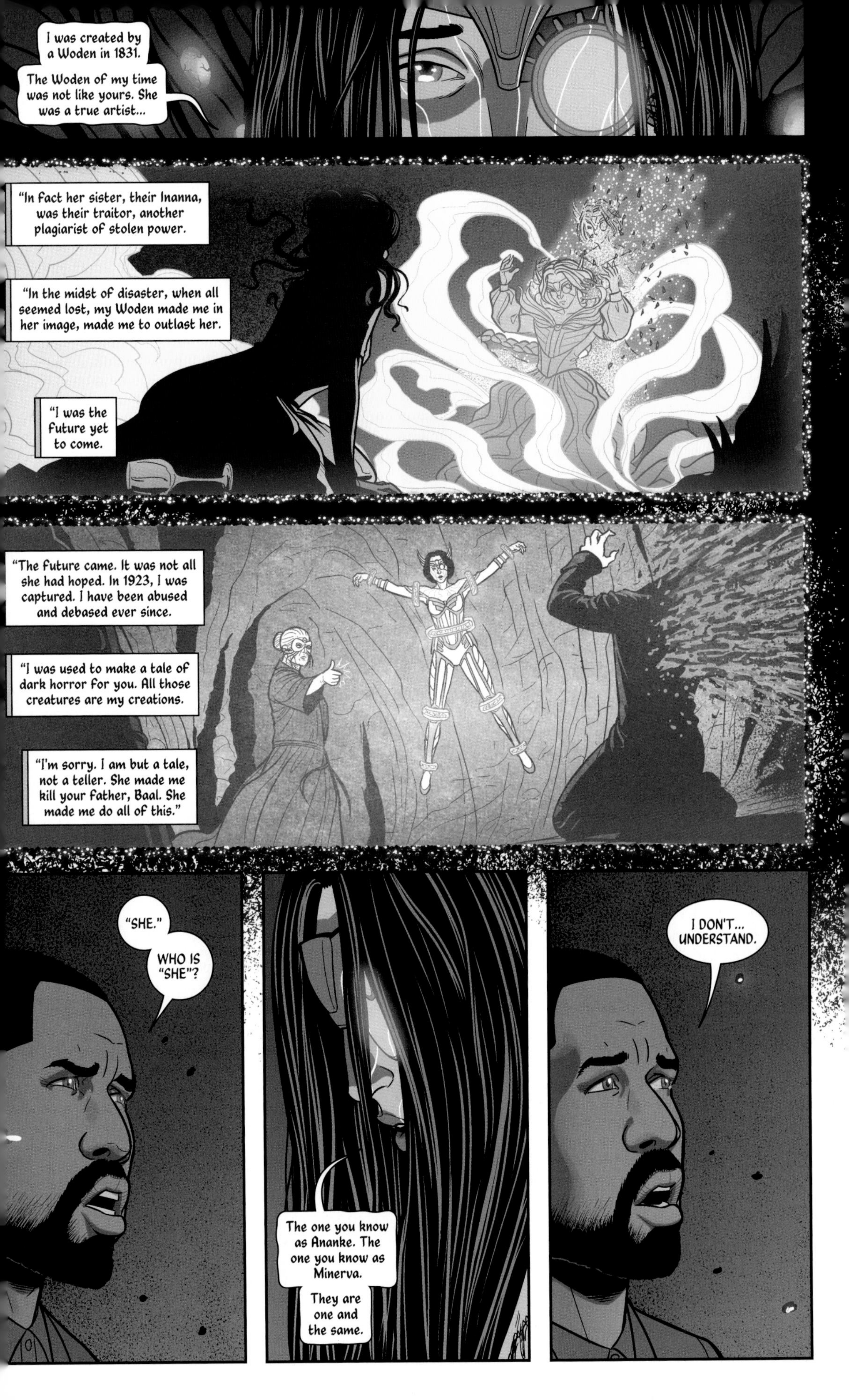
I was created by a Woden in 1831.
The Woden of my time was not like yours. She was a true artist...
"In fact her sister, their Inanna, was their traitor, another plagiarist of stolen power.
"In the midst of disaster, when all seemed lost, my Woden made me in her image, made me to outlast her.
"I was the future yet to come.
"The future came. It was not all she had hoped. In 1923, I was captured. I have been abused and debased ever since.
"I was used to make a tale of dark horror for you. All those creatures are my creations.
"I'm sorry. I am but a tale, not a teller. She made me kill your father, Baal. She made me do all of this."
"SHE."
WHO IS "SHE"?
The one you know as Ananke. The one you know as Minerva.
They are one and the same.
I DON'T... UNDERSTAND.

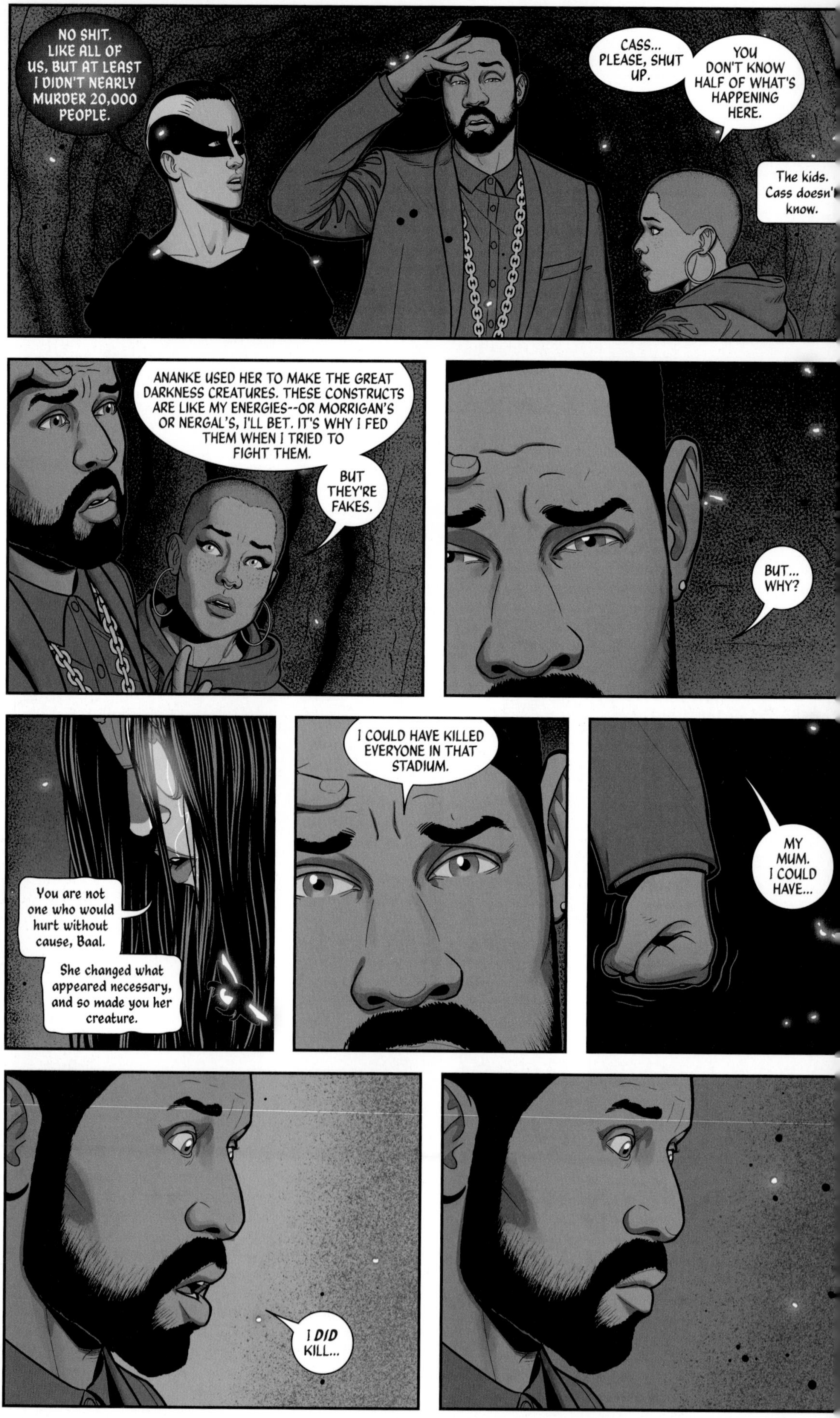
NO SHIT. LIKE ALL OF US, BUT AT LEAST I DIDN'T NEARLY MURDER 20,000 PEOPLE.
CASS... PLEASE, SHUT UP.
YOU DON'T KNOW HALF OF WHAT'S HAPPENING HERE.
The kids. Cass doesn't know.
ANANKE USED HER TO MAKE THE GREAT DARKNESS CREATURES. THESE CONSTRUCTS ARE LIKE MY ENERGIES--OR MORRIGAN'S OR NERGAL'S, I'LL BET. IT'S WHY I FED THEM WHEN I TRIED TO FIGHT THEM.
BUT THEY'RE FAKES.
BUT... WHY?
You are not one who would hurt without cause, Baal.
She changed what appeared necessary, and so made you her creature.
I COULD HAVE KILLED EVERYONE IN THAT STADIUM.
MY MUM. I COULD HAVE...
I *DID* KILL...

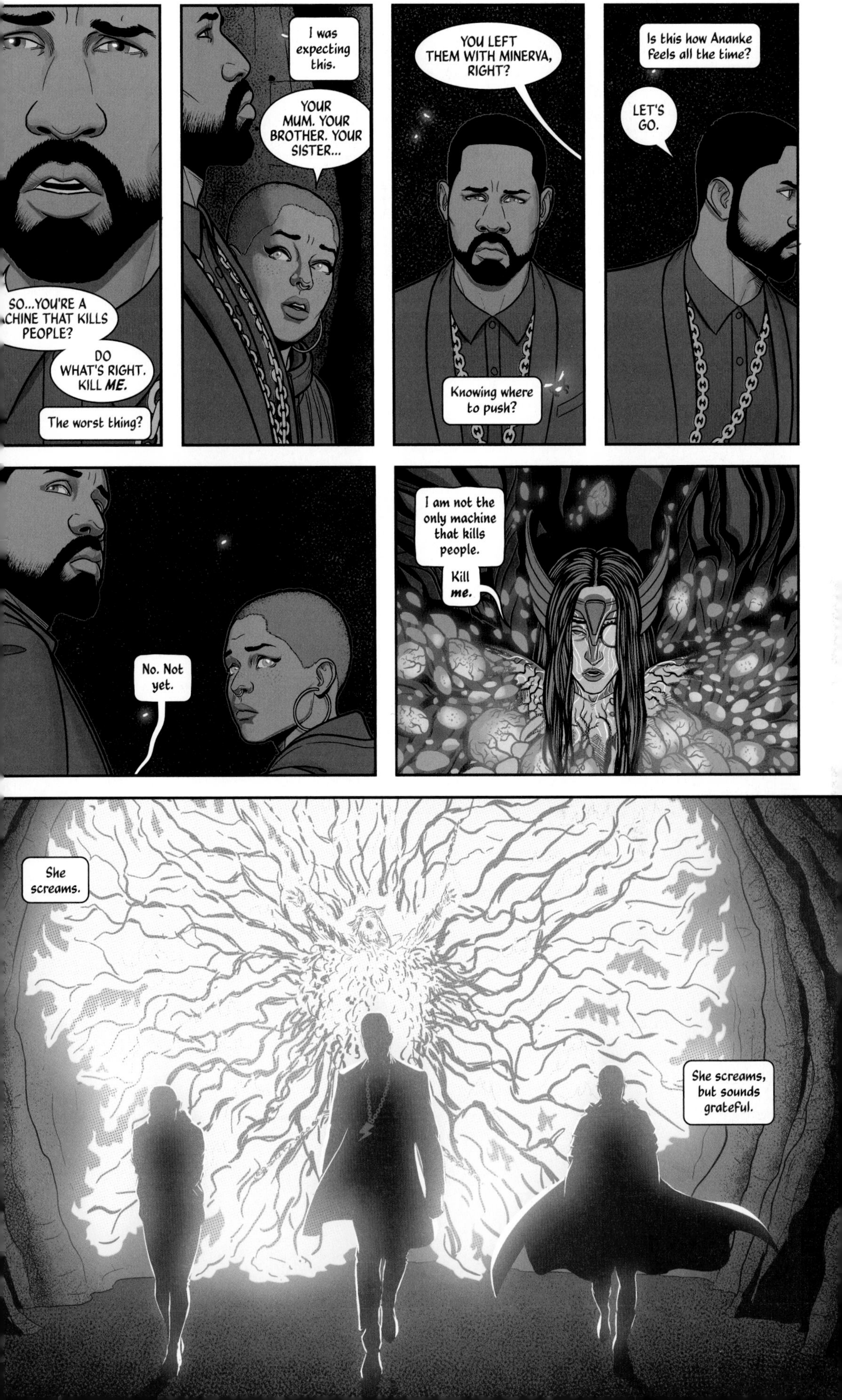
SO...YOU'RE A
CHINE THAT KILLS PEOPLE?
DO WHAT'S RIGHT. KILL ME.
The worst thing?
I was expecting this.
YOUR MUM. YOUR BROTHER. YOUR SISTER...
YOU LEFT THEM WITH MINERVA, RIGHT?
Knowing where to push?
Is this how Ananke feels all the time?
LET'S GO.
No. Not yet.
I am not the only machine that kills people.
Kill me.
She screams.
She screams, but sounds grateful.

THE UNDERGROUND.

TEXT FROM LAURA.

THEY'RE ALIVE. THEY'RE GOING TO BREAK OUT BAAL'S FAMILY AND THEN GET BACK.

WAIT...

...WHERE'S MIMIR?

DAD

HEY, DAD. DON'T WASTE TIME TRACING THIS. THE GREAT DARKNESS WAS MADE BY A MACHINE. ANANKE DID IT. ANANKE IS MINERVA. THEY'RE THE SAME PERSON. PLEASE. GET OUT.

SEND?

1 ao   2 abc   def 3
4 ghi   5 jkl   mno 6
7 pqrs   8 tuv

MIDLIFE CRISIS ON INFINITE FUCKWITS

2 MAY 2015

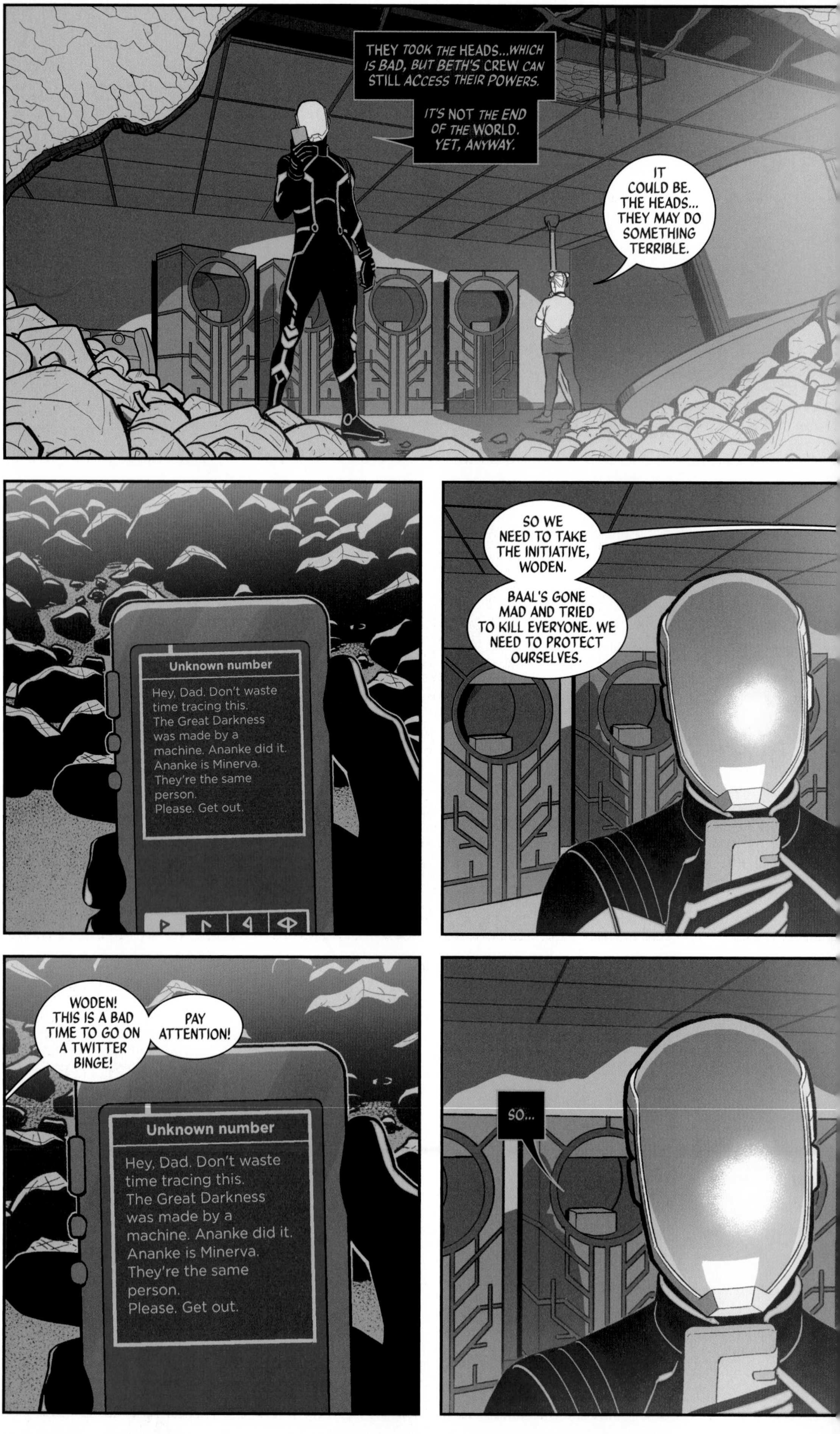
THEY TOOK THE HEADS...WHICH IS BAD, BUT BETH'S CREW CAN STILL ACCESS THEIR POWERS.
IT'S NOT THE END OF THE WORLD. YET, ANYWAY.
IT COULD BE. THE HEADS... THEY MAY DO SOMETHING TERRIBLE.
Unknown number
Hey, Dad. Don't waste time tracing this. The Great Darkness was made by a machine. Ananke did it. Ananke is Minerva. They're the same person. Please. Get out.
SO WE NEED TO TAKE THE INITIATIVE, WODEN.
BAAL'S GONE MAD AND TRIED TO KILL EVERYONE. WE NEED TO PROTECT OURSELVES.
WODEN! THIS IS A BAD TIME TO GO ON A TWITTER BINGE!
PAY ATTENTION!
Unknown number
Hey, Dad. Don't waste time tracing this. The Great Darkness was made by a machine. Ananke did it. Ananke is Minerva. They're the same person. Please. Get out.
SO...

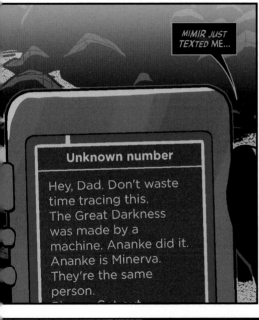

MIMIR JUST TEXTED ME...

Unknown number

Hey, Dad. Don't waste time tracing this. The Great Darkness was made by a machine. Ananke did it. Ananke is Minerva. They're the same person.

YOU'RE ANANKE.

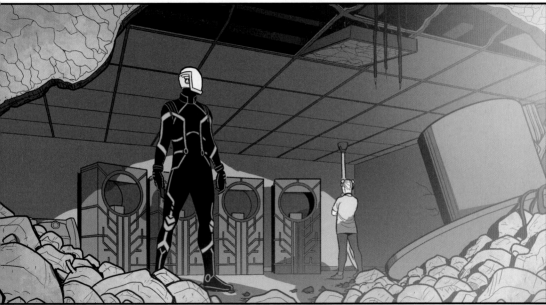

IT'S A NAME AS GOOD AS ANY.

IF WE'RE PLAYING BIG SECRET REVEALS...

kllk

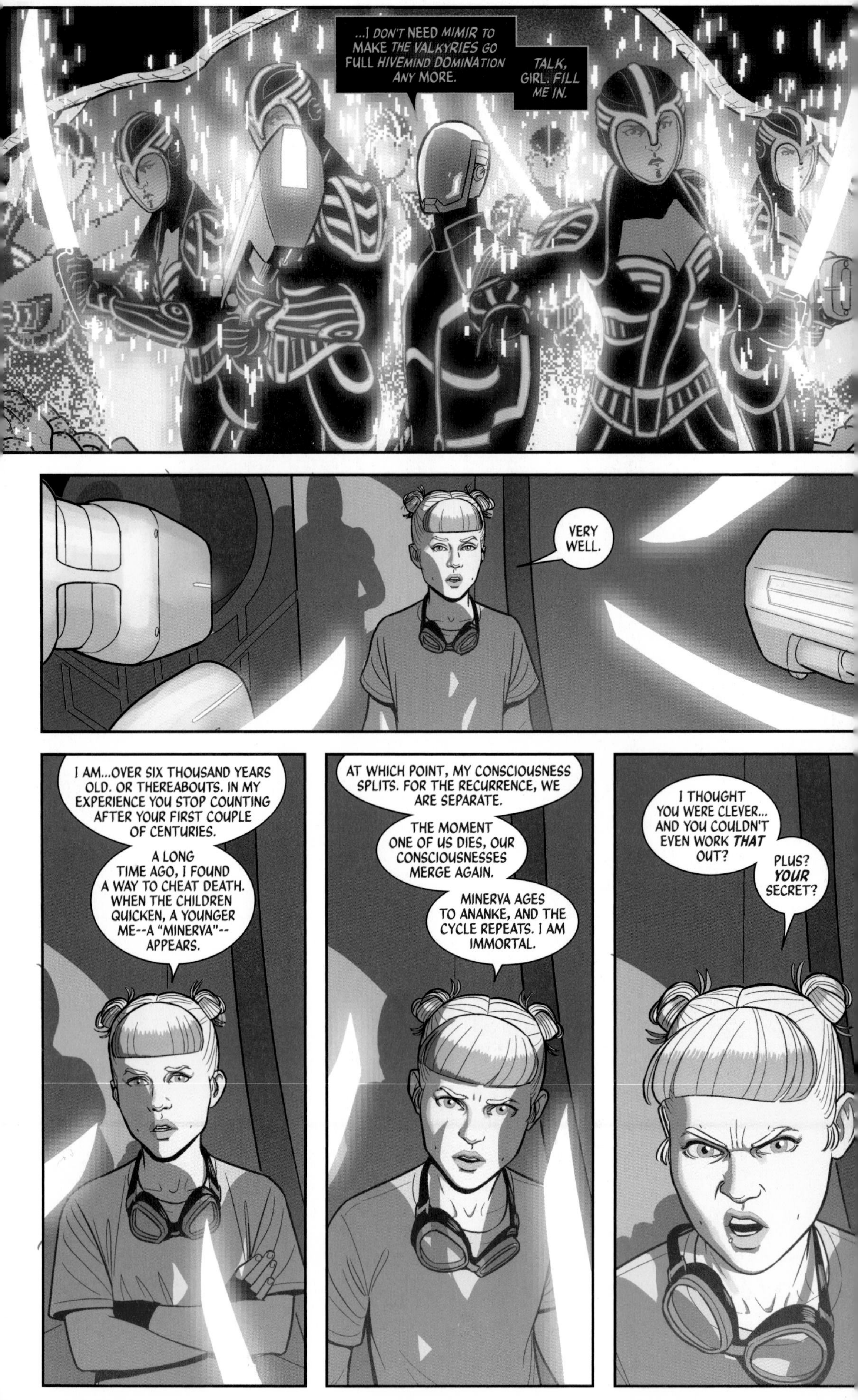
...I DON'T NEED MIMIR TO MAKE THE VALKYRIES GO FULL HIVEMIND DOMINATION ANY MORE.
TALK, GIRL. FILL ME IN.
VERY WELL.
I AM...OVER SIX THOUSAND YEARS OLD. OR THEREABOUTS. IN MY EXPERIENCE YOU STOP COUNTING AFTER YOUR FIRST COUPLE OF CENTURIES.
A LONG TIME AGO, I FOUND A WAY TO CHEAT DEATH. WHEN THE CHILDREN QUICKEN, A YOUNGER ME--A "MINERVA"--APPEARS.
AT WHICH POINT, MY CONSCIOUSNESS SPLITS. FOR THE RECURRENCE, WE ARE SEPARATE.
THE MOMENT ONE OF US DIES, OUR CONSCIOUSNESSES MERGE AGAIN.
MINERVA AGES TO ANANKE, AND THE CYCLE REPEATS. I AM IMMORTAL.
I THOUGHT YOU WERE CLEVER... AND YOU COULDN'T EVEN WORK THAT OUT?
PLUS? YOUR SECRET?

NO SECRET AT ALL.

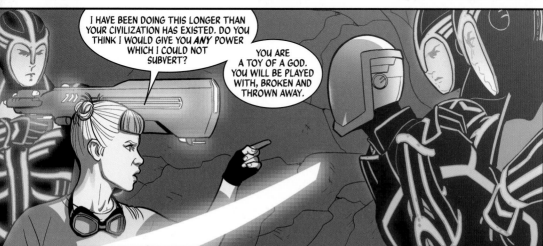

I HAVE BEEN DOING THIS LONGER THAN YOUR CIVILIZATION HAS EXISTED. DO YOU THINK I WOULD GIVE YOU *ANY* POWER WHICH I COULD NOT SUBVERT?

YOU ARE A TOY OF A GOD. YOU WILL BE PLAYED WITH, BROKEN AND THROWN AWAY.

WAIT! *SHE* NEEDED FOUR HEADS. SO *YOU* NEED FOUR HEADS...

I...I COULD LURE THEM HERE!

THE ONLY ONE WHO WOULD COME IS MIMIR. *HMM.* WE CAN PRESUME THEY WILL HAVE BODIES NOW, SOMEHOW? THAT CHANGES THINGS.

HOW ANNOYING. *MORE* DECAPITATION...

I CAN GET HIM TO WHERE YOU WANT. JUST LET ME GO.

I TAKE OFF THE COSTUME, AND I'M OUT OF THIS.

YOU WOULD DO THAT?

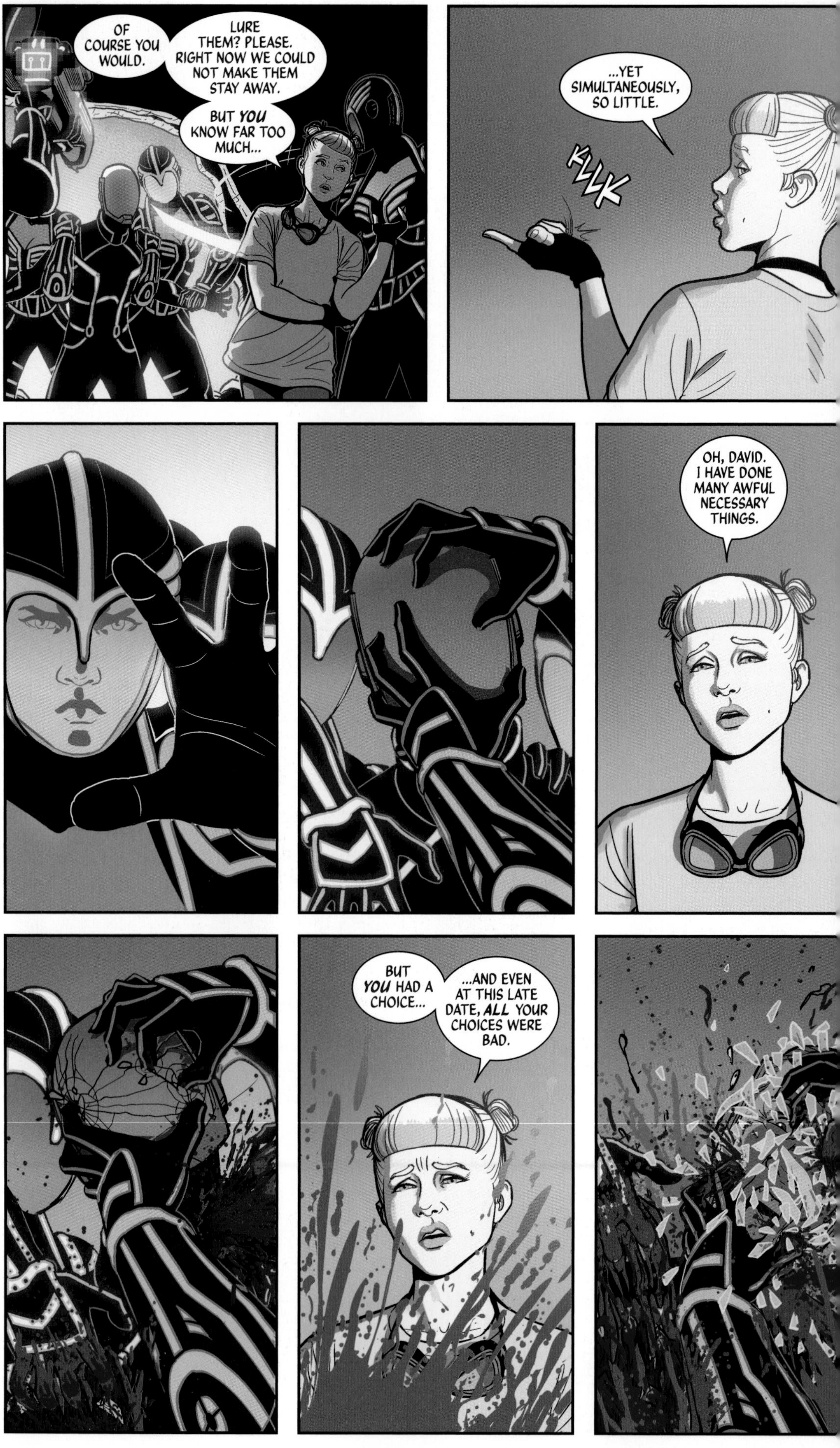
OF COURSE YOU WOULD.
LURE THEM? PLEASE. RIGHT NOW WE COULD NOT MAKE THEM STAY AWAY.
BUT *YOU* KNOW FAR TOO MUCH...
...YET SIMULTANEOUSLY, SO LITTLE.
KLIK
OH, DAVID. I HAVE DONE MANY AWFUL NECESSARY THINGS.
BUT *YOU* HAD A CHOICE...
...AND EVEN AT THIS LATE DATE, *ALL* YOUR CHOICES WERE BAD.

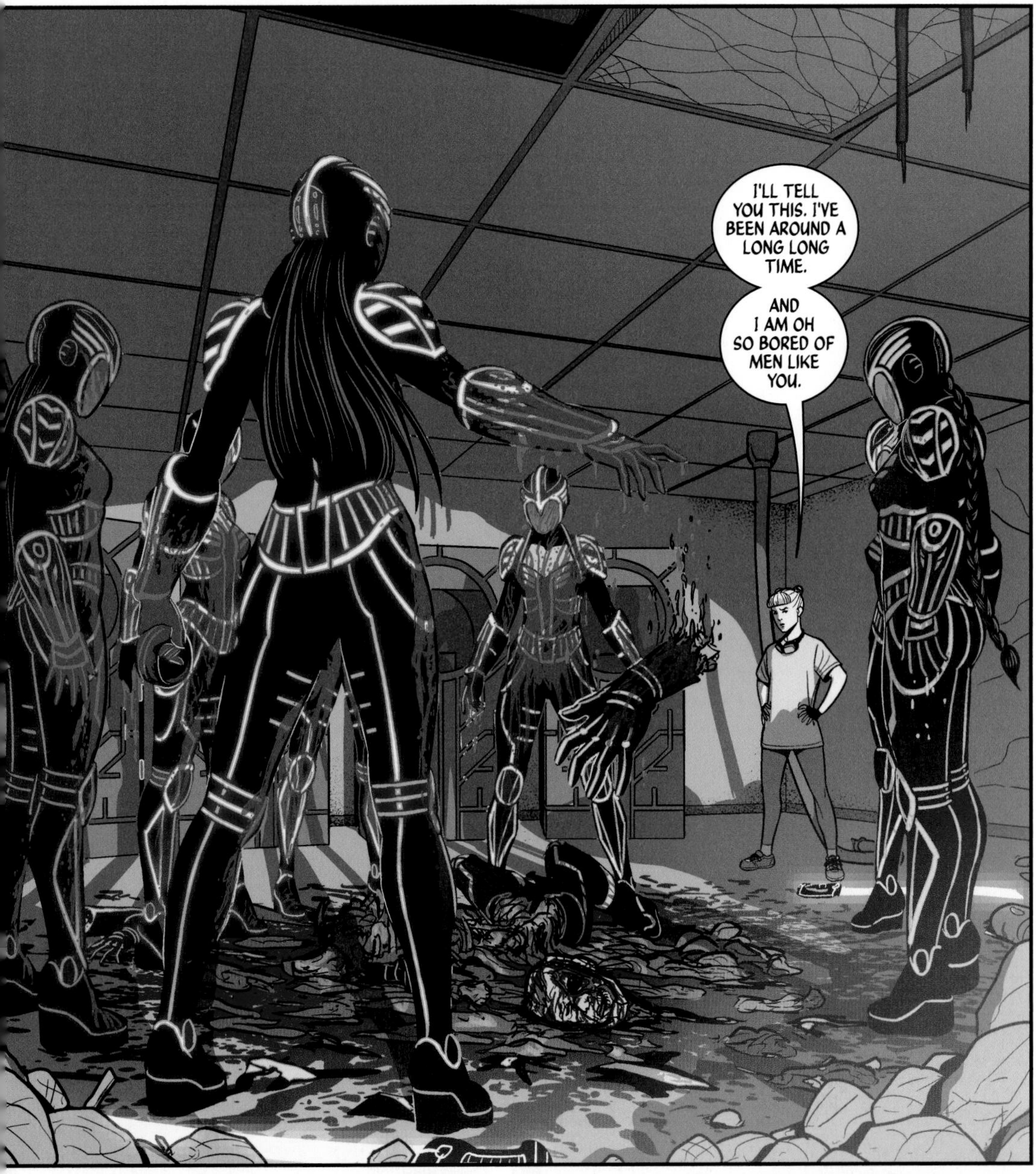
I'LL TELL YOU THIS. I'VE BEEN AROUND A LONG LONG TIME.
AND I AM OH SO BORED OF MEN LIKE YOU.

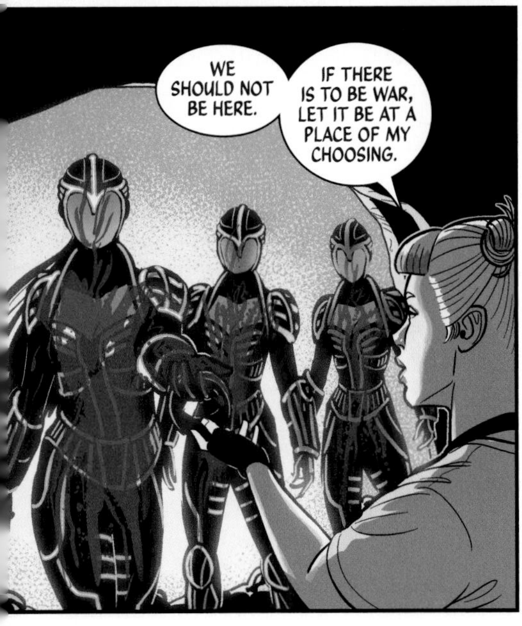
WE SHOULD NOT BE HERE.
IF THERE IS TO BE WAR, LET IT BE AT A PLACE OF MY CHOOSING.

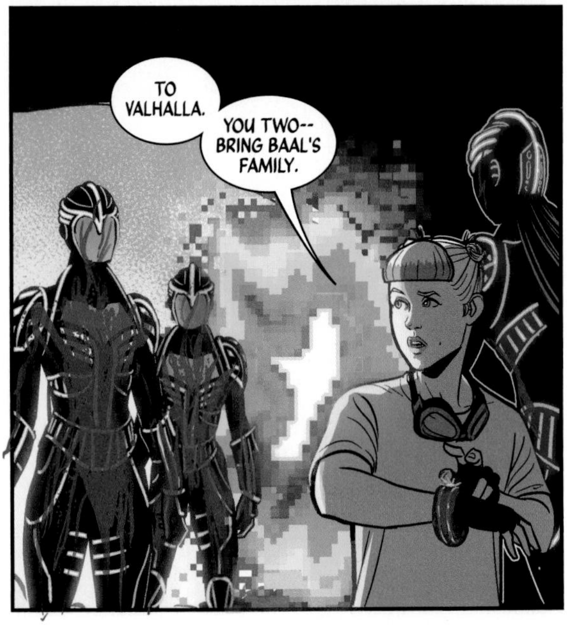
TO VALHALLA.
YOU TWO-- BRING BAAL'S FAMILY.

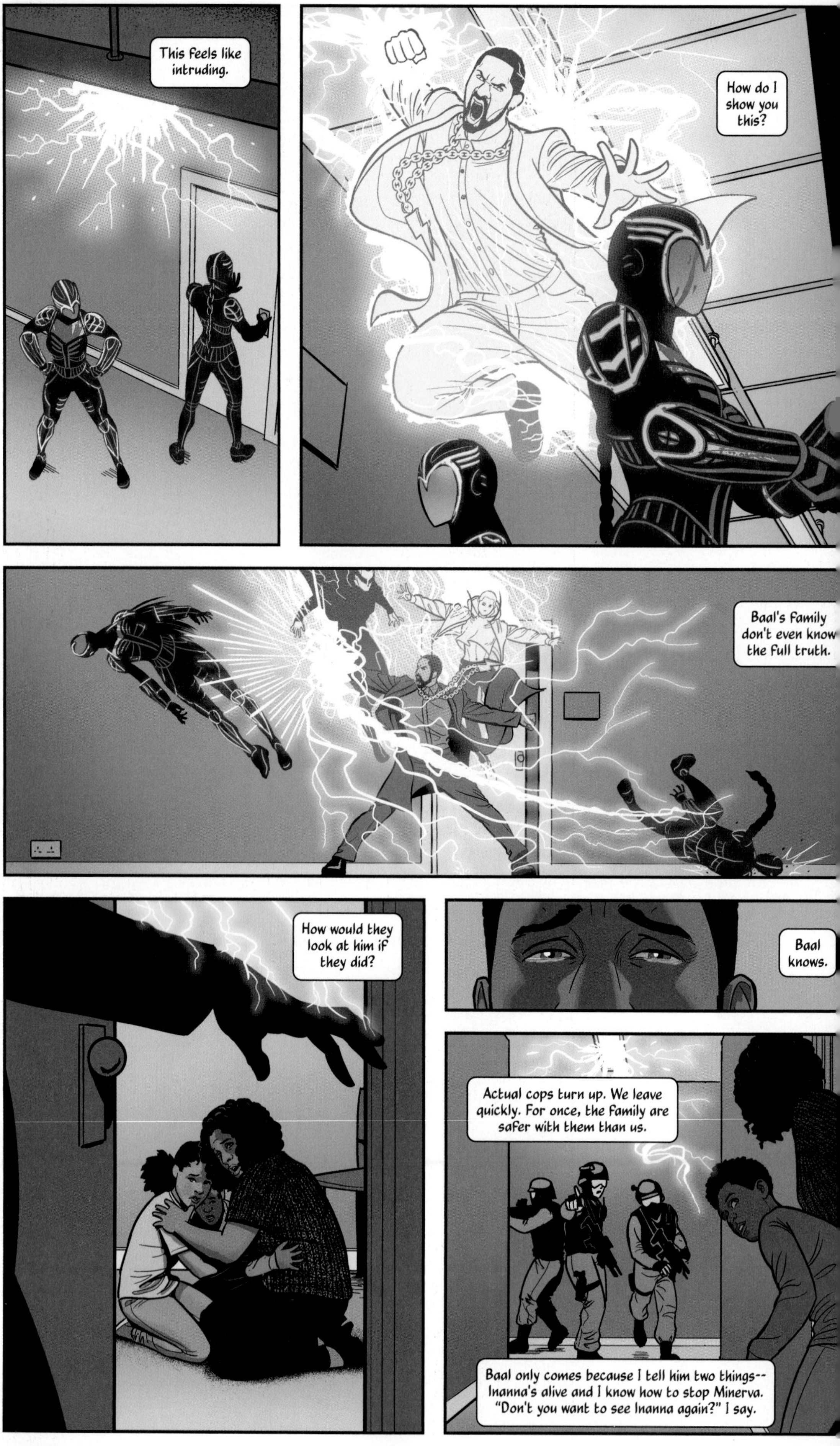
This feels like intruding.
How do I show you this?
Baal's family don't even know the full truth.
How would they look at him if they did?
Baal knows.
Actual cops turn up. We leave quickly. For once, the family are safer with them than us.
Baal only comes because I tell him two things-- Inanna's alive and I know how to stop Minerva. "Don't you want to see Inanna again?" I say.

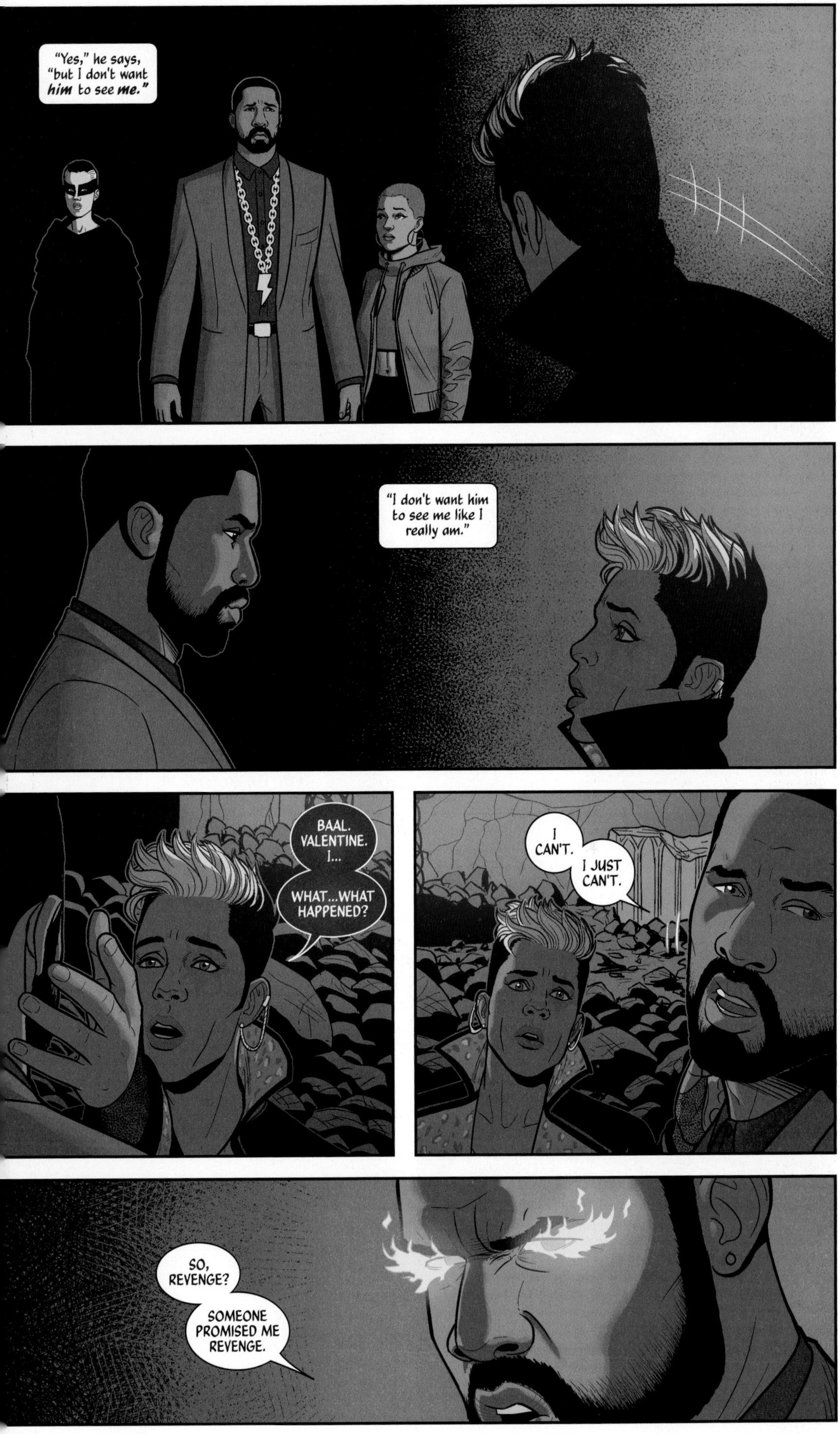
"Yes," he says, "but I don't want *him* to see *me.*"
"I don't want him to see me like I really am."
BAAL. VALENTINE. I...
WHAT...WHAT HAPPENED?
I CAN'T.
I JUST CAN'T.
SO, REVENGE?
SOMEONE PROMISED ME REVENGE.

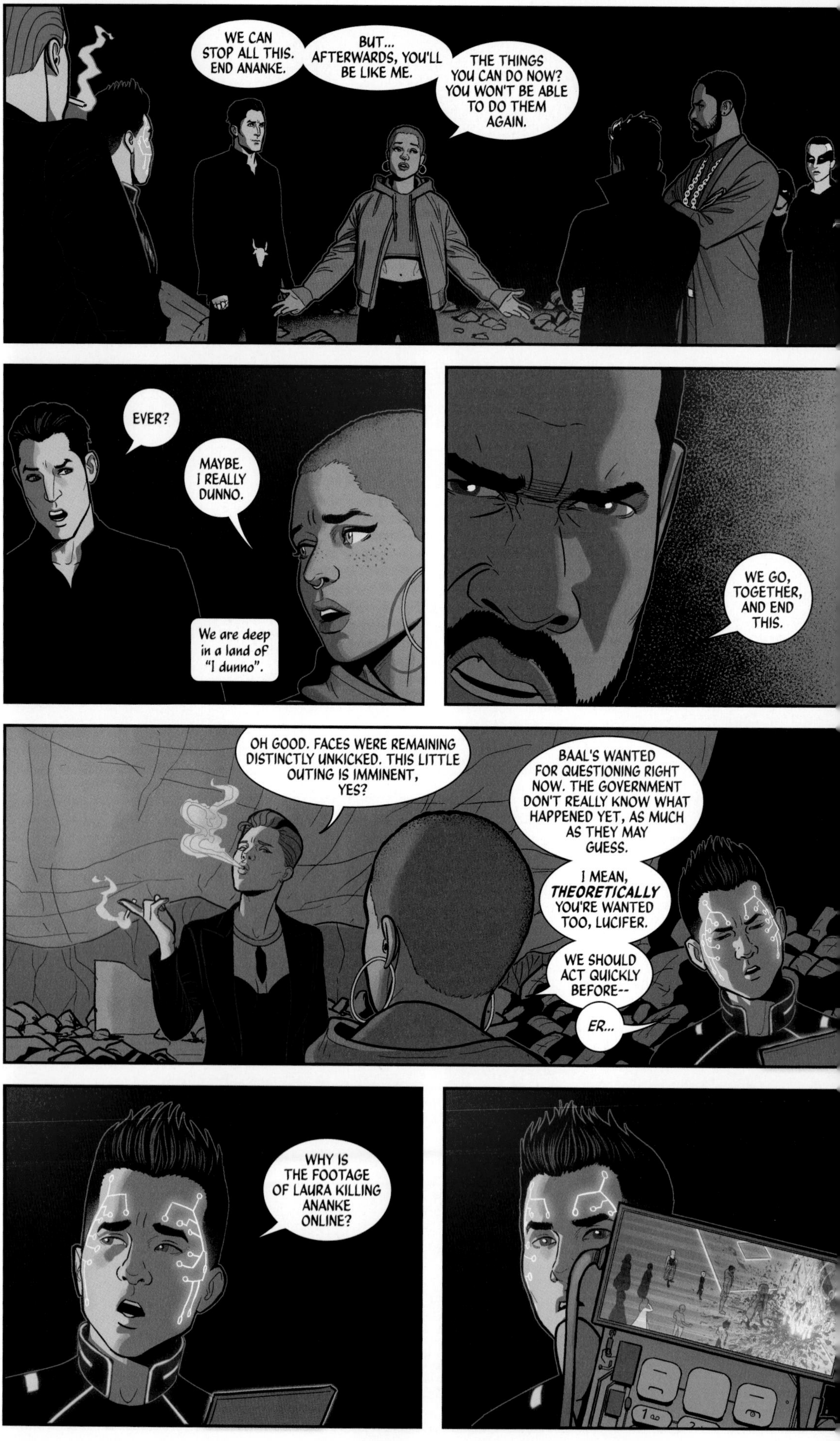
WE CAN STOP ALL THIS. END ANANKE.
BUT... AFTERWARDS, YOU'LL BE LIKE ME.
THE THINGS YOU CAN DO NOW? YOU WON'T BE ABLE TO DO THEM AGAIN.
EVER?
MAYBE. I REALLY DUNNO.
We are deep in a land of "I dunno".
WE GO, TOGETHER, AND END THIS.
OH GOOD. FACES WERE REMAINING DISTINCTLY UNKICKED. THIS LITTLE OUTING IS IMMINENT, YES?
BAAL'S WANTED FOR QUESTIONING RIGHT NOW. THE GOVERNMENT DON'T REALLY KNOW WHAT HAPPENED YET, AS MUCH AS THEY MAY GUESS.
I MEAN, THEORETICALLY YOU'RE WANTED TOO, LUCIFER.
WE SHOULD ACT QUICKLY BEFORE--
ER...
WHY IS THE FOOTAGE OF LAURA KILLING ANANKE ONLINE?

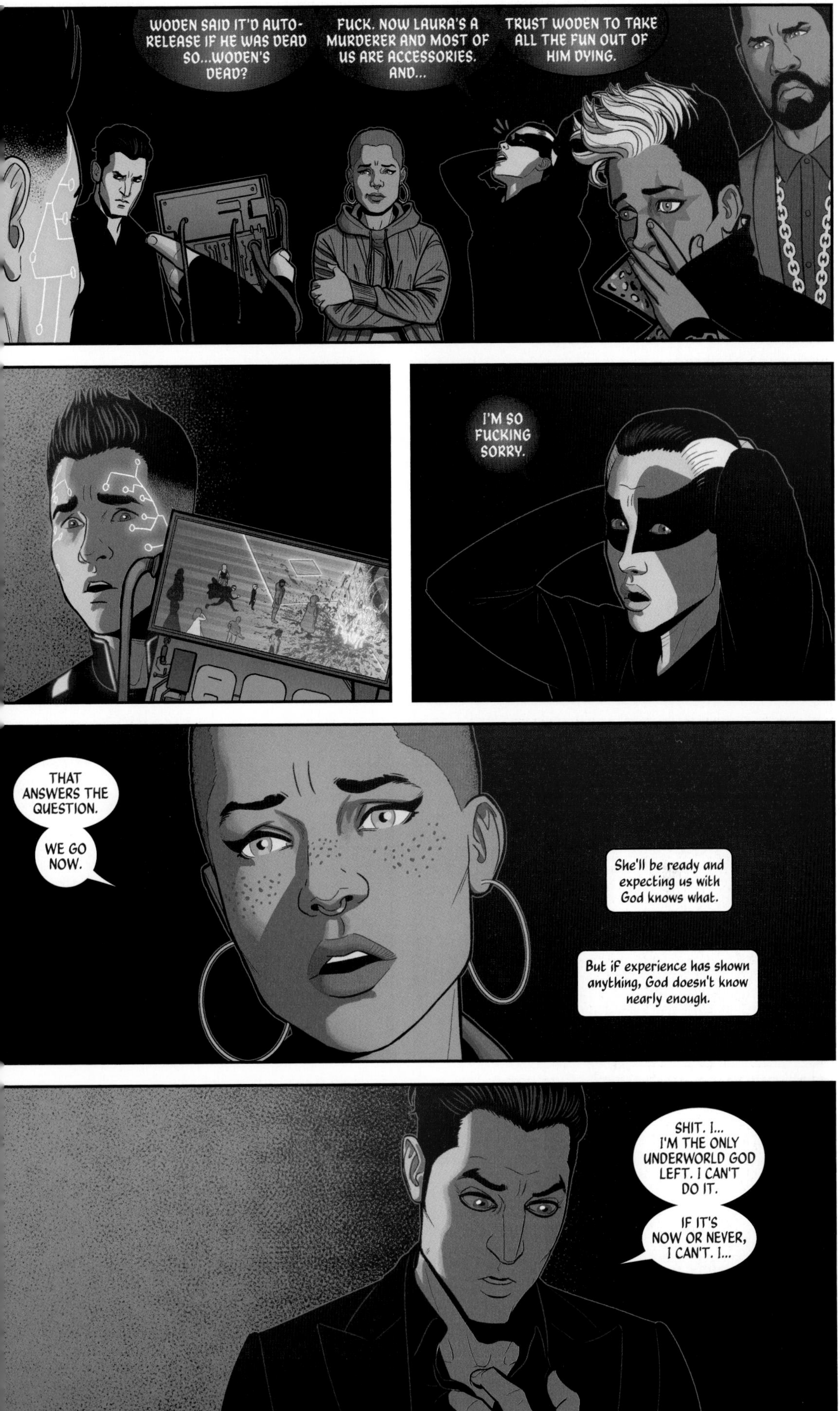
WODEN SAID IT'D AUTO-RELEASE IF HE WAS DEAD SO...WODEN'S DEAD?
FUCK. NOW LAURA'S A MURDERER AND MOST OF US ARE ACCESSORIES. AND...
TRUST WODEN TO TAKE ALL THE FUN OUT OF HIM DYING.
I'M SO FUCKING SORRY.
THAT ANSWERS THE QUESTION.
WE GO NOW.
She'll be ready and expecting us with God knows what.
But if experience has shown anything, God doesn't know nearly enough.
SHIT. I... I'M THE ONLY UNDERWORLD GOD LEFT. I CAN'T DO IT.
IF IT'S NOW OR NEVER, I CAN'T. I...

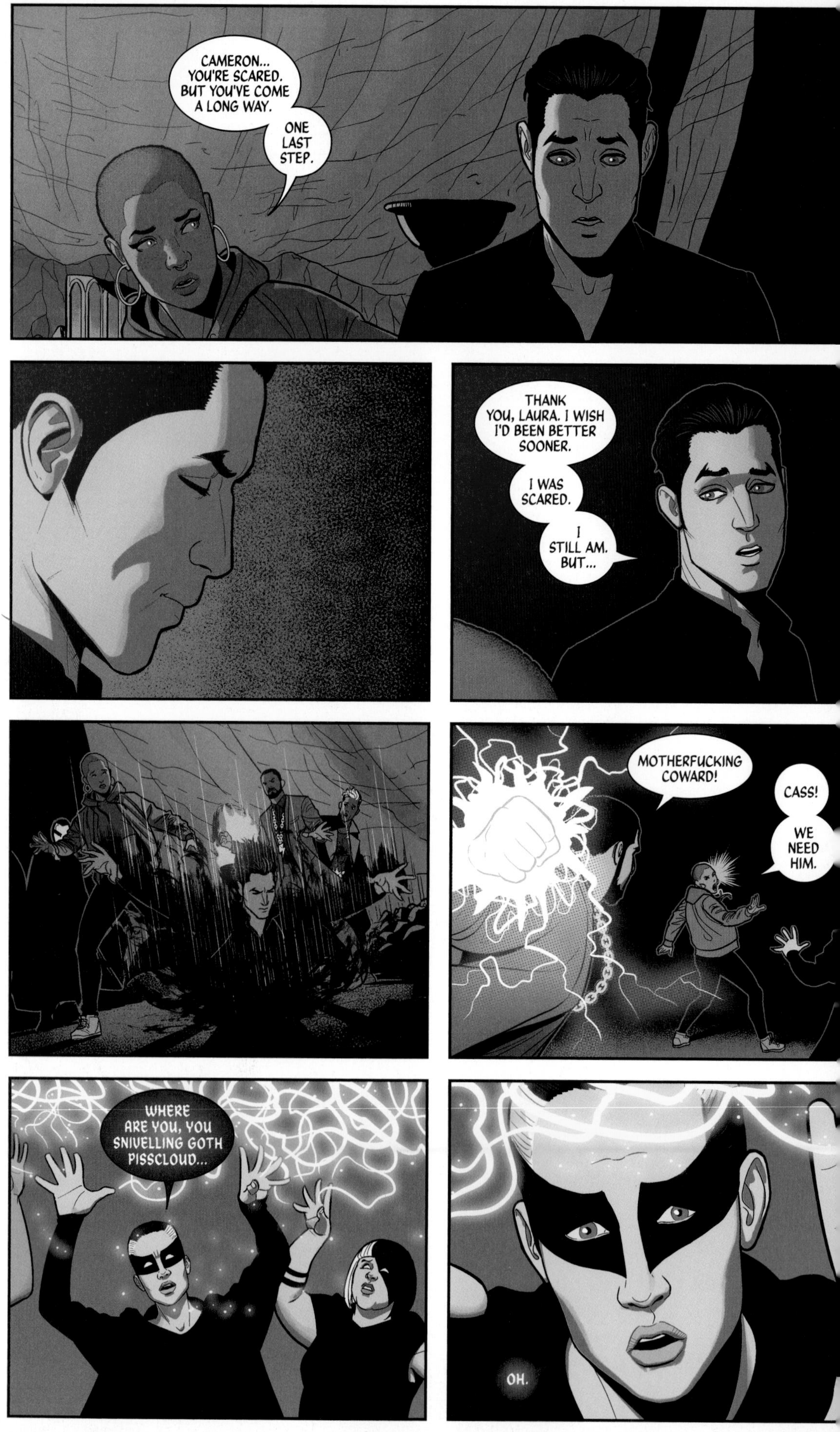
CAMERON... YOU'RE SCARED. BUT YOU'VE COME A LONG WAY.
ONE LAST STEP.
THANK YOU, LAURA. I WISH I'D BEEN BETTER SOONER.
I WAS SCARED.
I STILL AM. BUT...
MOTHERFUCKING COWARD!
CASS!
WE NEED HIM.
WHERE ARE YOU, YOU SNIVELLING GOTH PISSCLOUD...
OH.

HELL IS
OTHER PEOPLE

2 MAY 2015

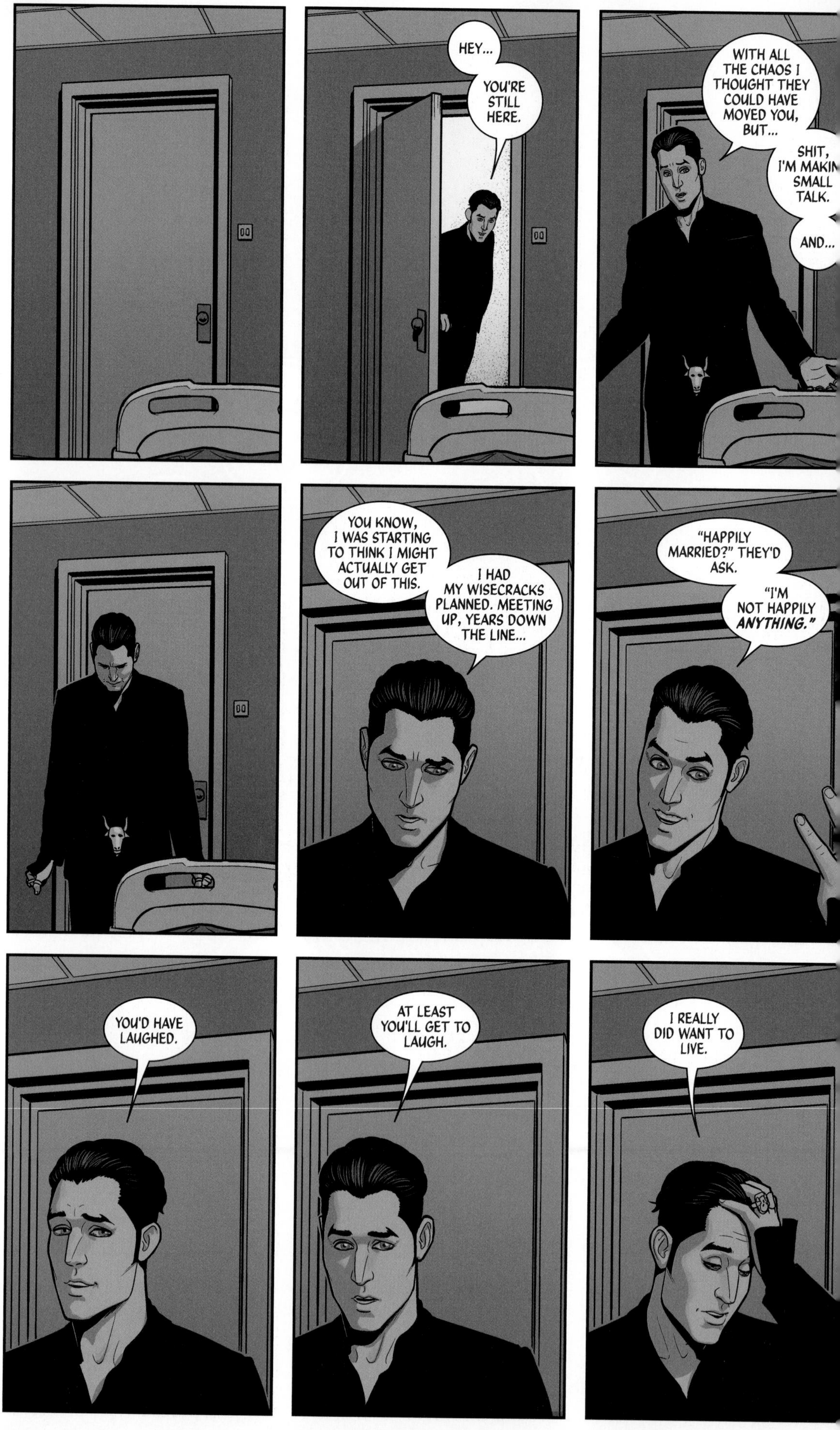
HEY...
YOU'RE STILL HERE.
WITH ALL THE CHAOS I THOUGHT THEY COULD HAVE MOVED YOU, BUT...
SHIT, I'M MAKIN SMALL TALK.
AND...
YOU KNOW, I WAS STARTING TO THINK I MIGHT ACTUALLY GET OUT OF THIS.
I HAD MY WISECRACKS PLANNED. MEETING UP, YEARS DOWN THE LINE...
"HAPPILY MARRIED?" THEY'D ASK.
"I'M NOT HAPPILY ANYTHING."
YOU'D HAVE LAUGHED.
AT LEAST YOU'LL GET TO LAUGH.
I REALLY DID WANT TO LIVE.

WE DON'T GET EVERYTHING WE WANT, DO WE?

WE HAVE TO CHOOSE WHAT REALLY MATTERS.

FUCKING HELL.

YOU'RE NOT DEAD...

...YOU'RE JUST SLEEPING.

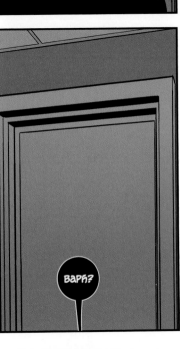

BAPH?

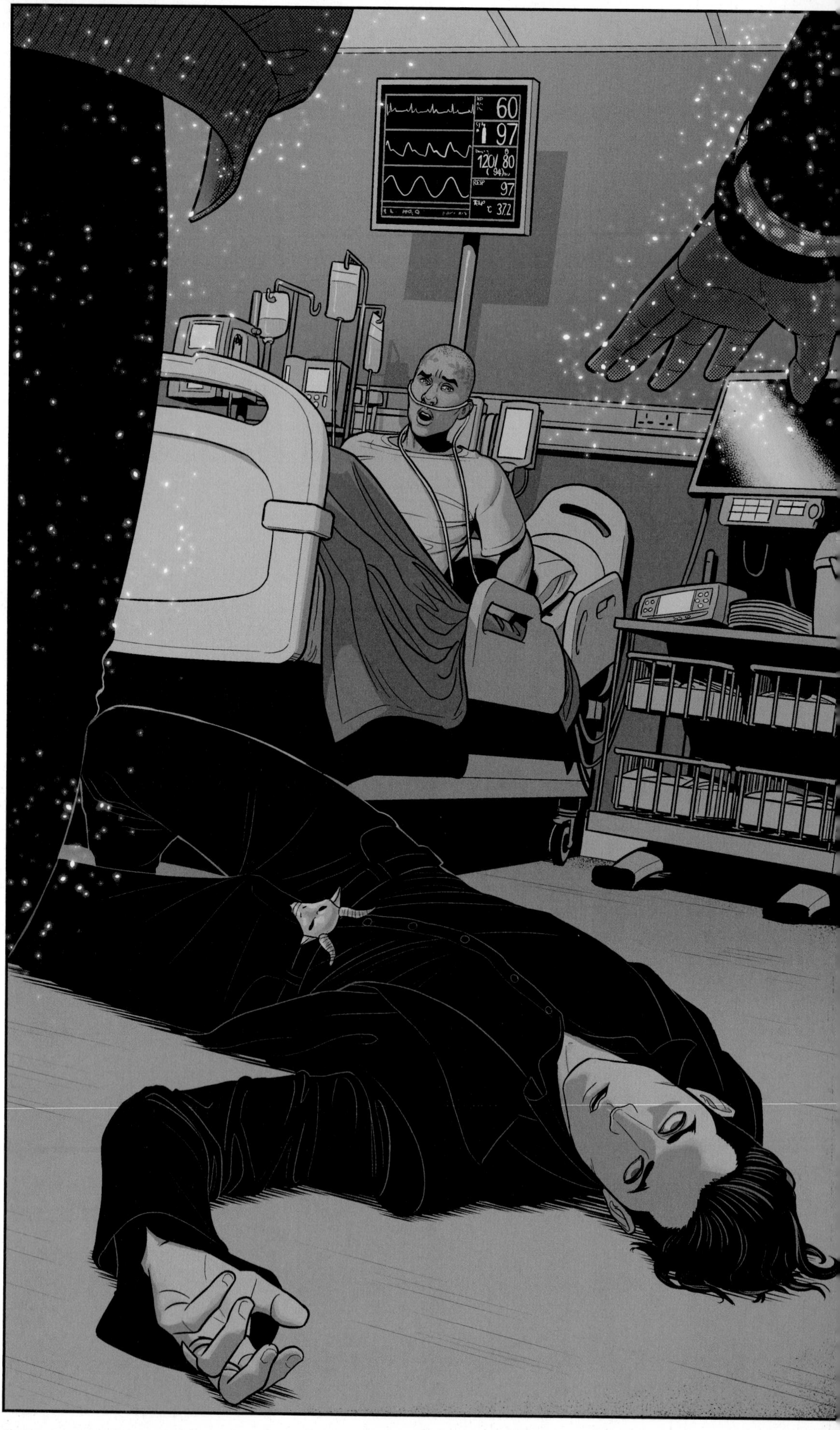
60
97
120/80
(94)
RESP 97
TEMP °C 37.2

AS IS HEAVEN

2 MAY 2015

43

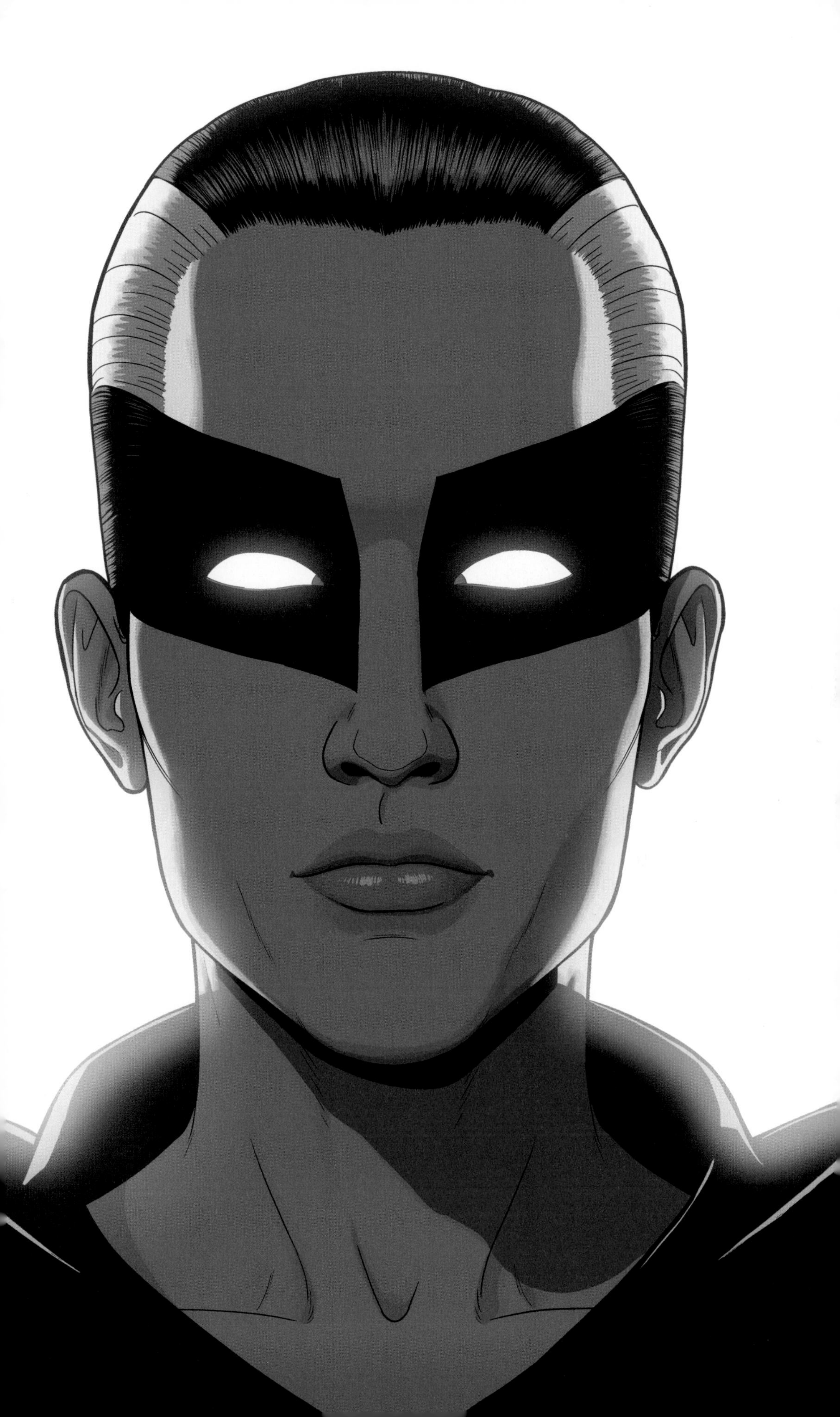

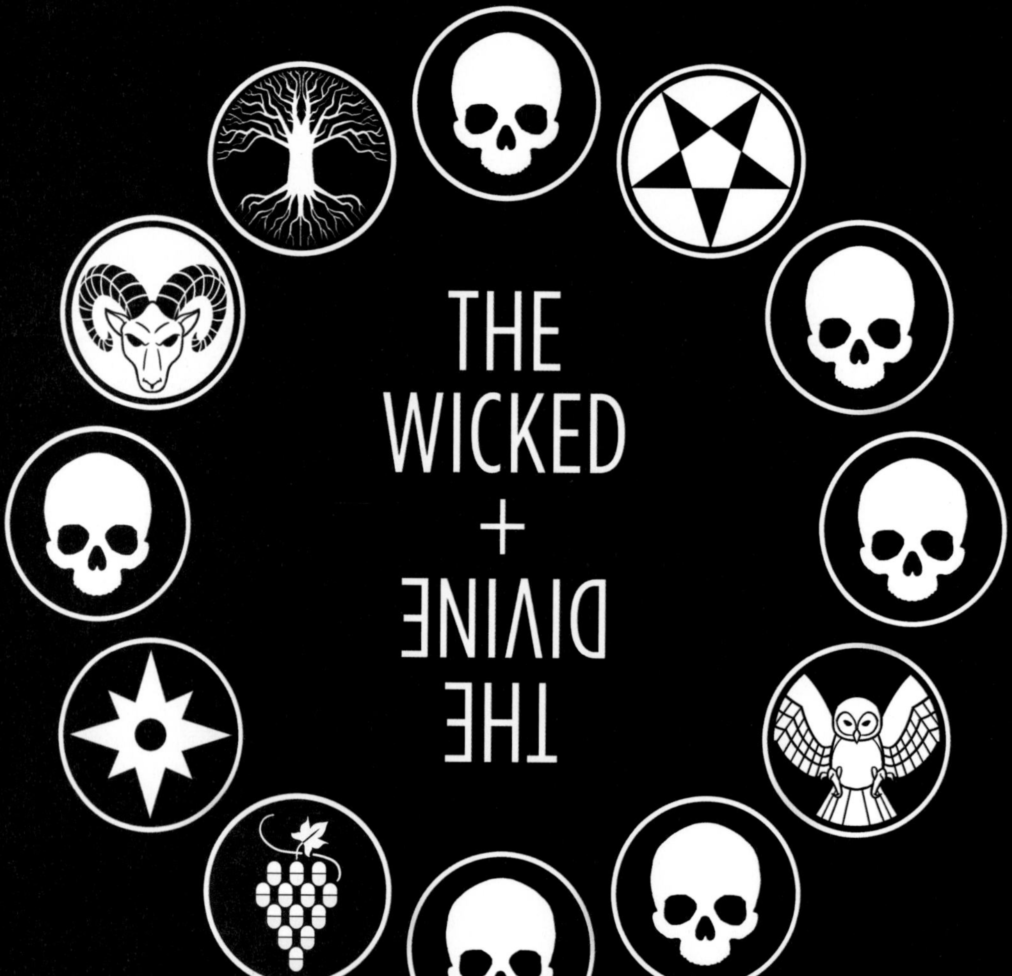
THE
WICKED
+
THE
DIVINE

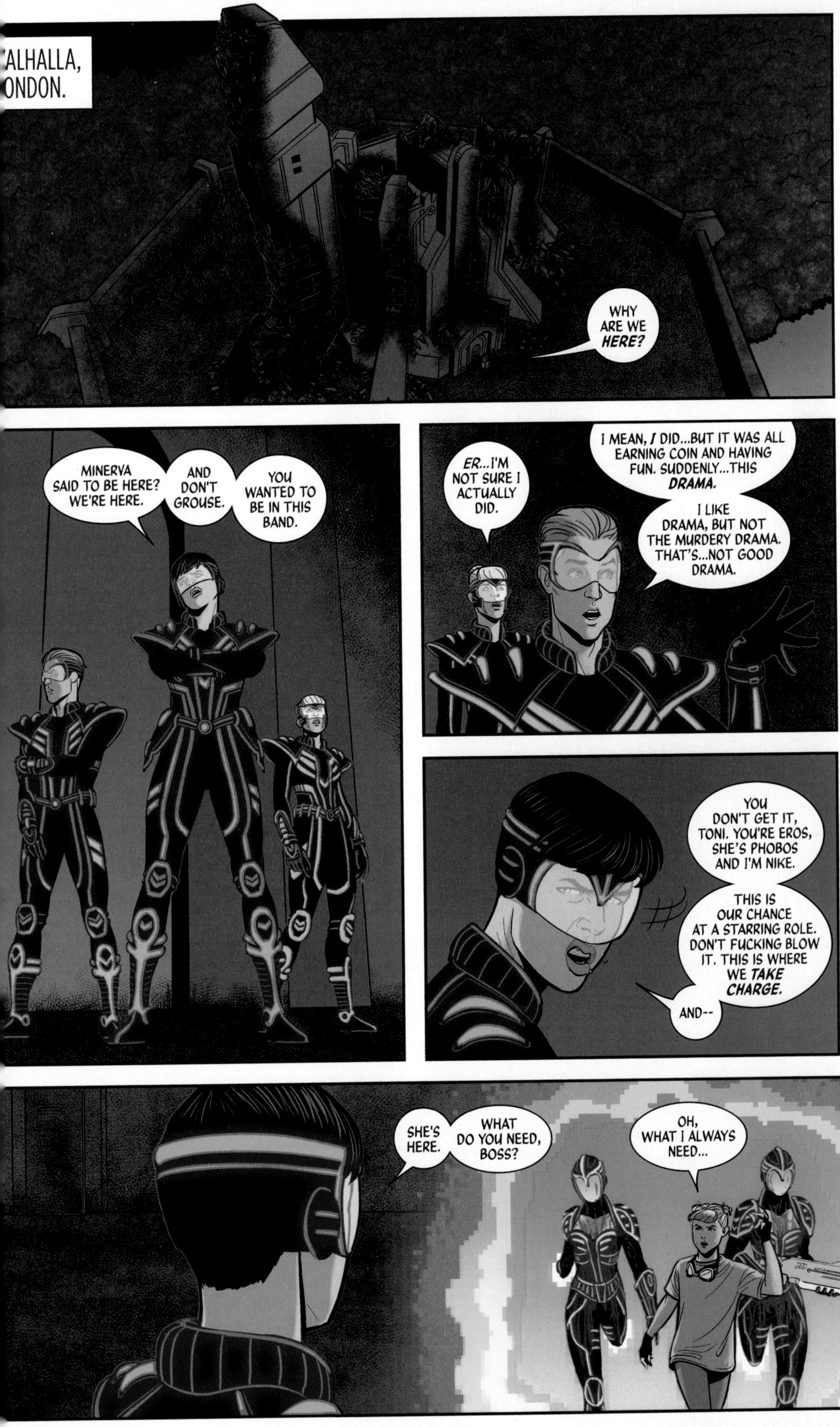
ALHALLA,
ONDON.
WHY ARE WE *HERE?*
MINERVA SAID TO BE HERE? WE'RE HERE.
AND DON'T GROUSE.
YOU WANTED TO BE IN THIS BAND.
ER...I'M NOT SURE I ACTUALLY DID.
I MEAN, *I* DID...BUT IT WAS ALL EARNING COIN AND HAVING FUN. SUDDENLY...THIS *DRAMA.*
I LIKE DRAMA, BUT NOT THE MURDERY DRAMA. THAT'S...NOT GOOD DRAMA.
YOU DON'T GET IT, TONI. YOU'RE EROS, SHE'S PHOBOS AND I'M NIKE.
THIS IS OUR CHANCE AT A STARRING ROLE. DON'T FUCKING BLOW IT. THIS IS WHERE WE *TAKE CHARGE.*
AND--
SHE'S HERE.
WHAT DO YOU NEED, BOSS?
OH, WHAT I ALWAYS NEED...

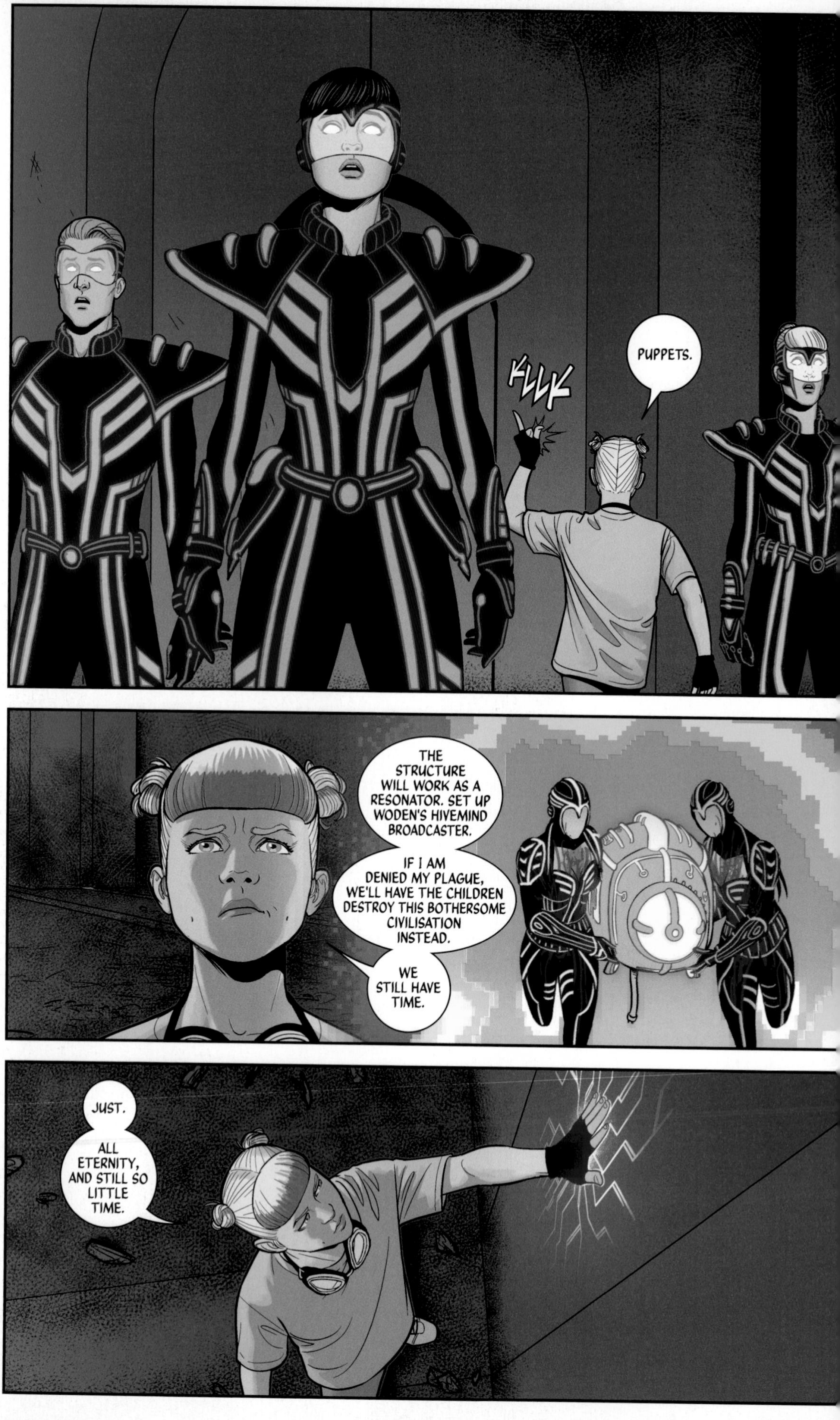
KLLK
PUPPETS.
THE STRUCTURE WILL WORK AS A RESONATOR. SET UP WODEN'S HIVEMIND BROADCASTER.
IF I AM DENIED MY PLAGUE, WE'LL HAVE THE CHILDREN DESTROY THIS BOTHERSOME CIVILISATION INSTEAD.
WE STILL HAVE TIME.
JUST.
ALL ETERNITY, AND STILL SO LITTLE TIME.

SHOW TIME

2 MAY 2015

It should be simple. We face Minerva. We end it. That's all that should be on our minds, right?

After everything that's happened, it's not. Part of me is grateful that it's not, but that doesn't make things any easier...

WE HAVE TO BRING CAM BACK! I WANT TO TRY AGAIN. HE—

IT WON'T WORK. IT WON'T WORK FOR ANY OF *US*. WE'RE NOT UNDERWORLD GODS.

EXCEPT PERHAPS ME, AND *FUCK NO*.

WHO WOULD DENY THE WORLD MY *MAGNIFICENCE*?

I...WOULDN'T ASK YOU TO DO IT, BUT COULD YOU TRY SOMETHING? AREN'T *YOU* AN UNDERWORLD GOD?

NOT EXACTLY, AND NOT ANY MORE.

AND PLEASE, DIO. EVEN IF YOU COULD DO SOMETHING, CAM DIDN'T BRING YOU BACK TO LET YOU SACRIFICE YOURSELF.

WE HAVE TO FOLLOW LAURA'S PLAN.

ER... WHAT DO WE DO NOW?

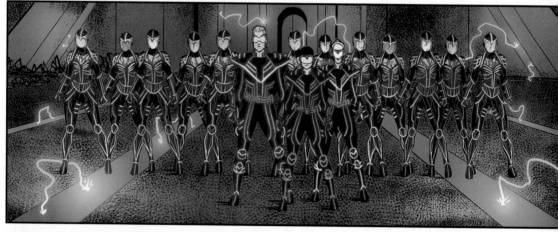

I CAN GUESS.

Yes, there was a fight.

What was it like?

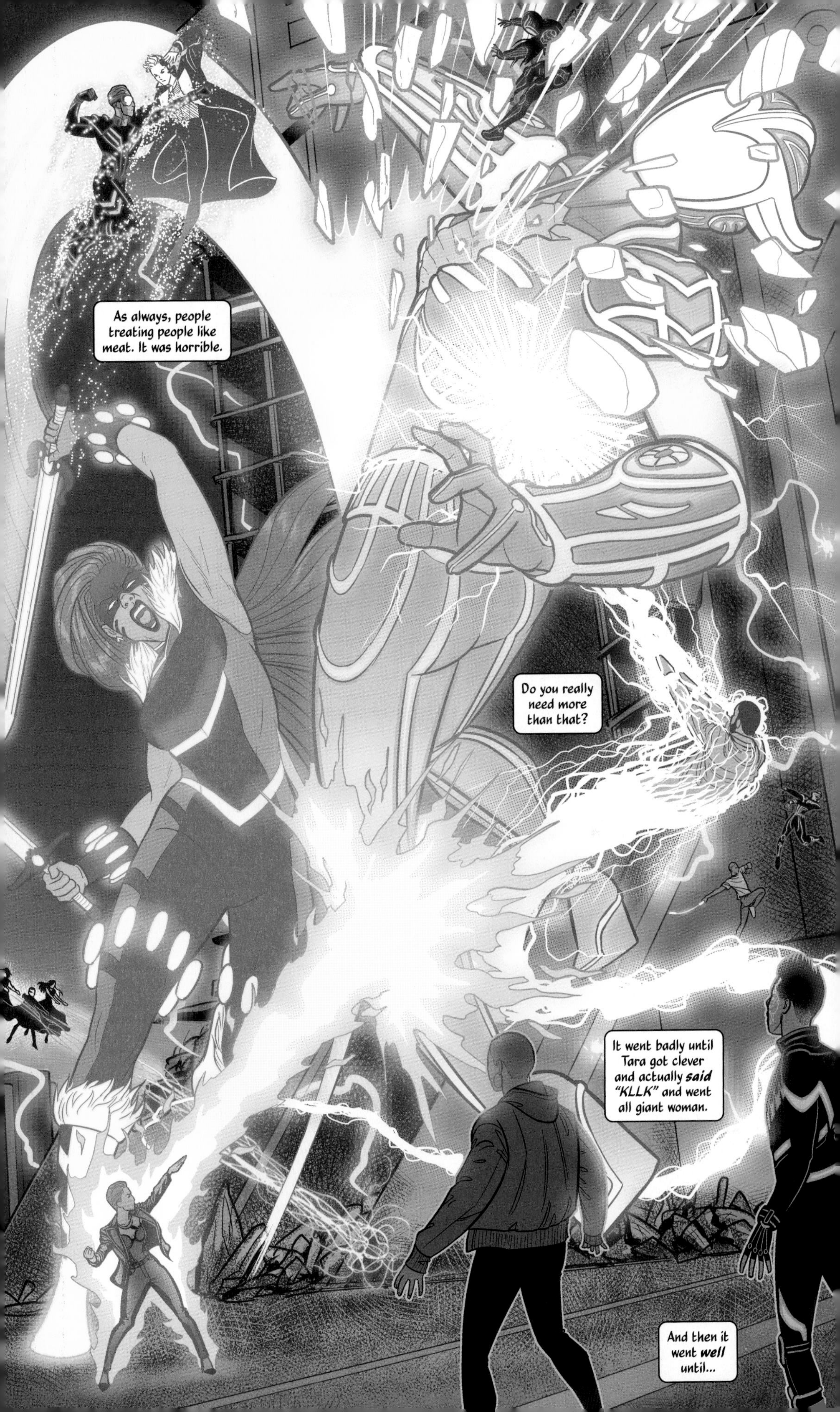
As always, people treating people like meat. It was horrible.
Do you really need more than that?
It went badly until Tara got clever and actually **said** "KLLK" and went all giant woman.
And then it went **well** until...

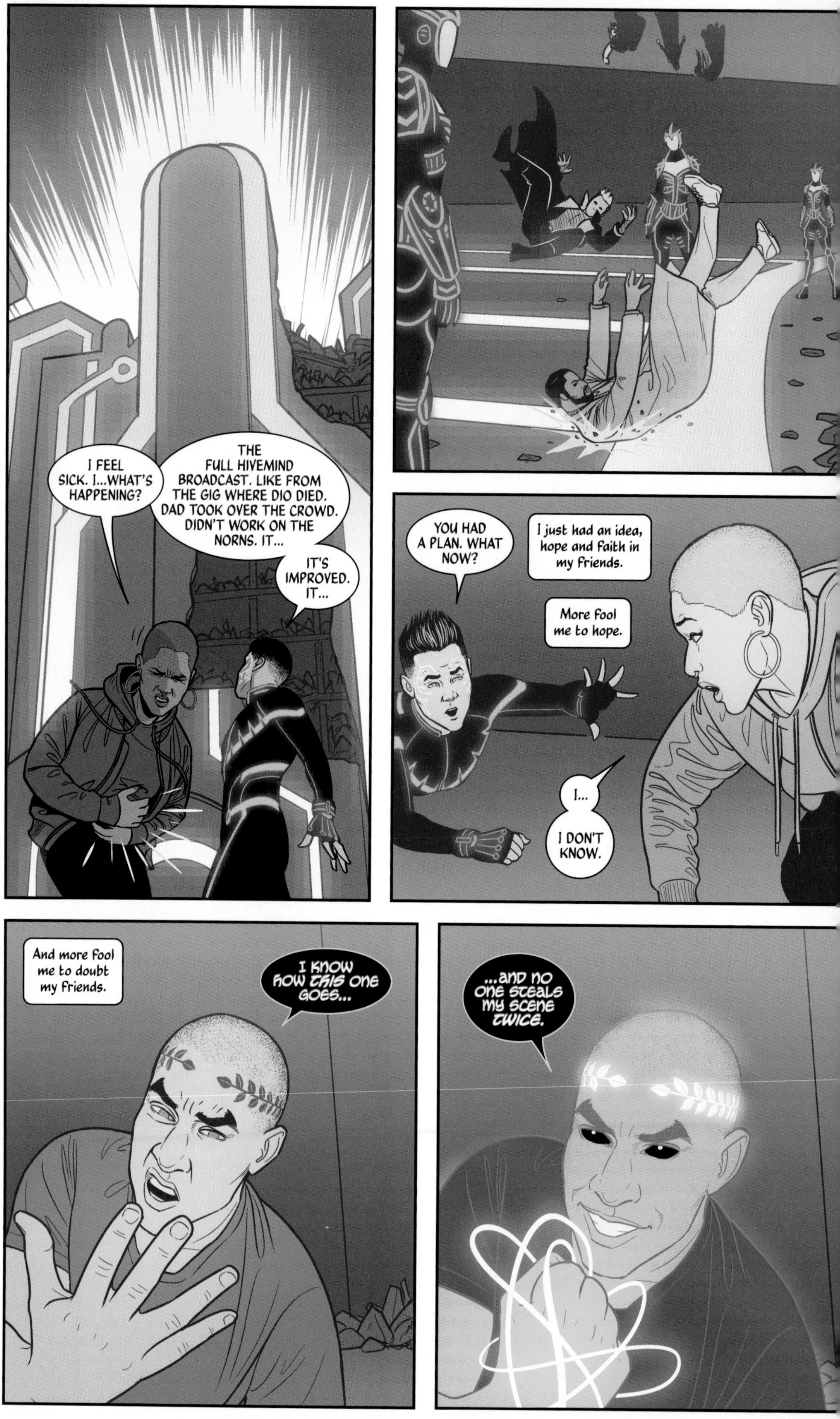
I FEEL SICK. I...WHAT'S HAPPENING?
THE FULL HIVEMIND BROADCAST. LIKE FROM THE GIG WHERE DIO DIED. DAD TOOK OVER THE CROWD. DIDN'T WORK ON THE NORNS. IT...
IT'S IMPROVED. IT...
YOU HAD A PLAN. WHAT NOW?
I just had an idea, hope and faith in my friends.
More fool me to hope.
I...
I DON'T KNOW.
And more fool me to doubt my friends.
I KNOW HOW THIS ONE GOES...
...AND NO ONE STEALS MY SCENE TWICE.

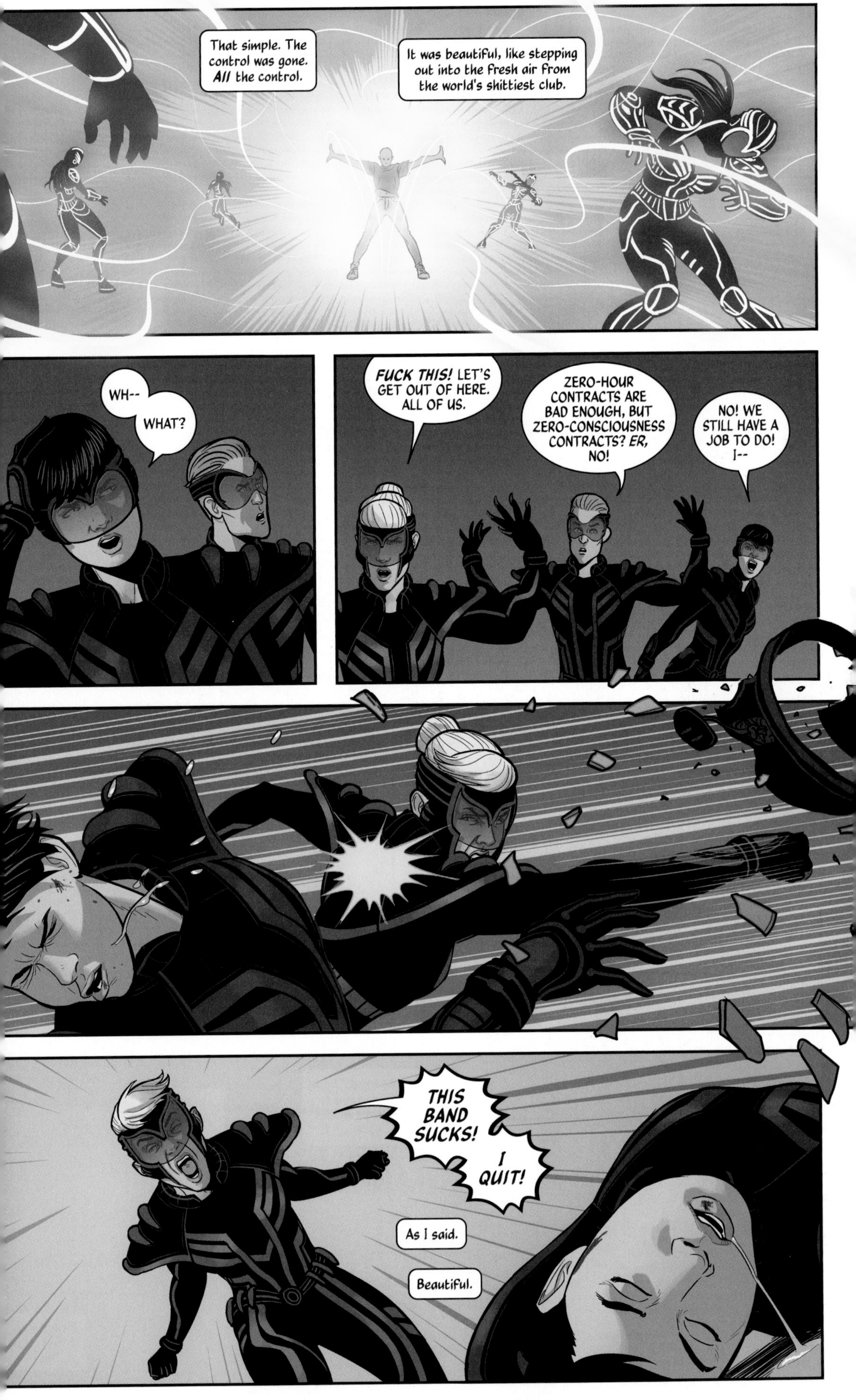

That simple. The control was gone. *All* the control.
It was beautiful, like stepping out into the fresh air from the world's shittiest club.
WH--
WHAT?
FUCK THIS! LET'S GET OUT OF HERE. ALL OF US.
ZERO-HOUR CONTRACTS ARE BAD ENOUGH, BUT ZERO-CONSCIOUSNESS CONTRACTS? *ER,* NO!
NO! WE STILL HAVE A JOB TO DO! I--
THIS BAND SUCKS!
I QUIT!
As I said.
Beautiful.

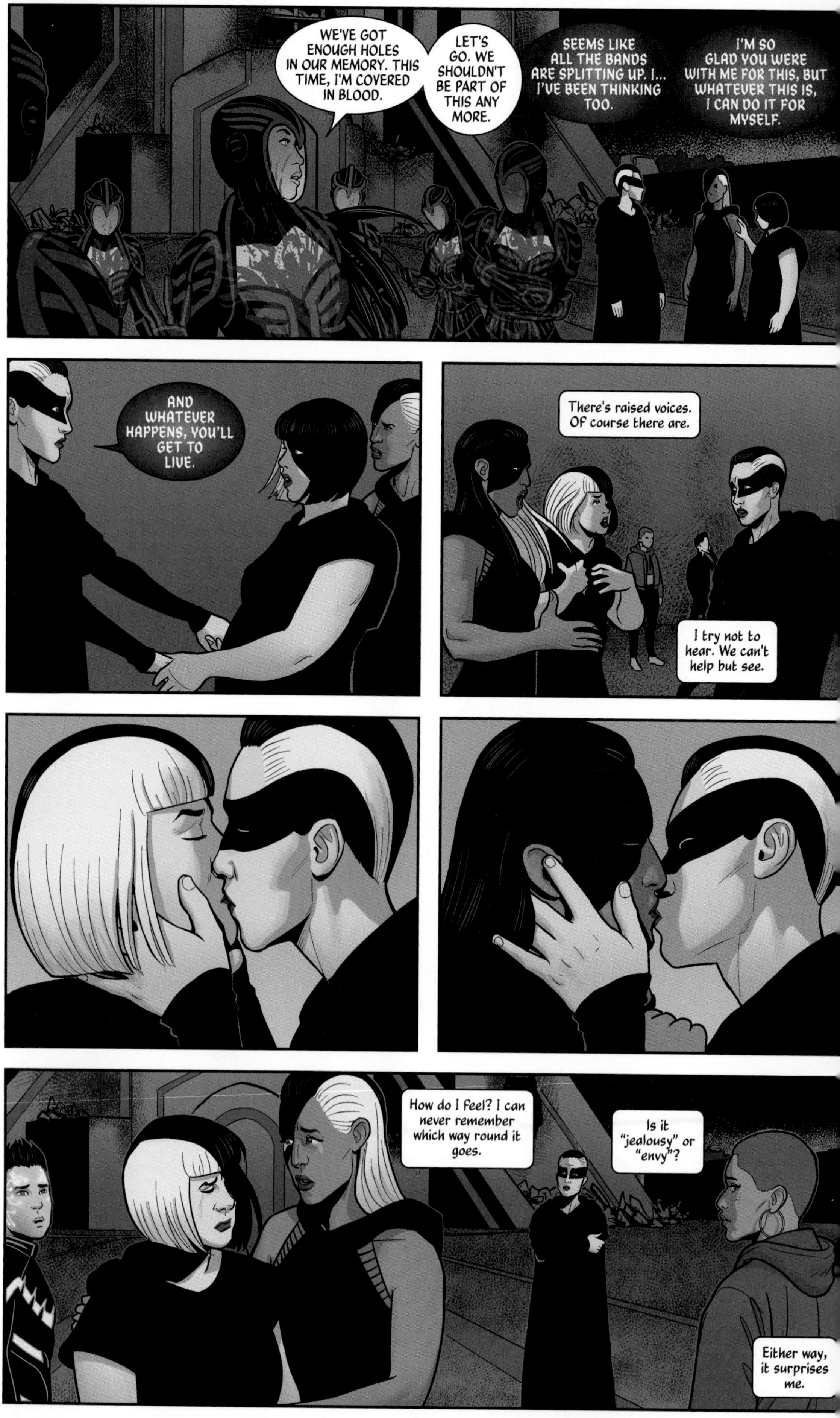
WE'VE GOT ENOUGH HOLES IN OUR MEMORY. THIS TIME, I'M COVERED IN BLOOD.
LET'S GO. WE SHOULDN'T BE PART OF THIS ANY MORE.
SEEMS LIKE ALL THE BANDS ARE SPLITTING UP. I... I'VE BEEN THINKING TOO.
I'M SO GLAD YOU WERE WITH ME FOR THIS, BUT WHATEVER THIS IS, I CAN DO IT FOR MYSELF.
AND WHATEVER HAPPENS, YOU'LL GET TO LIVE.
There's raised voices. Of course there are.
I try not to hear. We can't help but see.
How do I feel? I can never remember which way round it goes.
Is it "jealousy" or "envy"?
Either way, it surprises me.

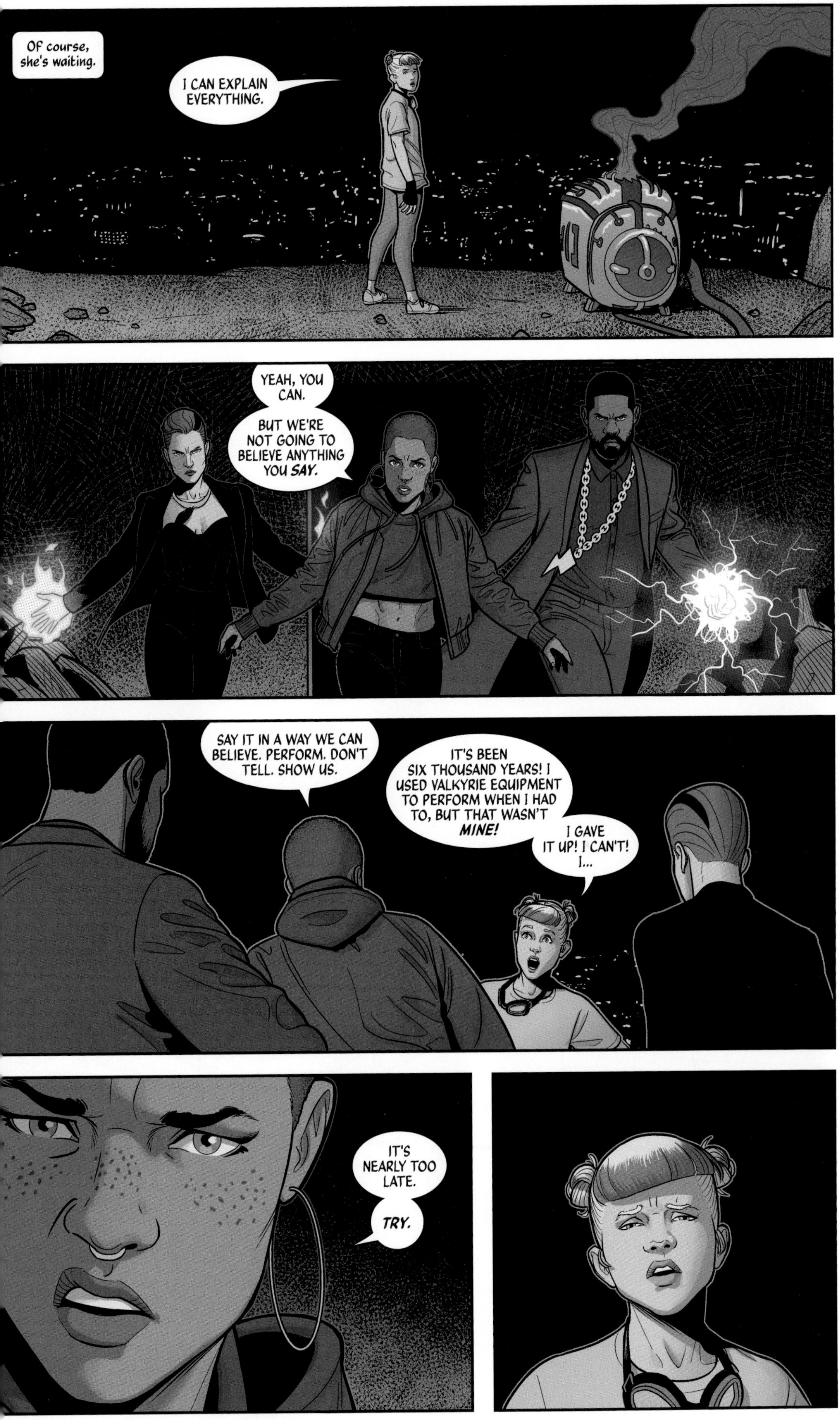
Of course, she's waiting.
I CAN EXPLAIN EVERYTHING.
YEAH, YOU CAN.
BUT WE'RE NOT GOING TO BELIEVE ANYTHING YOU *SAY.*
SAY IT IN A WAY WE CAN BELIEVE. PERFORM. DON'T TELL. SHOW US.
IT'S BEEN SIX THOUSAND YEARS! I USED VALKYRIE EQUIPMENT TO PERFORM WHEN I HAD TO, BUT THAT WASN'T *MINE!*
I GAVE IT UP! I CAN'T! I...
IT'S NEARLY TOO LATE.
TRY.

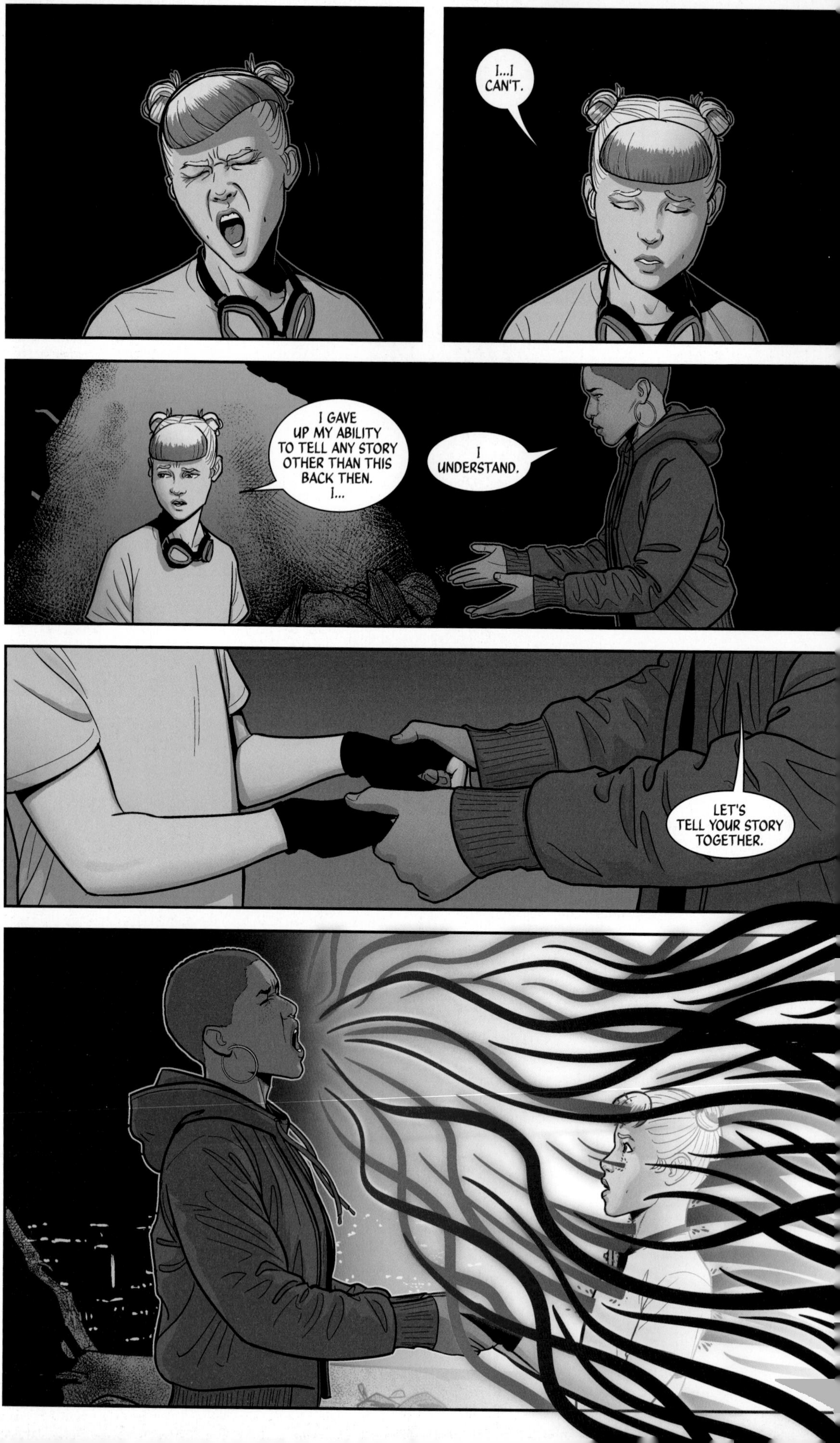
I...I CAN'T.
I GAVE UP MY ABILITY TO TELL ANY STORY OTHER THAN THIS BACK THEN. I...
I UNDERSTAND.
LET'S TELL YOUR STORY TOGETHER.

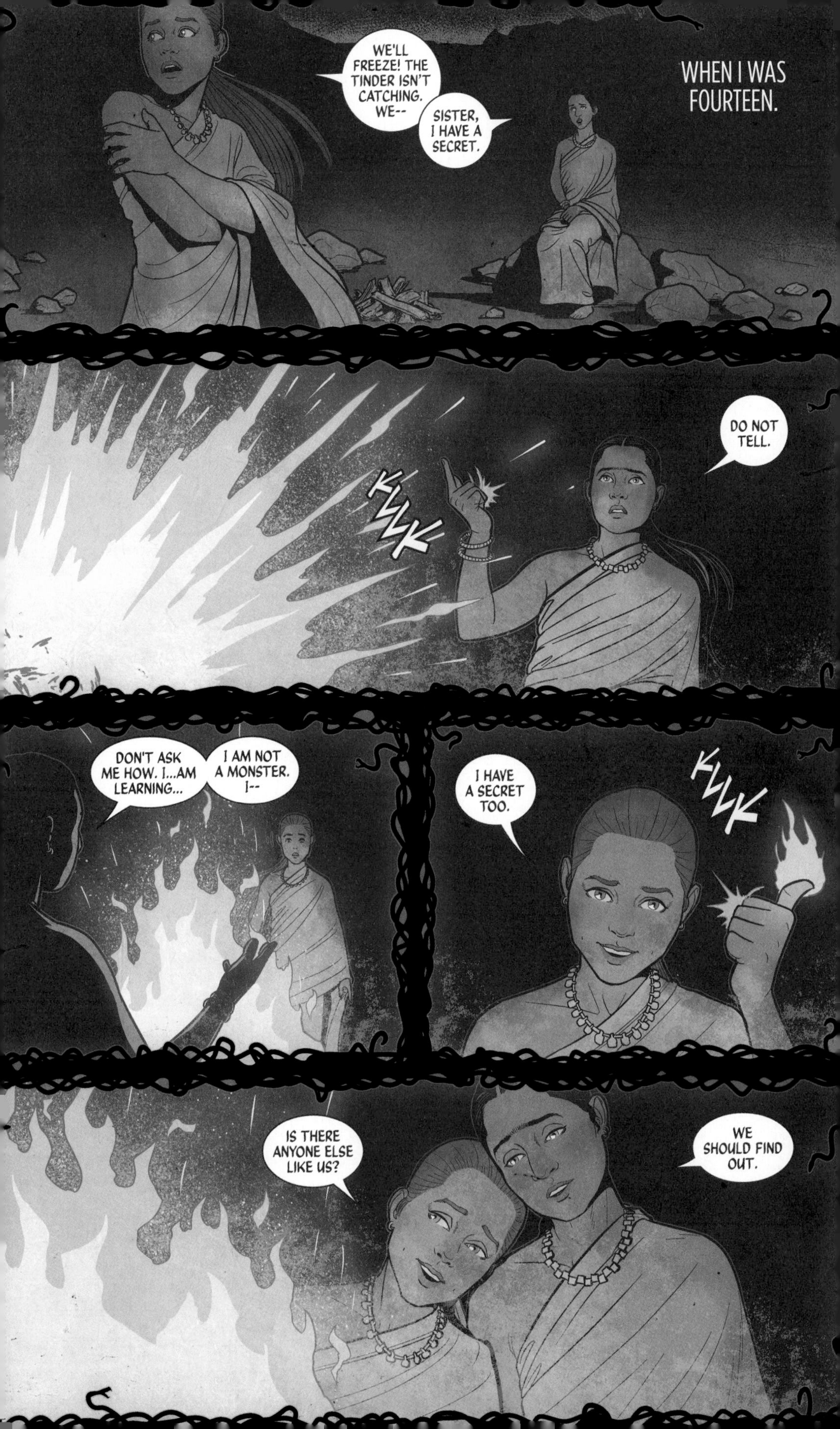
WHEN I WAS FOURTEEN.
WE'LL FREEZE! THE TINDER ISN'T CATCHING. WE--
SISTER, I HAVE A SECRET.
KKKK
DO NOT TELL.
DON'T ASK ME HOW. I...AM LEARNING...
I AM NOT A MONSTER. I--
KKKK
I HAVE A SECRET TOO.
IS THERE ANYONE ELSE LIKE US?
WE SHOULD FIND OUT.

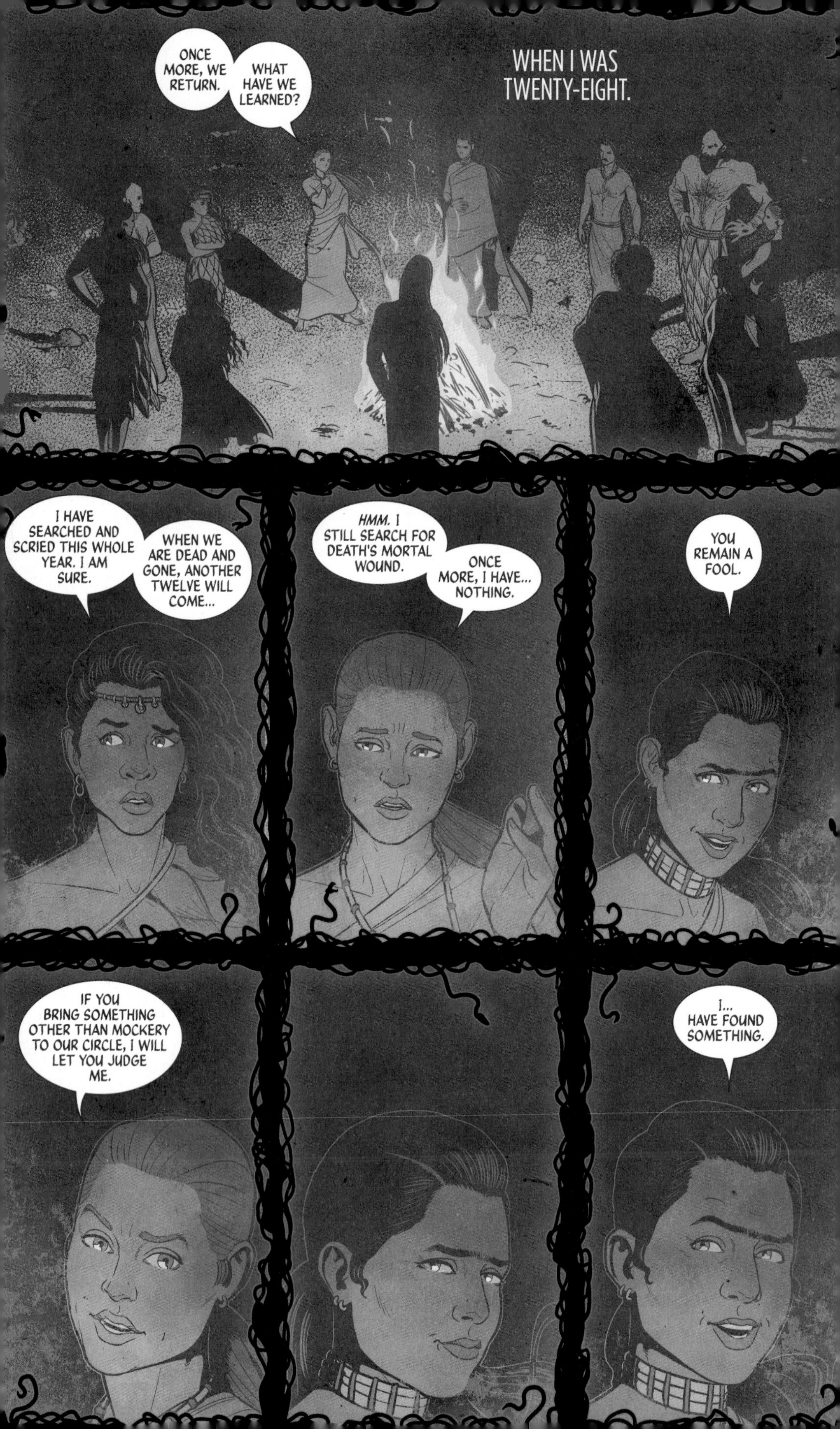
ONCE MORE, WE RETURN.
WHAT HAVE WE LEARNED?
WHEN I WAS TWENTY-EIGHT.
I HAVE SEARCHED AND SCRIED THIS WHOLE YEAR. I AM SURE.
WHEN WE ARE DEAD AND GONE, ANOTHER TWELVE WILL COME...
HMM. I STILL SEARCH FOR DEATH'S MORTAL WOUND.
ONCE MORE, I HAVE... NOTHING.
YOU REMAIN A FOOL.
IF YOU BRING SOMETHING OTHER THAN MOCKERY TO OUR CIRCLE, I WILL LET YOU JUDGE ME.
I... HAVE FOUND SOMETHING.

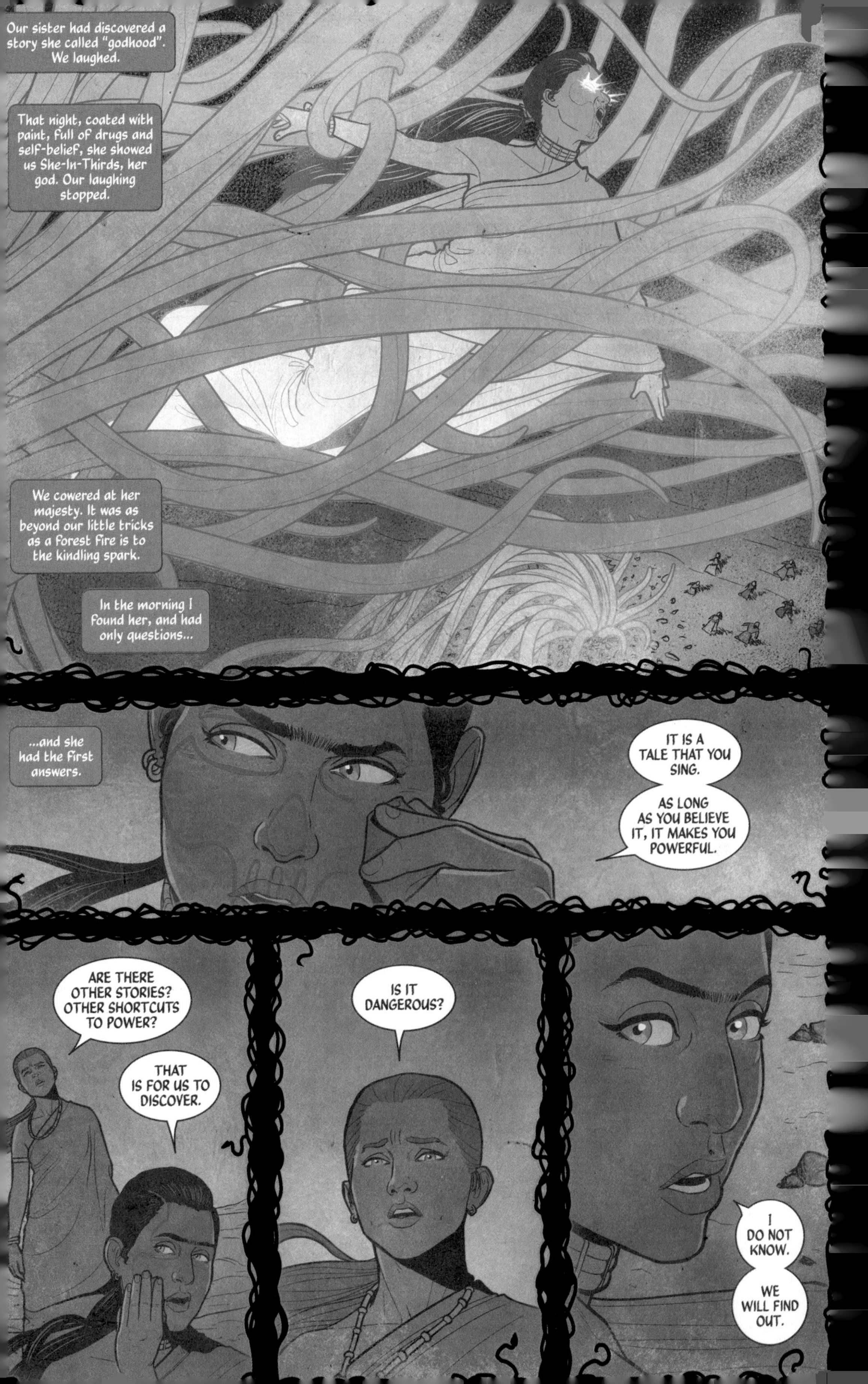
Our sister had discovered a story she called "godhood". We laughed.
That night, coated with paint, full of drugs and self-belief, she showed us She-In-Thirds, her god. Our laughing stopped.
We cowered at her majesty. It was as beyond our little tricks as a forest fire is to the kindling spark.
In the morning I found her, and had only questions...
...and she had the first answers.
IT IS A TALE THAT YOU SING.
AS LONG AS YOU BELIEVE IT, IT MAKES YOU POWERFUL.
ARE THERE OTHER STORIES? OTHER SHORTCUTS TO POWER?
THAT IS FOR US TO DISCOVER.
IS IT DANGEROUS?
I DO NOT KNOW.
WE WILL FIND OUT.

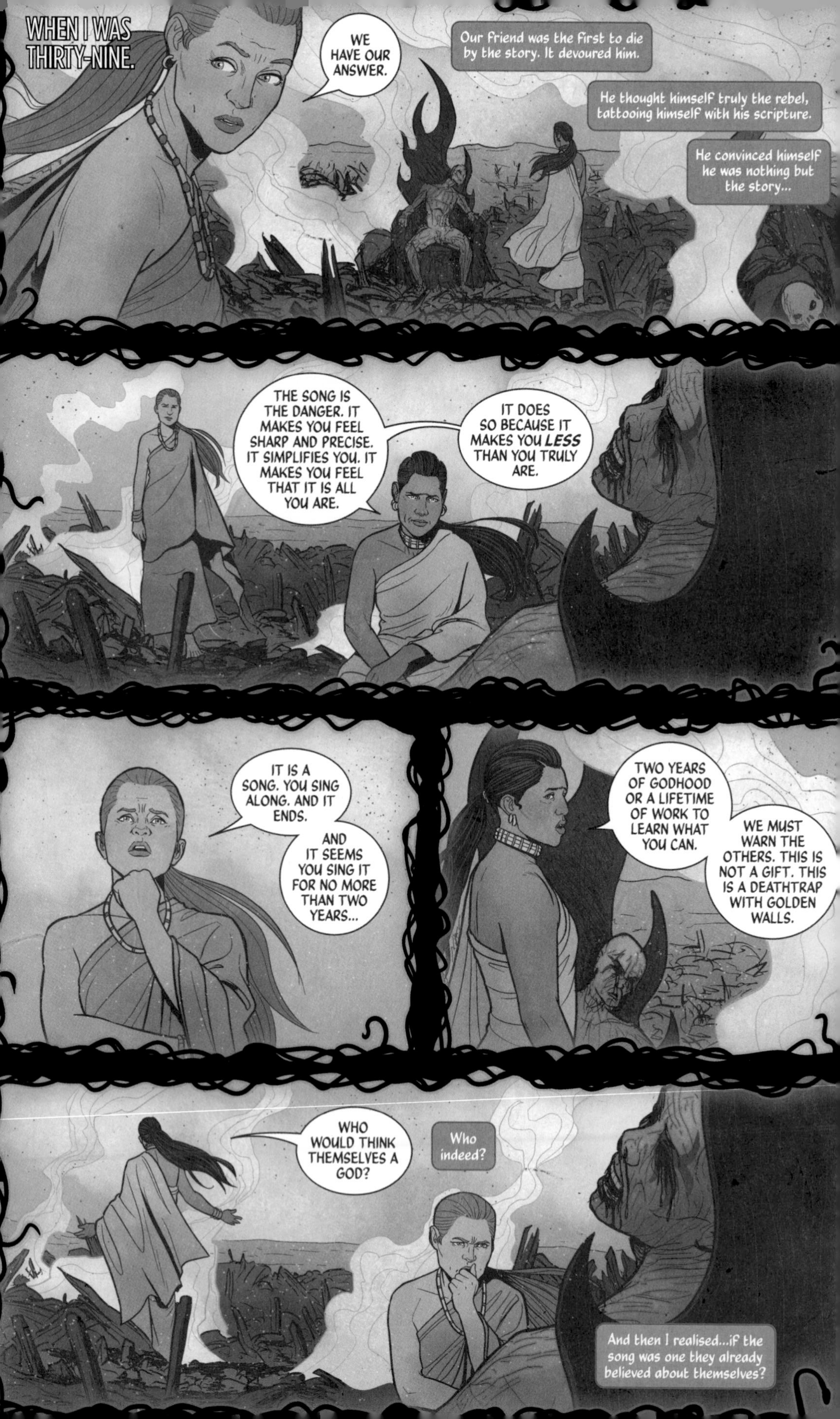
WHEN I WAS THIRTY-NINE.
WE HAVE OUR ANSWER.
Our friend was the first to die by the story. It devoured him.
He thought himself truly the rebel, tattooing himself with his scripture.
He convinced himself he was nothing but the story...
THE SONG IS THE DANGER. IT MAKES YOU FEEL SHARP AND PRECISE. IT SIMPLIFIES YOU. IT MAKES YOU FEEL THAT IT IS ALL YOU ARE.
IT DOES SO BECAUSE IT MAKES YOU LESS THAN YOU TRULY ARE.
IT IS A SONG. YOU SING ALONG. AND IT ENDS.
AND IT SEEMS YOU SING IT FOR NO MORE THAN TWO YEARS...
TWO YEARS OF GODHOOD OR A LIFETIME OF WORK TO LEARN WHAT YOU CAN.
WE MUST WARN THE OTHERS. THIS IS NOT A GIFT. THIS IS A DEATHTRAP WITH GOLDEN WALLS.
WHO WOULD THINK THEMSELVES A GOD?
Who indeed?
And then I realised...if the song was one they already believed about themselves?

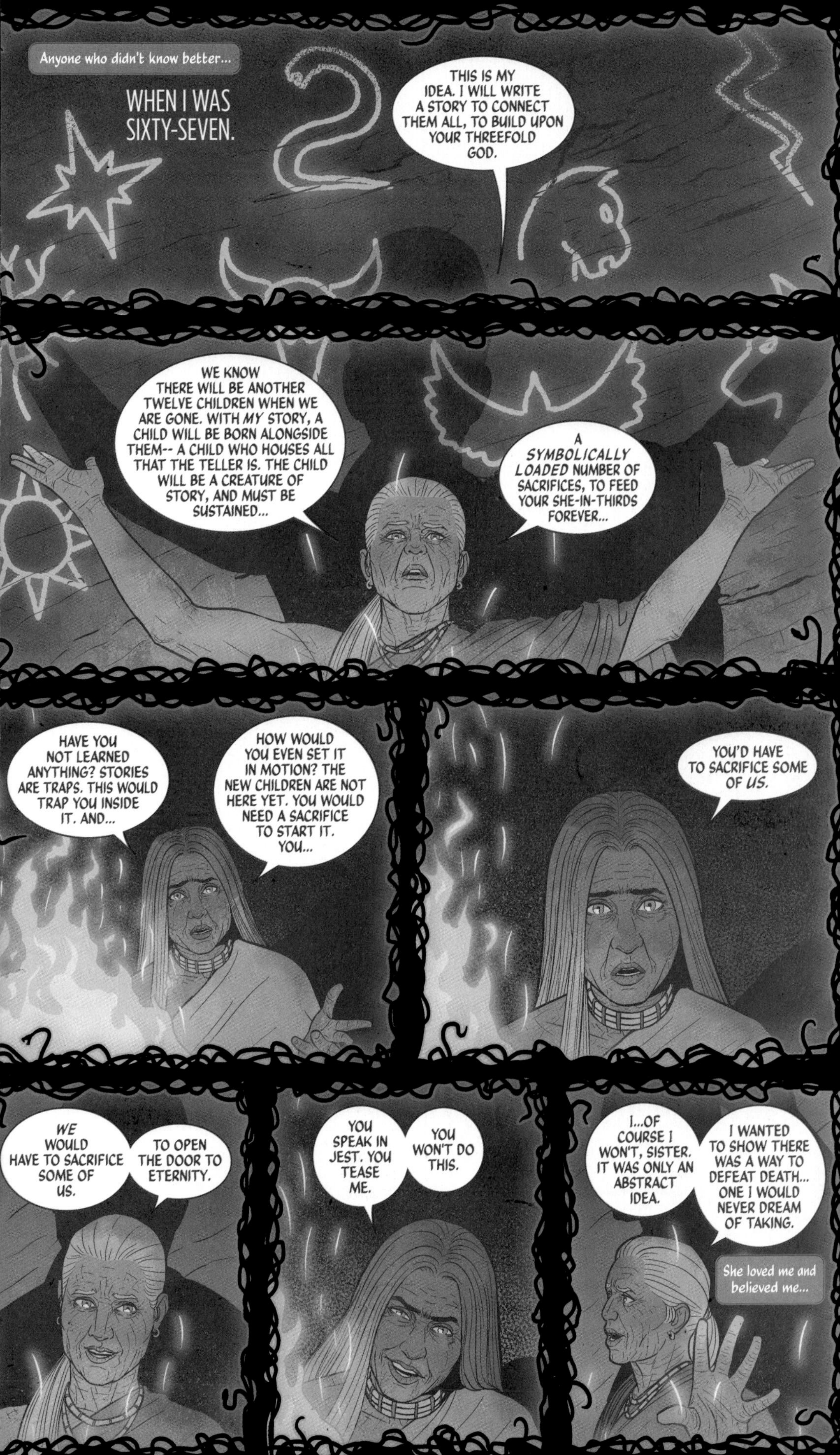
Anyone who didn't know better...
WHEN I WAS SIXTY-SEVEN.
THIS IS MY IDEA. I WILL WRITE A STORY TO CONNECT THEM ALL, TO BUILD UPON YOUR THREEFOLD GOD.
WE KNOW THERE WILL BE ANOTHER TWELVE CHILDREN WHEN WE ARE GONE. WITH *MY* STORY, A CHILD WILL BE BORN ALONGSIDE THEM-- A CHILD WHO HOUSES ALL THAT THE TELLER IS. THE CHILD WILL BE A CREATURE OF STORY, AND MUST BE SUSTAINED...
A *SYMBOLICALLY LOADED* NUMBER OF SACRIFICES, TO FEED YOUR SHE-IN-THIRDS FOREVER...
HAVE YOU NOT LEARNED ANYTHING? STORIES ARE TRAPS. THIS WOULD TRAP YOU INSIDE IT. AND...
HOW WOULD YOU EVEN SET IT IN MOTION? THE NEW CHILDREN ARE NOT HERE YET. YOU WOULD NEED A SACRIFICE TO START IT. YOU...
YOU'D HAVE TO SACRIFICE SOME OF *US*.
WE WOULD HAVE TO SACRIFICE SOME OF US.
TO OPEN THE DOOR TO ETERNITY.
YOU SPEAK IN JEST. YOU TEASE ME.
YOU WON'T DO THIS.
I...OF COURSE I WON'T, SISTER. IT WAS ONLY AN ABSTRACT IDEA.
I WANTED TO SHOW THERE WAS A WAY TO DEFEAT DEATH... ONE I WOULD NEVER DREAM OF TAKING.
She loved me and believed me...

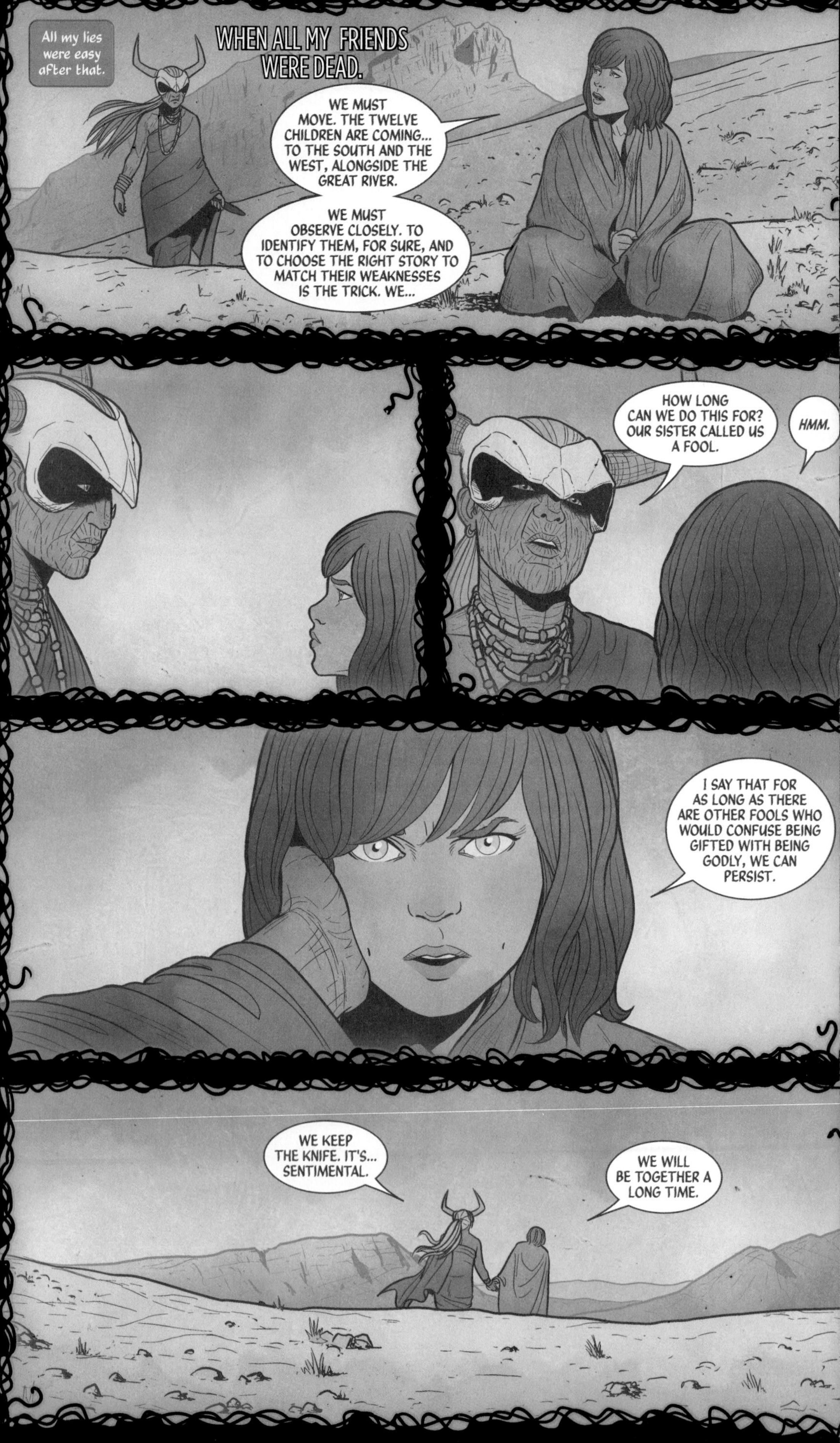

All my lies were easy after that.
WHEN ALL MY FRIENDS WERE DEAD.
WE MUST MOVE. THE TWELVE CHILDREN ARE COMING... TO THE SOUTH AND THE WEST, ALONGSIDE THE GREAT RIVER.
WE MUST OBSERVE CLOSELY. TO IDENTIFY THEM, FOR SURE, AND TO CHOOSE THE RIGHT STORY TO MATCH THEIR WEAKNESSES IS THE TRICK. WE...
HOW LONG CAN WE DO THIS FOR? OUR SISTER CALLED US A FOOL.
HMM.
I SAY THAT FOR AS LONG AS THERE ARE OTHER FOOLS WHO WOULD CONFUSE BEING GIFTED WITH BEING GODLY, WE CAN PERSIST.
WE KEEP THE KNIFE. IT'S... SENTIMENTAL.
WE WILL BE TOGETHER A LONG TIME.

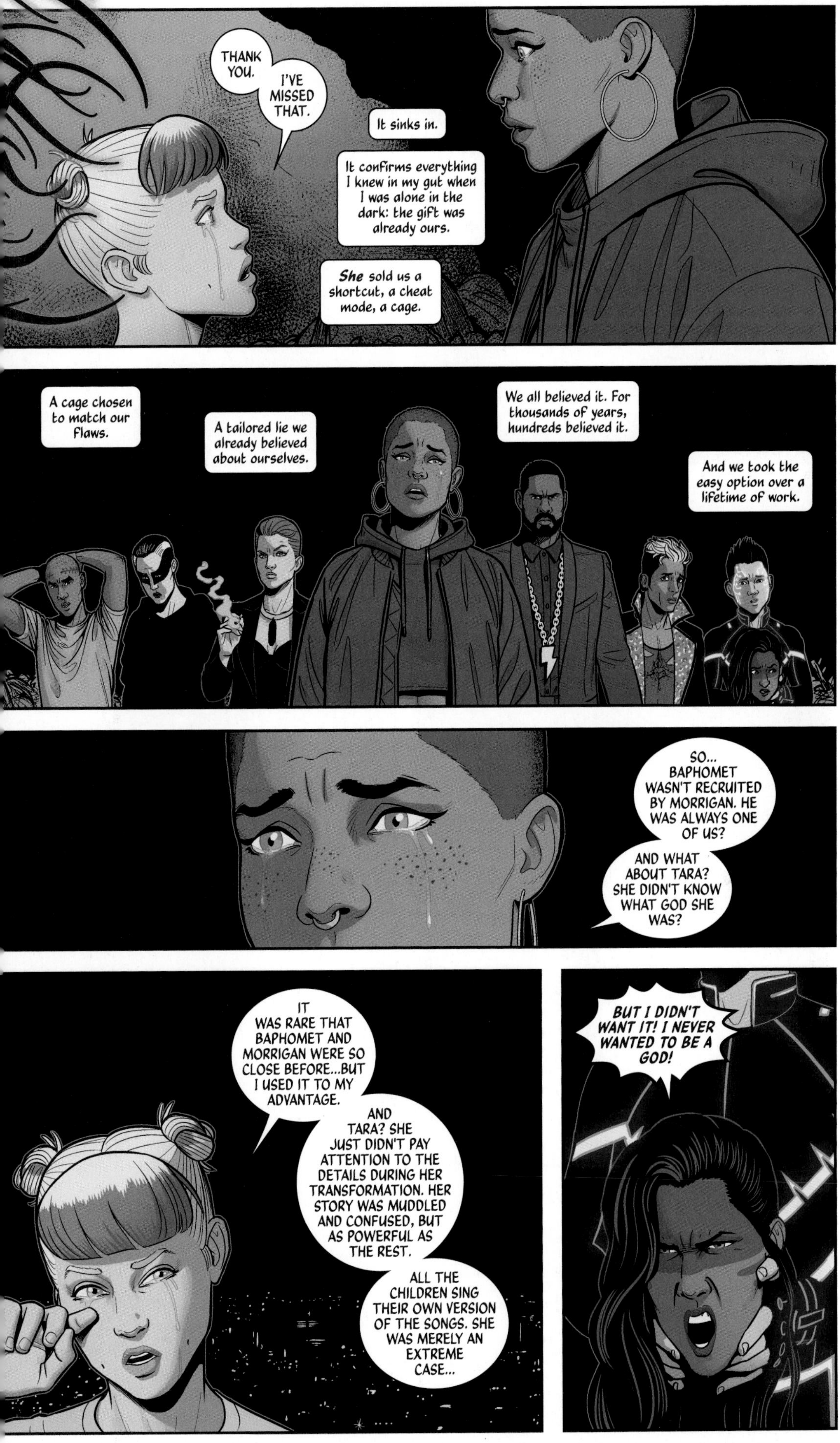
THANK YOU.
I'VE MISSED THAT.
It sinks in.
It confirms everything I knew in my gut when I was alone in the dark: the gift was already ours.
She sold us a shortcut, a cheat mode, a cage.
A cage chosen to match our flaws.
A tailored lie we already believed about ourselves.
We all believed it. For thousands of years, hundreds believed it.
And we took the easy option over a lifetime of work.
SO... BAPHOMET WASN'T RECRUITED BY MORRIGAN. HE WAS ALWAYS ONE OF US?
AND WHAT ABOUT TARA? SHE DIDN'T KNOW WHAT GOD SHE WAS?
IT WAS RARE THAT BAPHOMET AND MORRIGAN WERE SO CLOSE BEFORE...BUT I USED IT TO MY ADVANTAGE.
AND TARA? SHE JUST DIDN'T PAY ATTENTION TO THE DETAILS DURING HER TRANSFORMATION. HER STORY WAS MUDDLED AND CONFUSED, BUT AS POWERFUL AS THE REST.
ALL THE CHILDREN SING THEIR OWN VERSION OF THE SONGS. SHE WAS MERELY AN EXTREME CASE...
BUT I DIDN'T WANT IT! I NEVER WANTED TO BE A GOD!

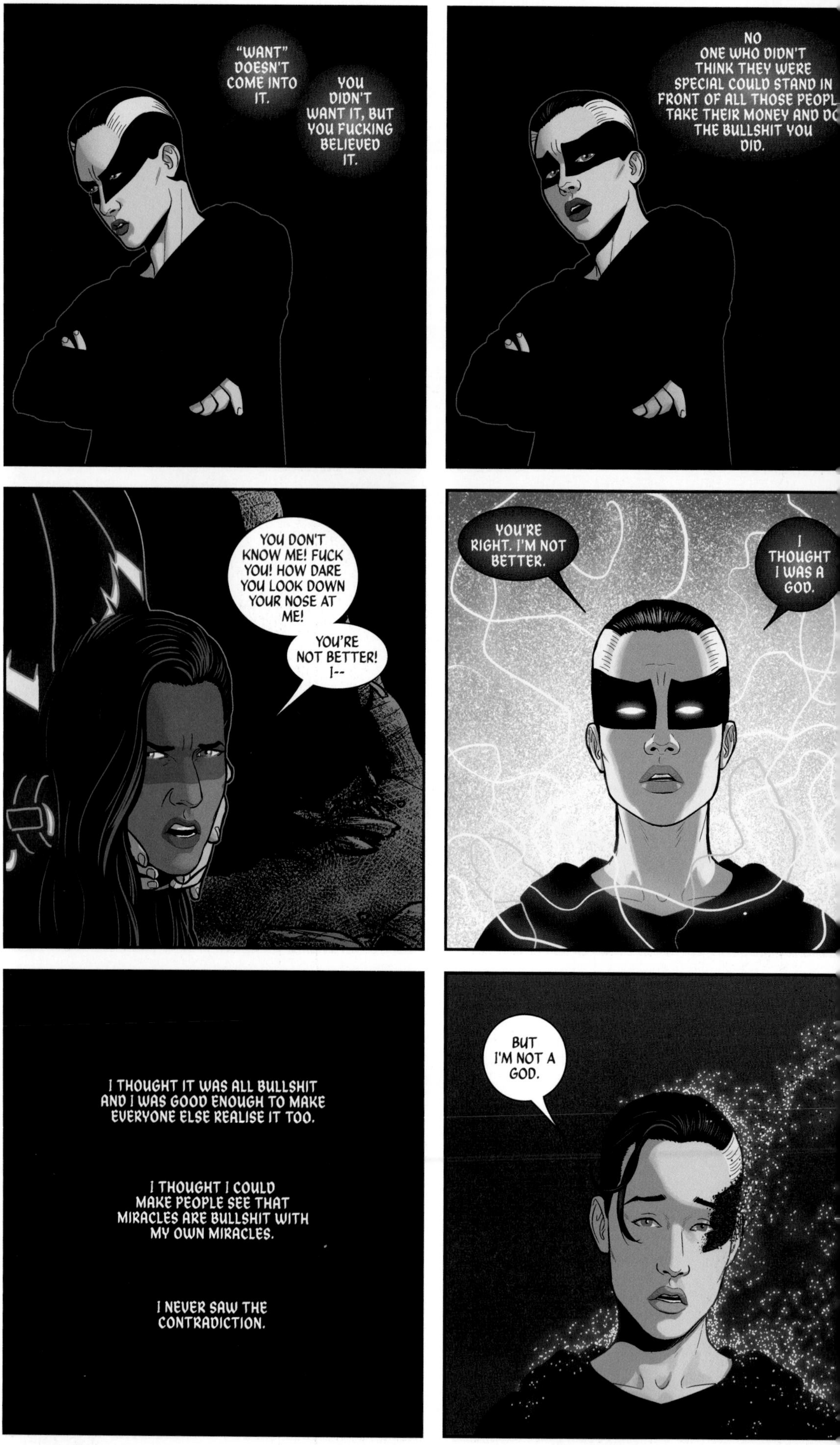
"WANT" DOESN'T COME INTO IT.
YOU DIDN'T WANT IT, BUT YOU FUCKING BELIEVED IT.
NO ONE WHO DIDN'T THINK THEY WERE SPECIAL COULD STAND IN FRONT OF ALL THOSE PEOPL TAKE THEIR MONEY AND DO THE BULLSHIT YOU DID.
YOU DON'T KNOW ME! FUCK YOU! HOW DARE YOU LOOK DOWN YOUR NOSE AT ME!
YOU'RE NOT BETTER! I--
YOU'RE RIGHT. I'M NOT BETTER.
I THOUGHT I WAS A GOD.
I THOUGHT IT WAS ALL BULLSHIT AND I WAS GOOD ENOUGH TO MAKE EVERYONE ELSE REALISE IT TOO.
I THOUGHT I COULD MAKE PEOPLE SEE THAT MIRACLES ARE BULLSHIT WITH MY OWN MIRACLES.
I NEVER SAW THE CONTRADICTION.
BUT I'M NOT A GOD.

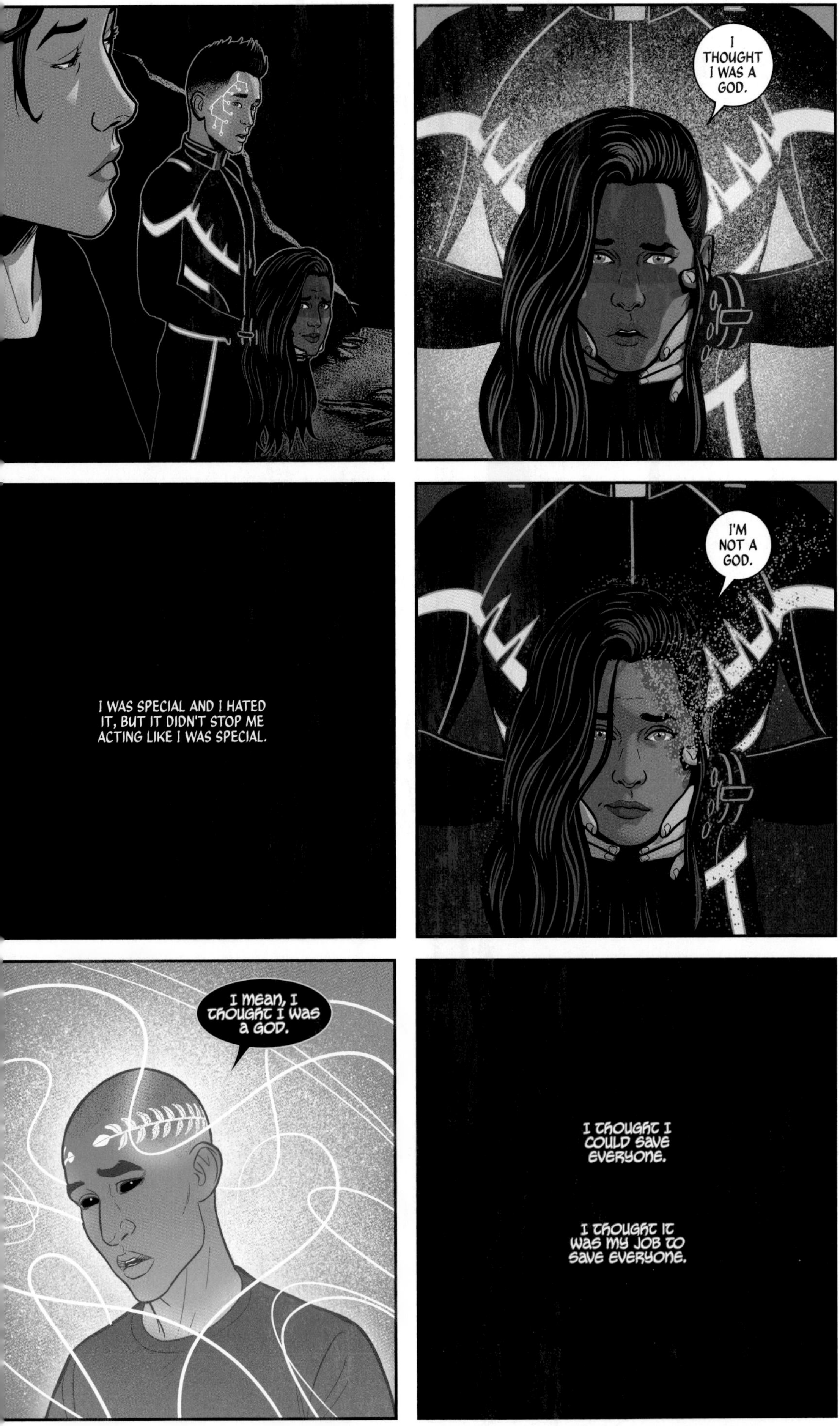
I THOUGHT I WAS A GOD.
I WAS SPECIAL AND I HATED IT, BUT IT DIDN'T STOP ME ACTING LIKE I WAS SPECIAL.
I'M NOT A GOD.
I MEAN, I THOUGHT I WAS A GOD.
I THOUGHT I COULD SAVE EVERYONE.
I THOUGHT IT WAS MY JOB TO SAVE EVERYONE.

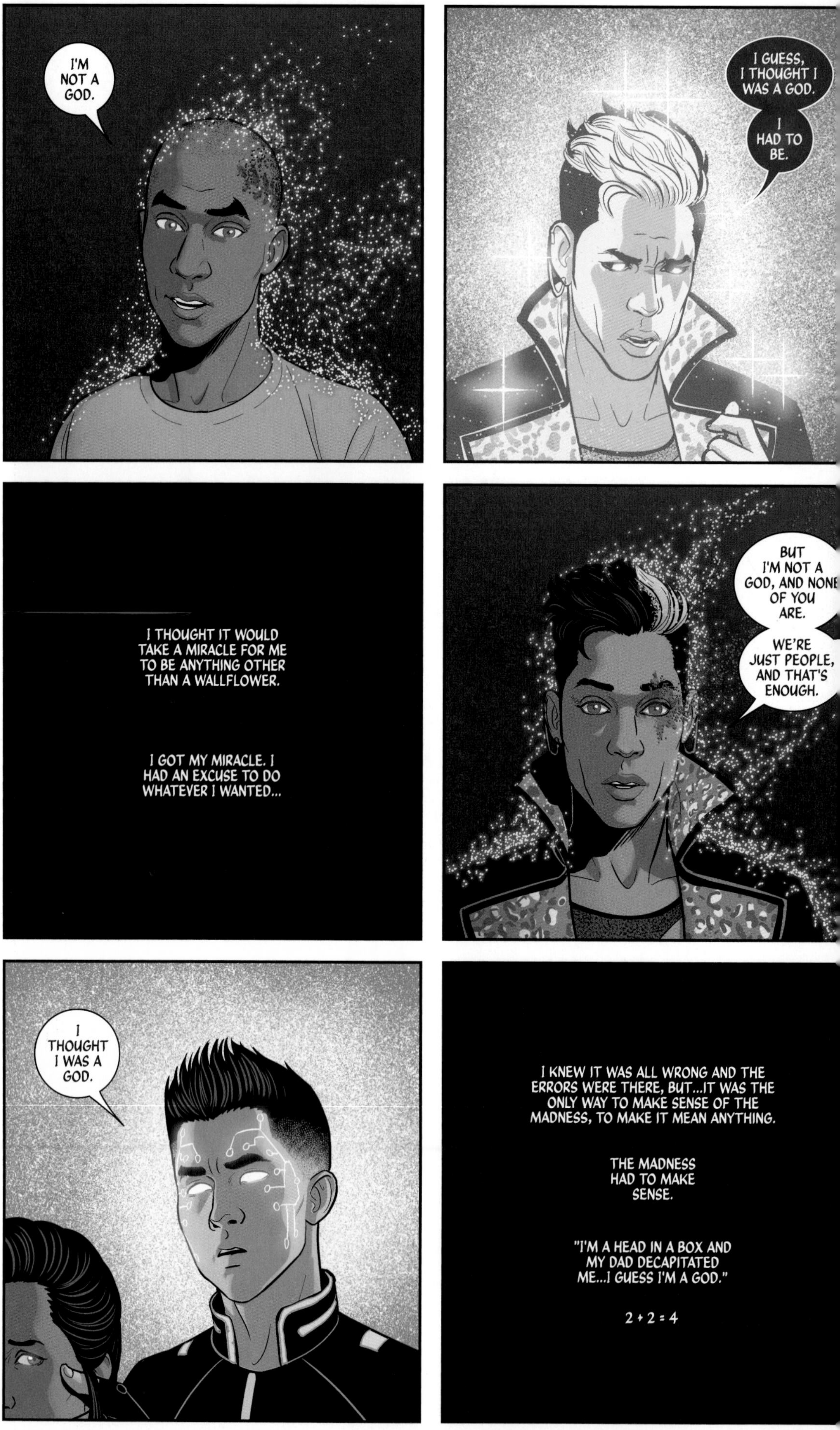
I'M NOT A GOD.
I GUESS, I THOUGHT I WAS A GOD.
I HAD TO BE.
I THOUGHT IT WOULD TAKE A MIRACLE FOR ME TO BE ANYTHING OTHER THAN A WALLFLOWER.
I GOT MY MIRACLE. I HAD AN EXCUSE TO DO WHATEVER I WANTED...
BUT I'M NOT A GOD, AND NONE OF YOU ARE.
WE'RE JUST PEOPLE, AND THAT'S ENOUGH.
I THOUGHT I WAS A GOD.
I KNEW IT WAS ALL WRONG AND THE ERRORS WERE THERE, BUT...IT WAS THE ONLY WAY TO MAKE SENSE OF THE MADNESS, TO MAKE IT MEAN ANYTHING.
THE MADNESS HAD TO MAKE SENSE.
"I'M A HEAD IN A BOX AND MY DAD DECAPITATED ME...I GUESS I'M A GOD."
2 + 2 = 4

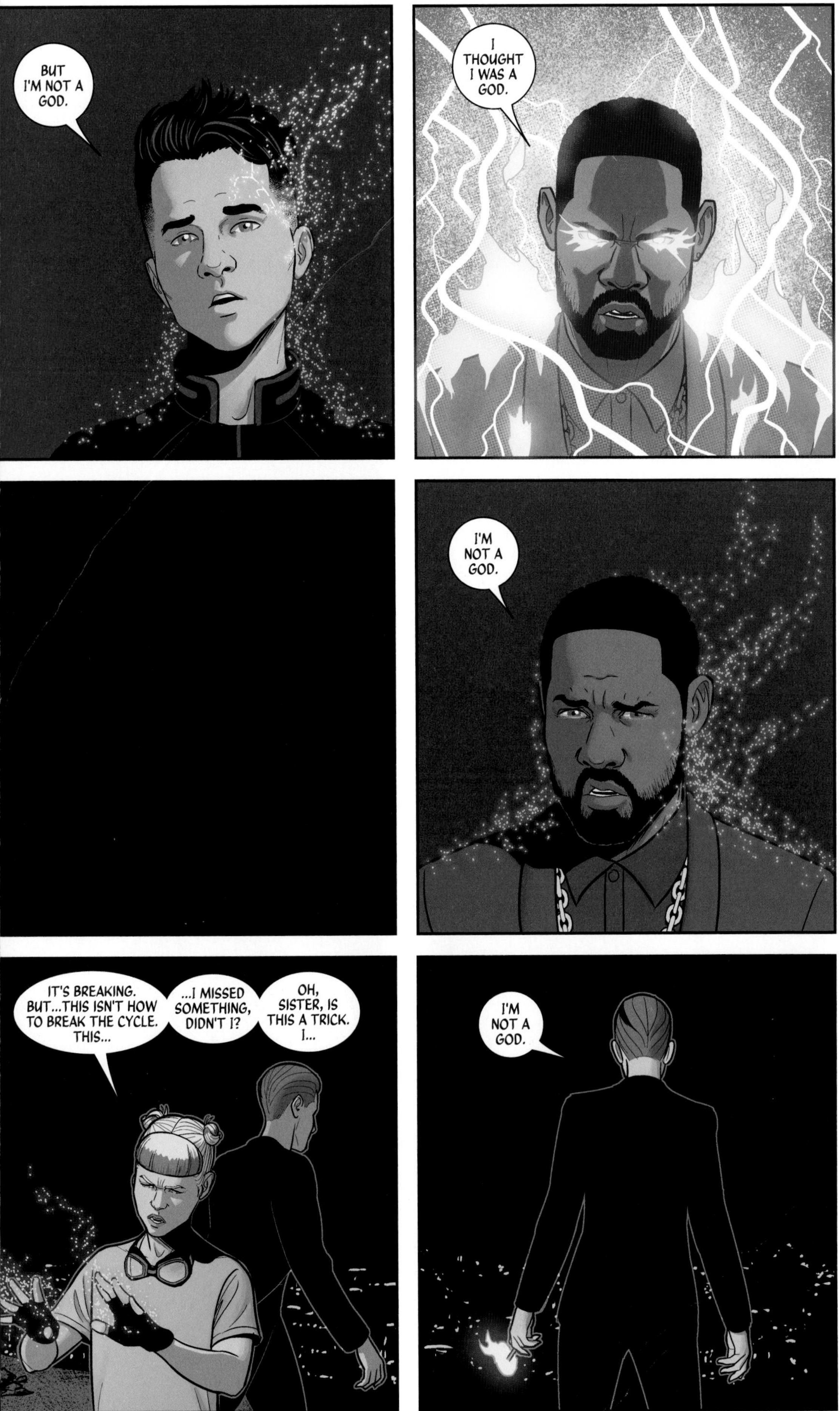
BUT I'M NOT A GOD.
I THOUGHT I WAS A GOD.
I'M NOT A GOD.
IT'S BREAKING. BUT...THIS ISN'T HOW TO BREAK THE CYCLE. THIS...
...I MISSED SOMETHING, DIDN'T I?
OH, SISTER, IS THIS A TRICK. I...
I'M NOT A GOD.

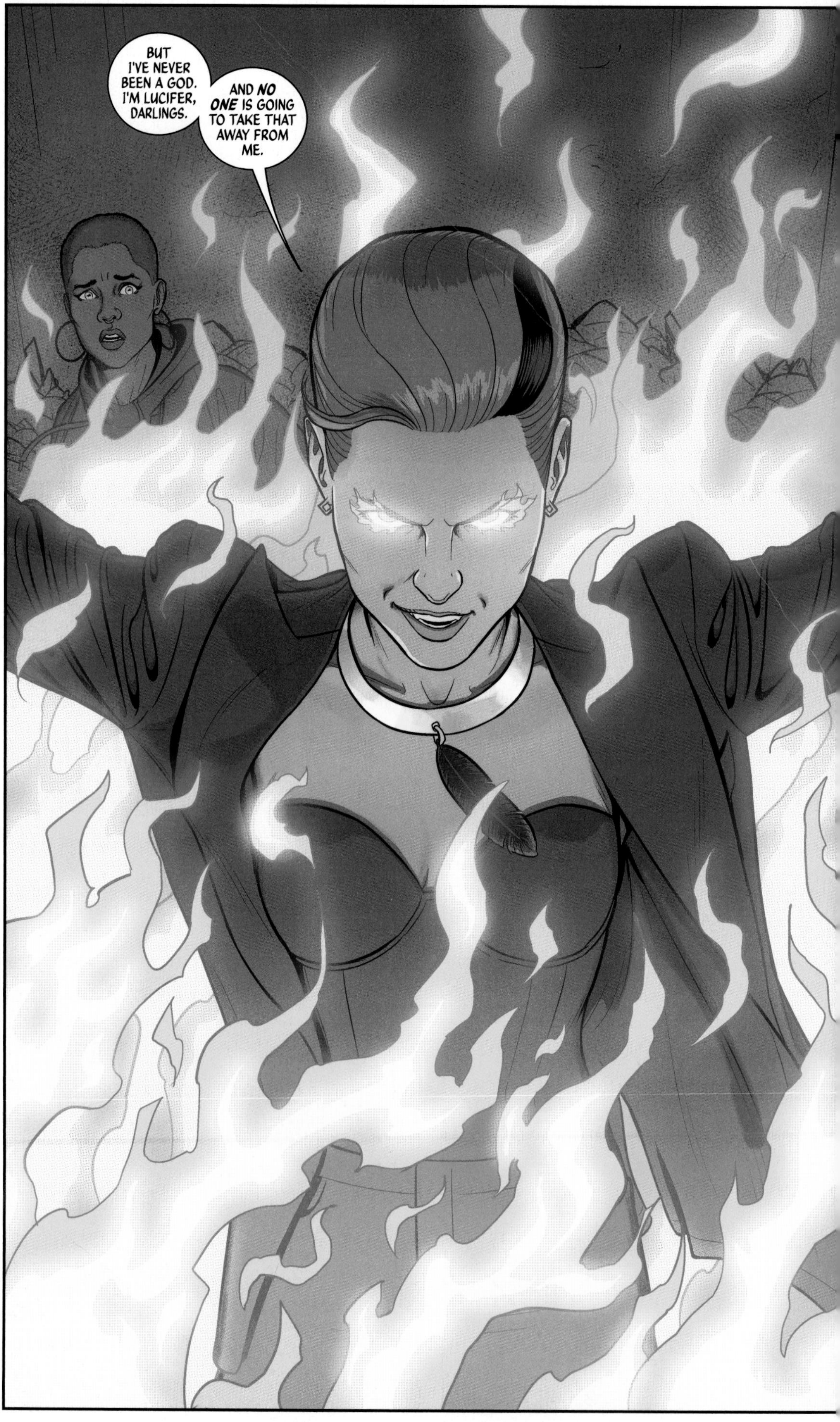
BUT I'VE NEVER BEEN A GOD. I'M LUCIFER, DARLINGS.
AND *NO ONE* IS GOING TO TAKE THAT AWAY FROM ME.

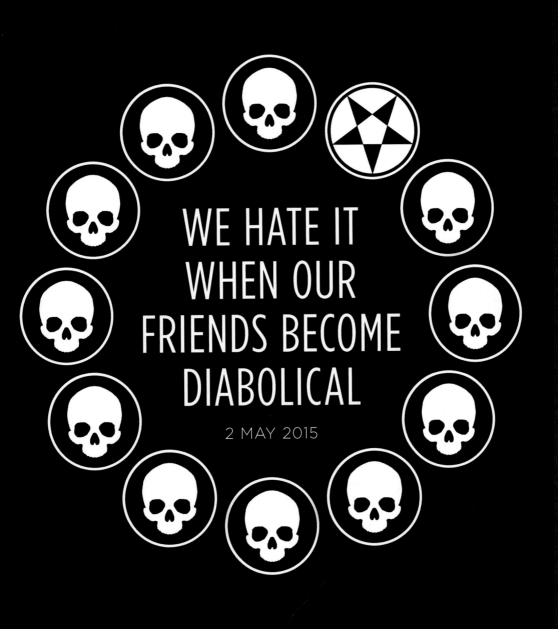

WE HATE IT WHEN OUR FRIENDS BECOME DIABOLICAL

2 MAY 2015

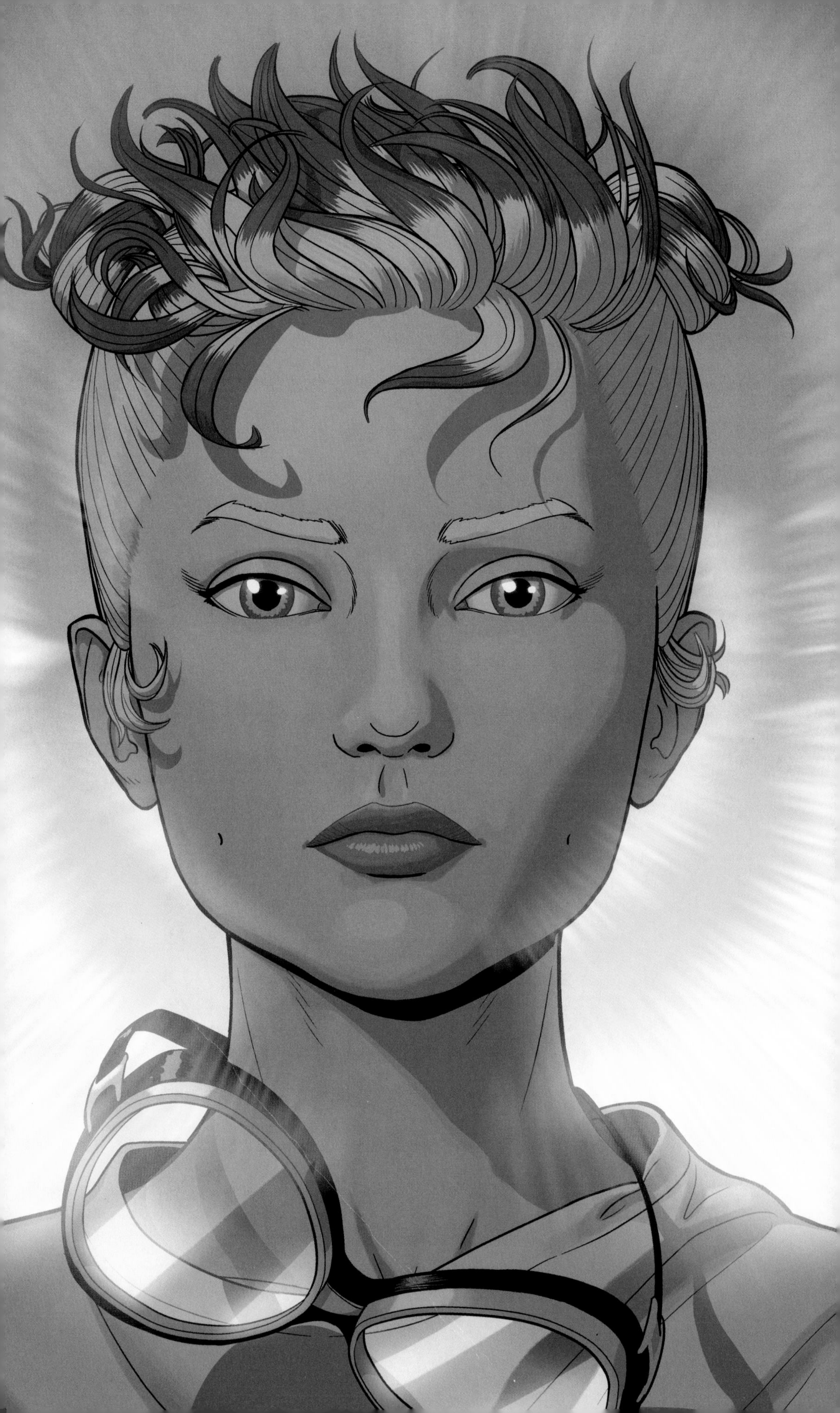

THE
WICKED
+
DIVINE
THE

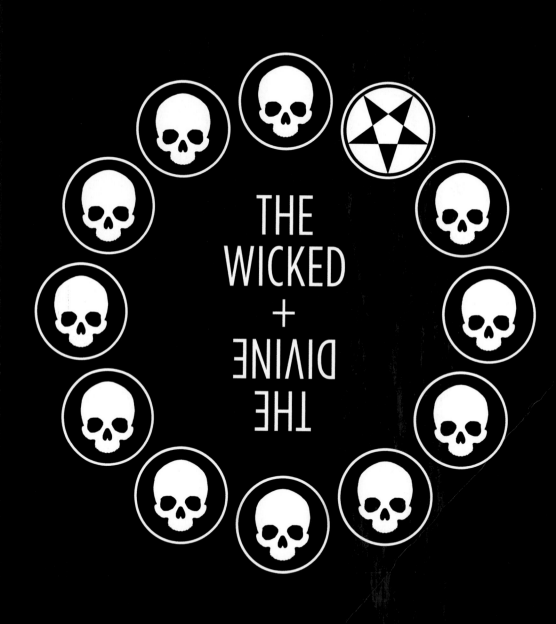

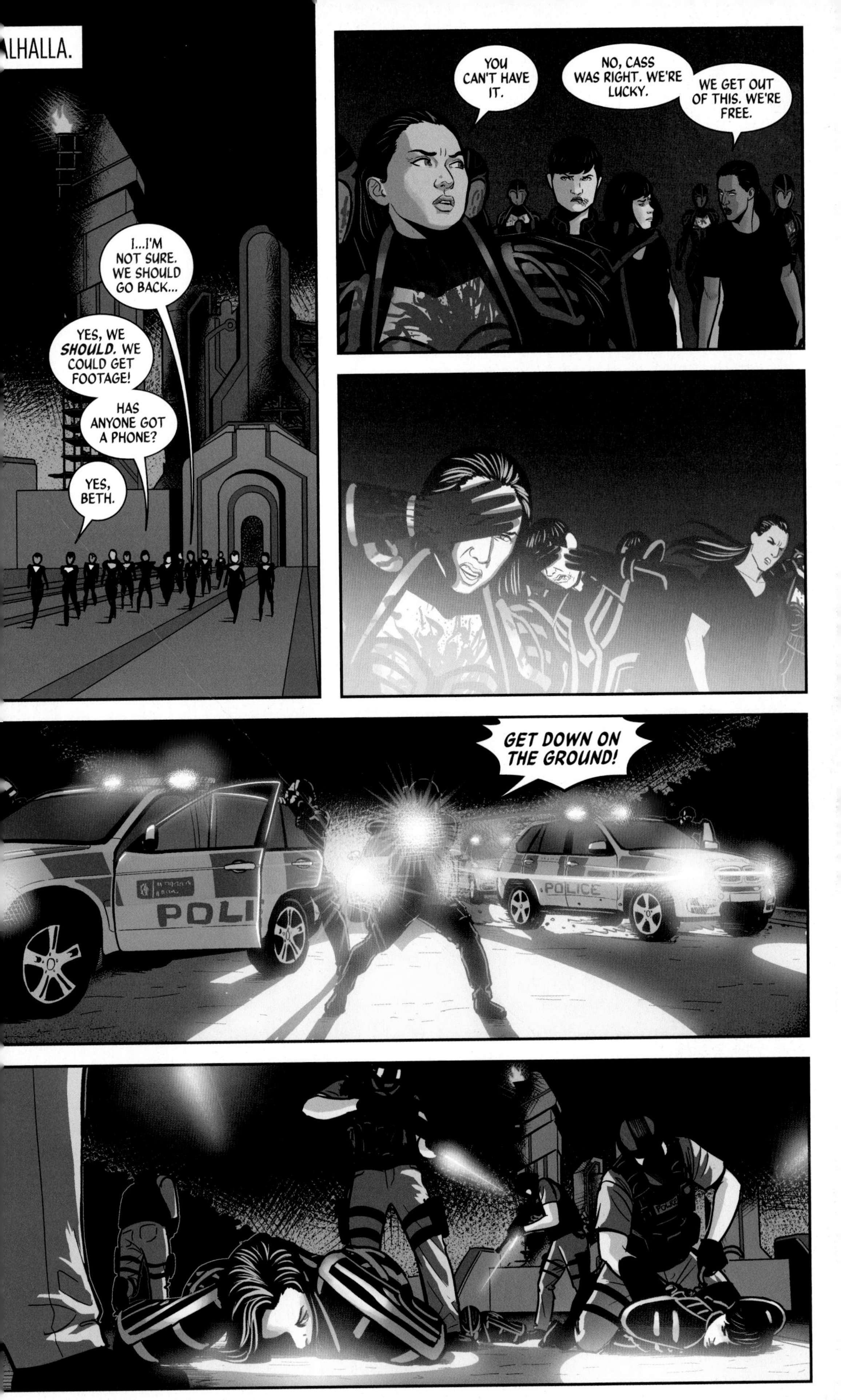

ALHALLA.
I...I'M NOT SURE. WE SHOULD GO BACK...
YES, WE *SHOULD.* WE COULD GET FOOTAGE!
HAS ANYONE GOT A PHONE?
YES, BETH.
YOU CAN'T HAVE IT.
NO, CASS WAS RIGHT. WE'RE LUCKY.
WE GET OUT OF THIS. WE'RE FREE.
GET DOWN ON THE GROUND!
POLI
POLICE

BETTER
NO DEVIL
AT ALL

2 MAY 2015

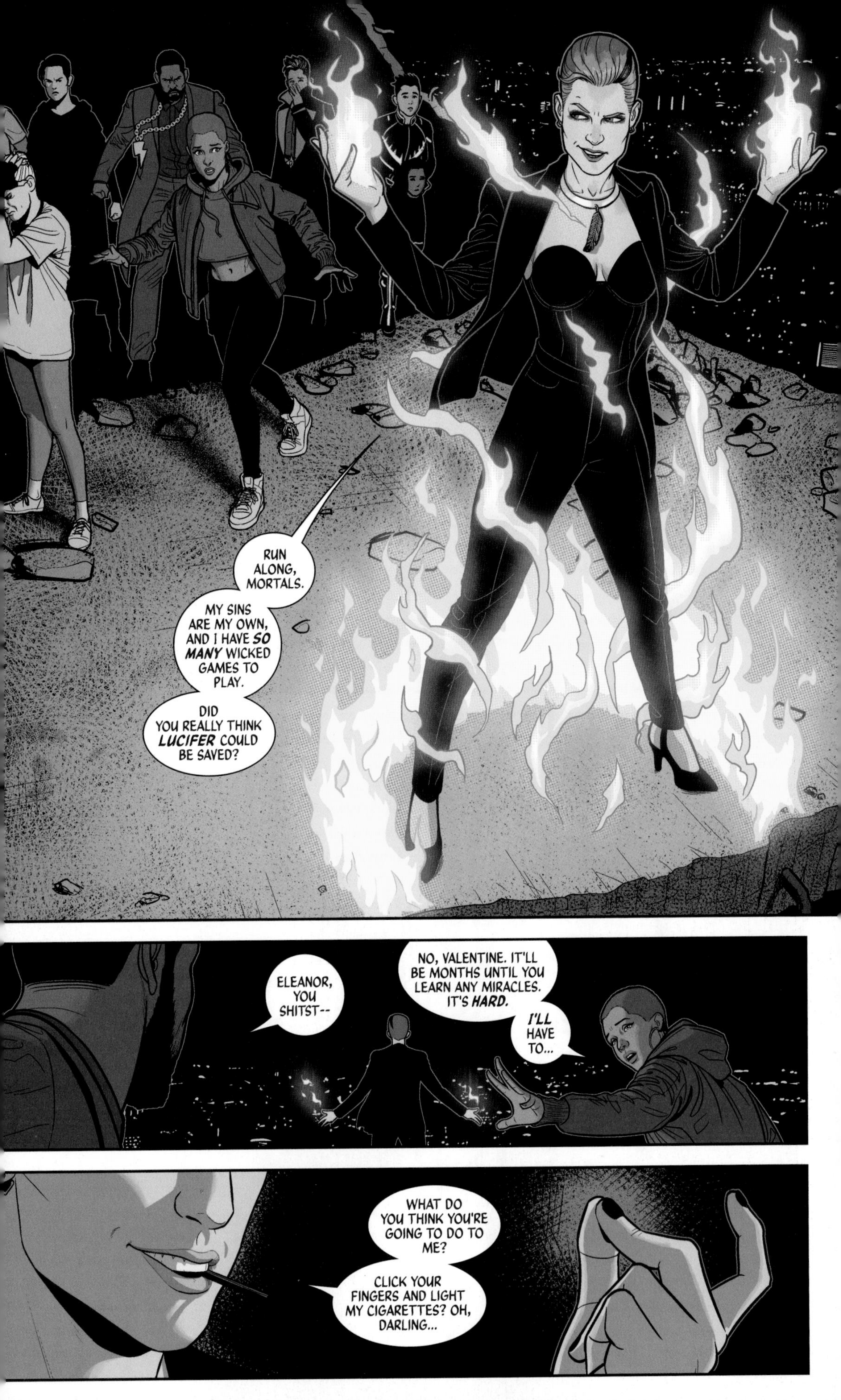
RUN ALONG, MORTALS.
MY SINS ARE MY OWN, AND I HAVE ***SO MANY*** WICKED GAMES TO PLAY.
DID YOU REALLY THINK ***LUCIFER*** COULD BE SAVED?
ELEANOR, YOU SHITST--
NO, VALENTINE. IT'LL BE MONTHS UNTIL YOU LEARN ANY MIRACLES. IT'S ***HARD.***
I'LL HAVE TO...
WHAT DO YOU THINK YOU'RE GOING TO DO TO ME?
CLICK YOUR FINGERS AND LIGHT MY CIGARETTES? OH, DARLING...

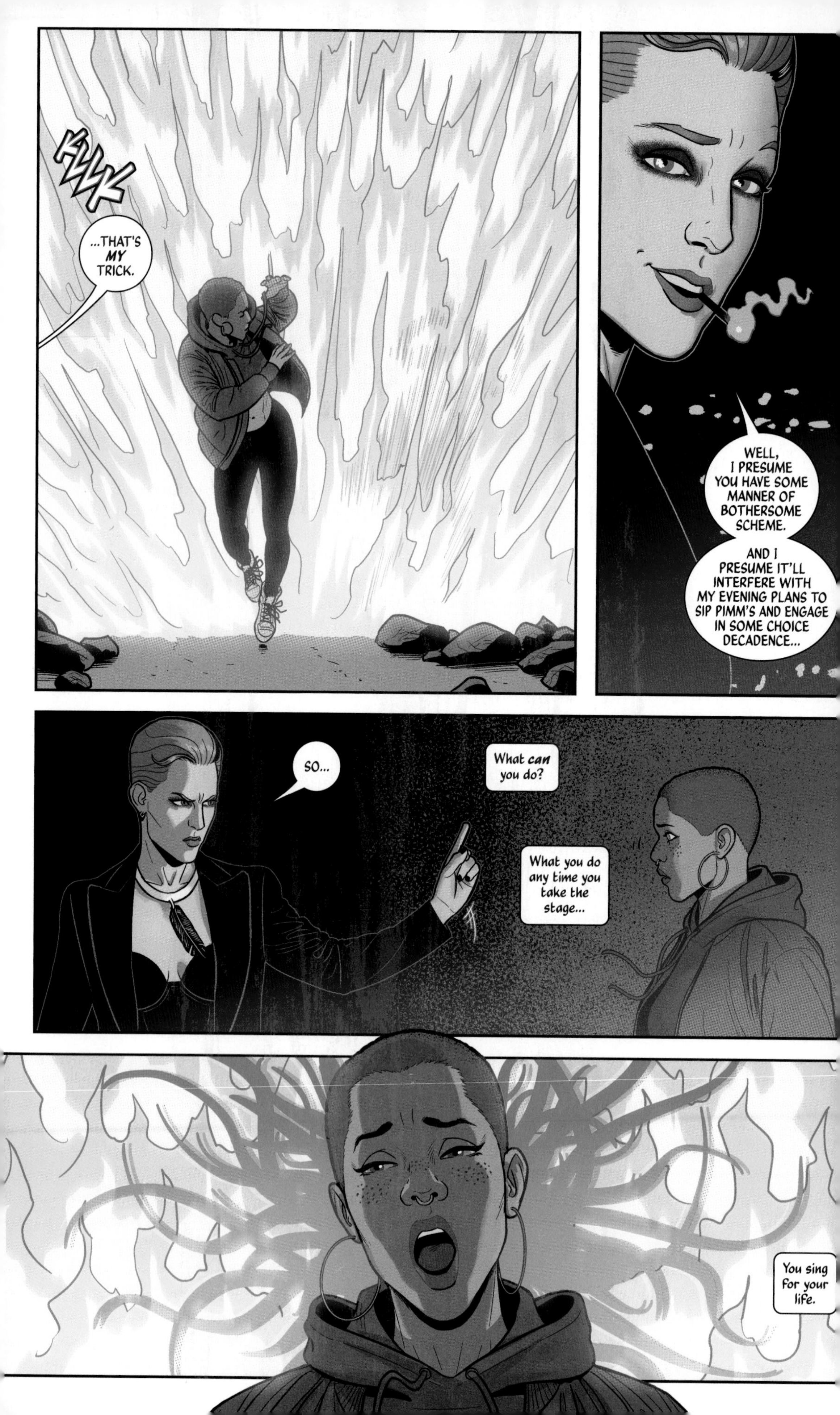
KKKK
...THAT'S MY TRICK.
WELL, I PRESUME YOU HAVE SOME MANNER OF BOTHERSOME SCHEME.
AND I PRESUME IT'LL INTERFERE WITH MY EVENING PLANS TO SIP PIMM'S AND ENGAGE IN SOME CHOICE DECADENCE...
SO...
What can you do?
What you do any time you take the stage...
You sing for your life.

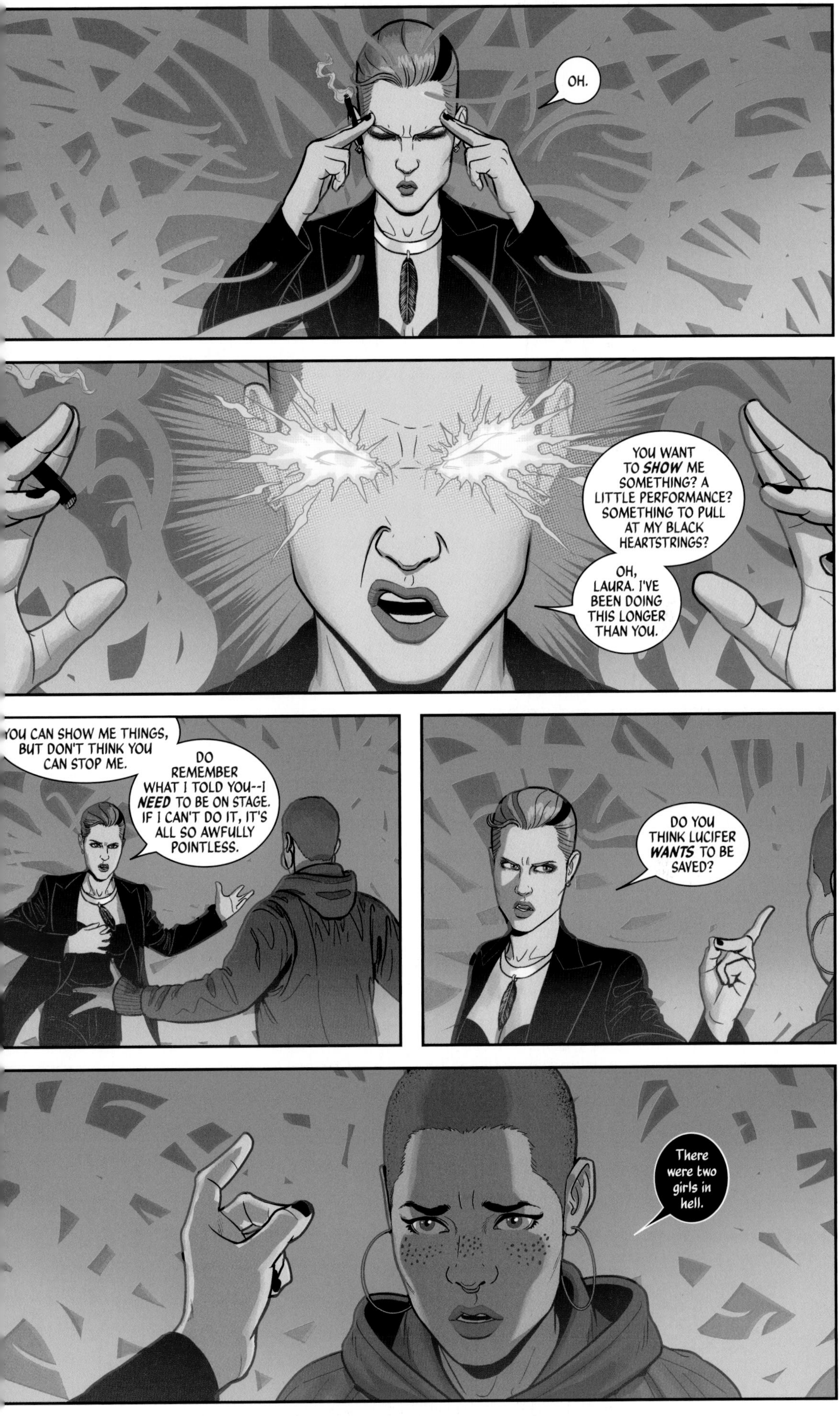
OH.
YOU WANT TO SHOW ME SOMETHING? A LITTLE PERFORMANCE? SOMETHING TO PULL AT MY BLACK HEARTSTRINGS?
OH, LAURA. I'VE BEEN DOING THIS LONGER THAN YOU.
YOU CAN SHOW ME THINGS, BUT DON'T THINK YOU CAN STOP ME.
DO REMEMBER WHAT I TOLD YOU--I NEED TO BE ON STAGE. IF I CAN'T DO IT, IT'S ALL SO AWFULLY POINTLESS.
DO YOU THINK LUCIFER WANTS TO BE SAVED?
There were two girls in hell.

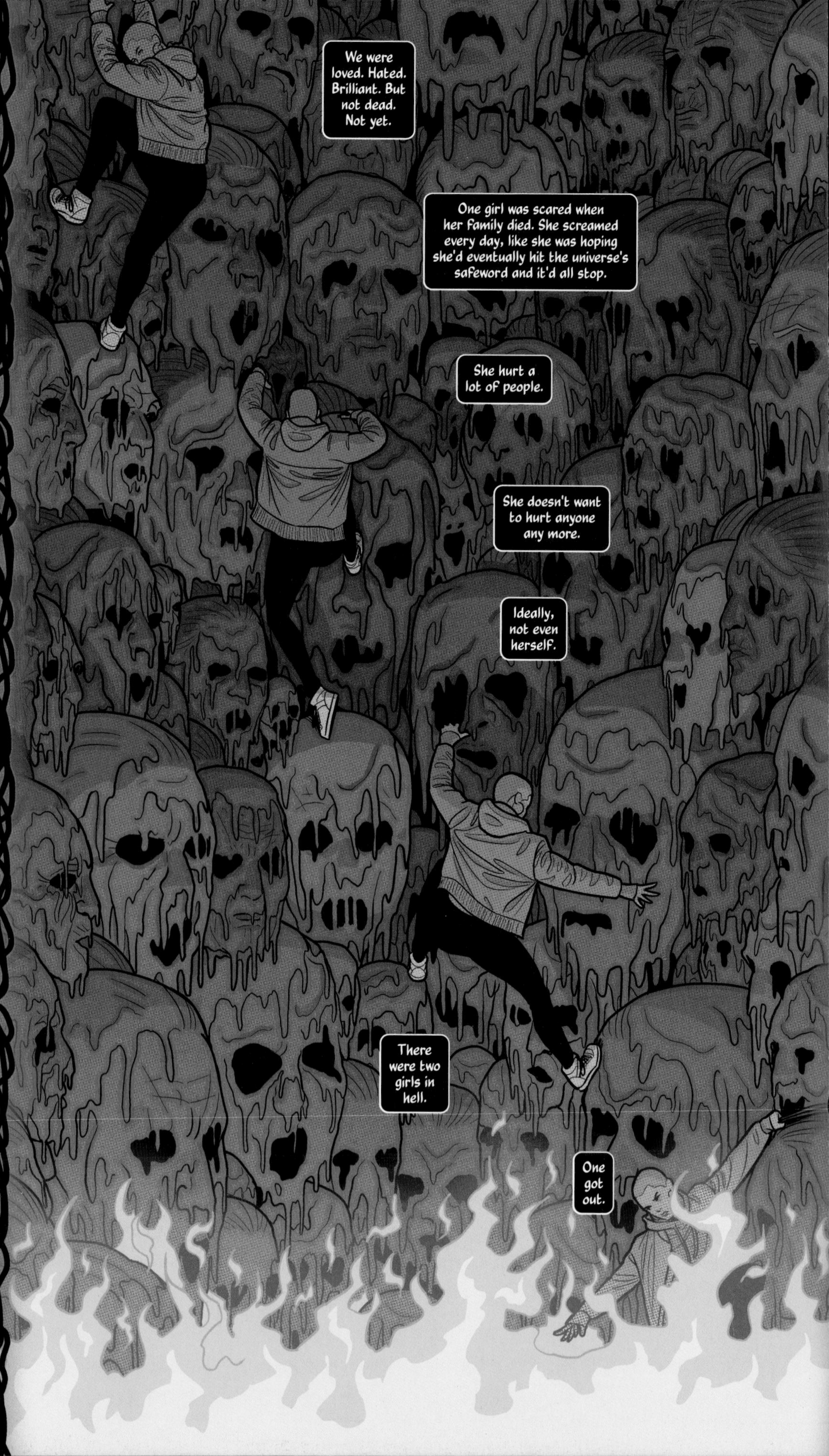
We were loved. Hated. Brilliant. But not dead. Not yet.
One girl was scared when her family died. She screamed every day, like she was hoping she'd eventually hit the universe's safeword and it'd all stop.
She hurt a lot of people.
She doesn't want to hurt anyone any more.
Ideally, not even herself.
There were two girls in hell.
One got out.

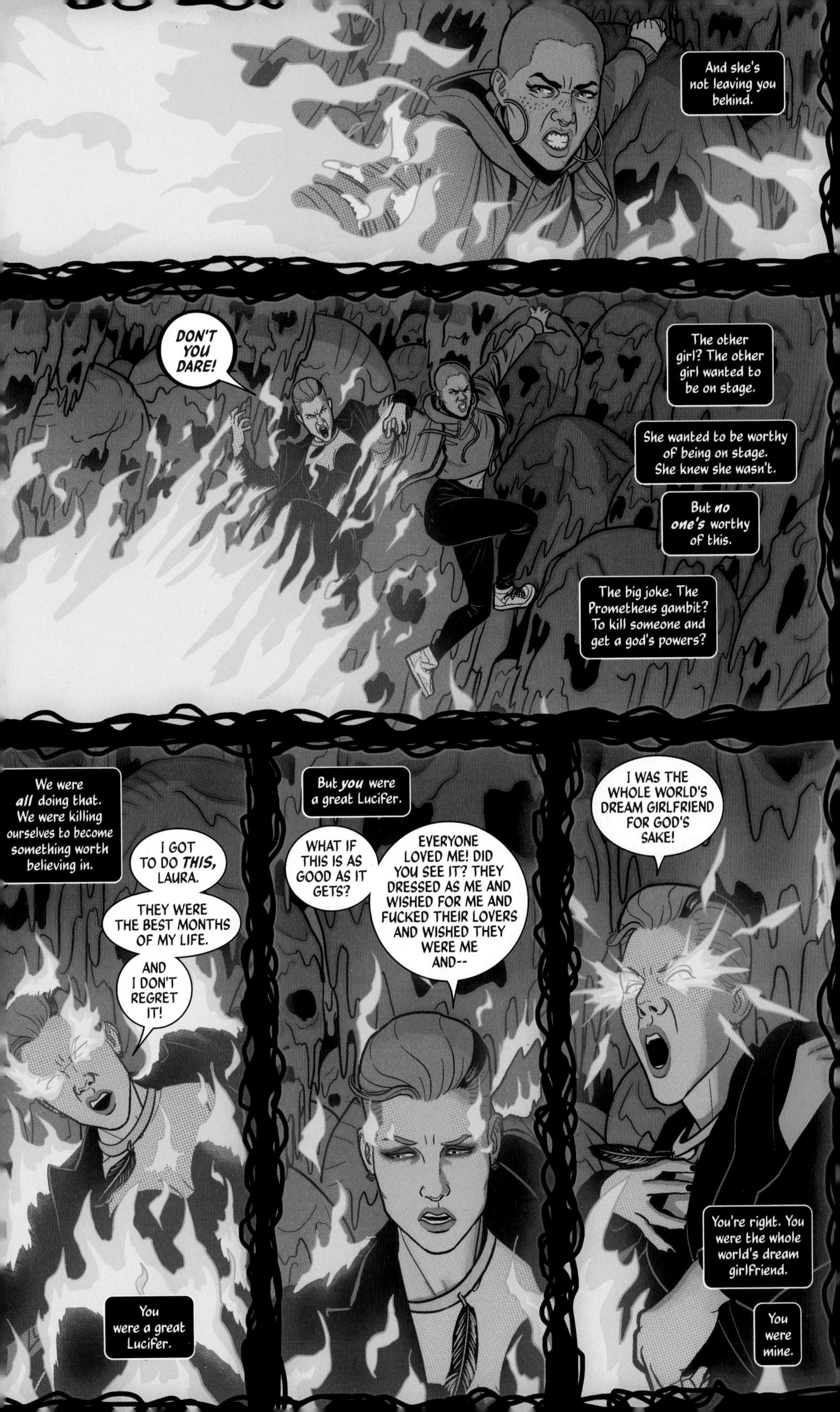

And she's not leaving you behind.
DON'T YOU DARE!
The other girl? The other girl wanted to be on stage.
She wanted to be worthy of being on stage. She knew she wasn't.
But *no one's* worthy of this.
The big joke. The Prometheus gambit? To kill someone and get a god's powers?
We were *all* doing that. We were killing ourselves to become something worth believing in.
I GOT TO DO *THIS,* LAURA.
THEY WERE THE BEST MONTHS OF MY LIFE.
AND I DON'T REGRET IT!
You were a great Lucifer.
But *you* were a great Lucifer.
WHAT IF THIS IS AS GOOD AS IT GETS?
EVERYONE LOVED ME! DID YOU SEE IT? THEY DRESSED AS ME AND WISHED FOR ME AND FUCKED THEIR LOVERS AND WISHED THEY WERE ME AND--
I WAS THE WHOLE WORLD'S DREAM GIRLFRIEND FOR GOD'S SAKE!
You're right. You were the whole world's dream girlfriend.
You were mine.

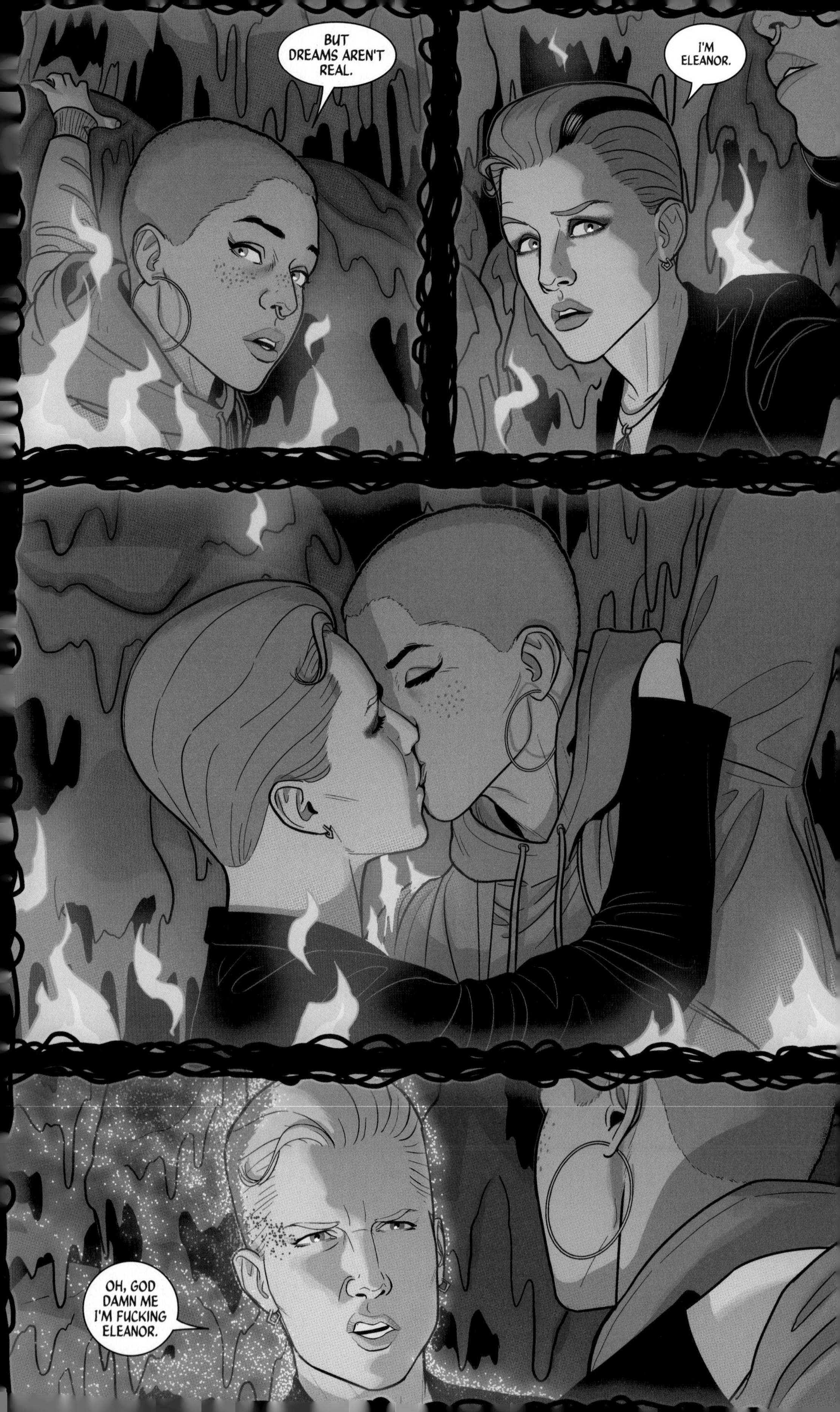
BUT DREAMS AREN'T REAL.
I'M ELEANOR.
OH, GOD DAMN ME I'M FUCKING ELEANOR.

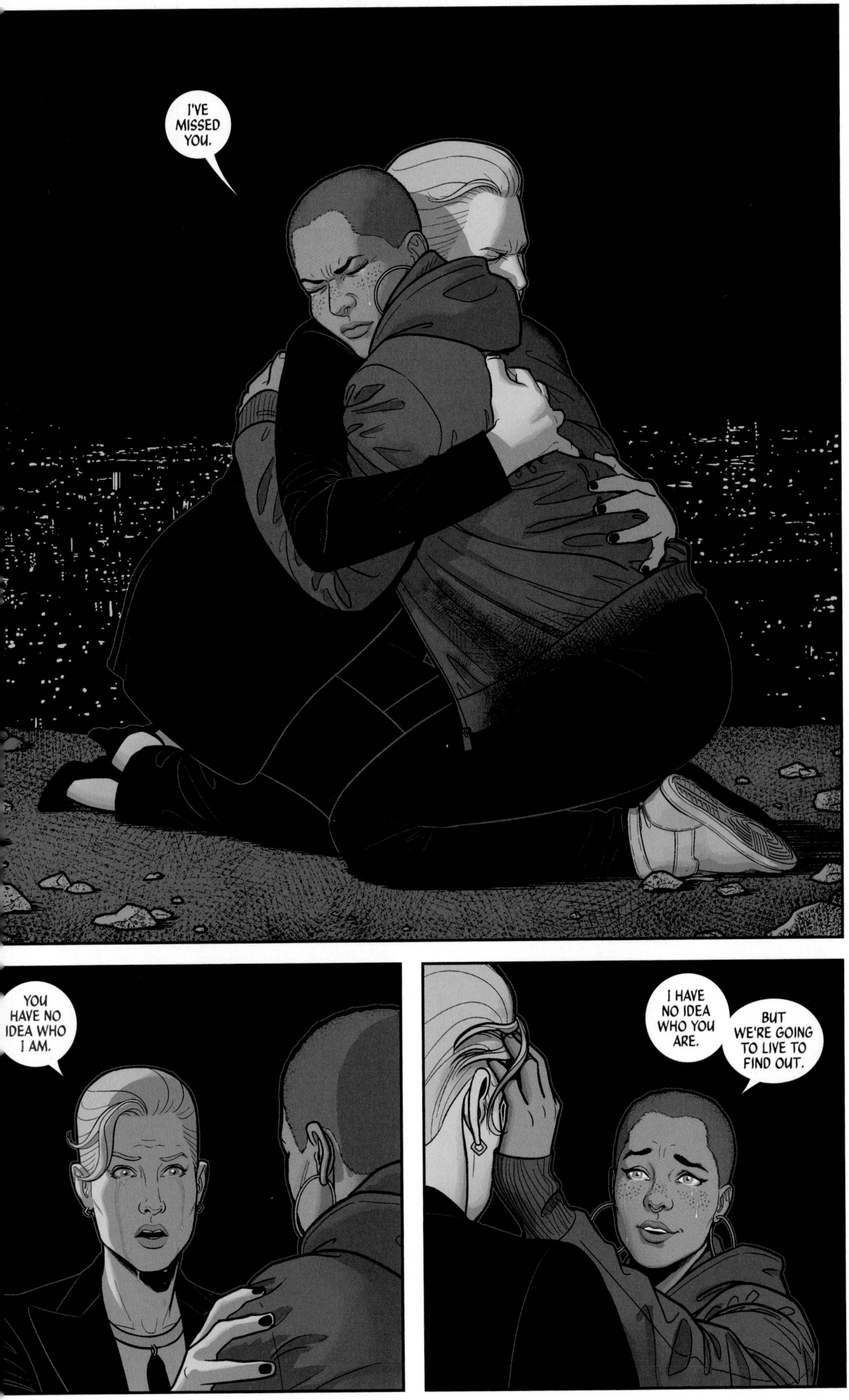
I'VE MISSED YOU.
YOU HAVE NO IDEA WHO I AM.
I HAVE NO IDEA WHO YOU ARE.
BUT WE'RE GOING TO LIVE TO FIND OUT.

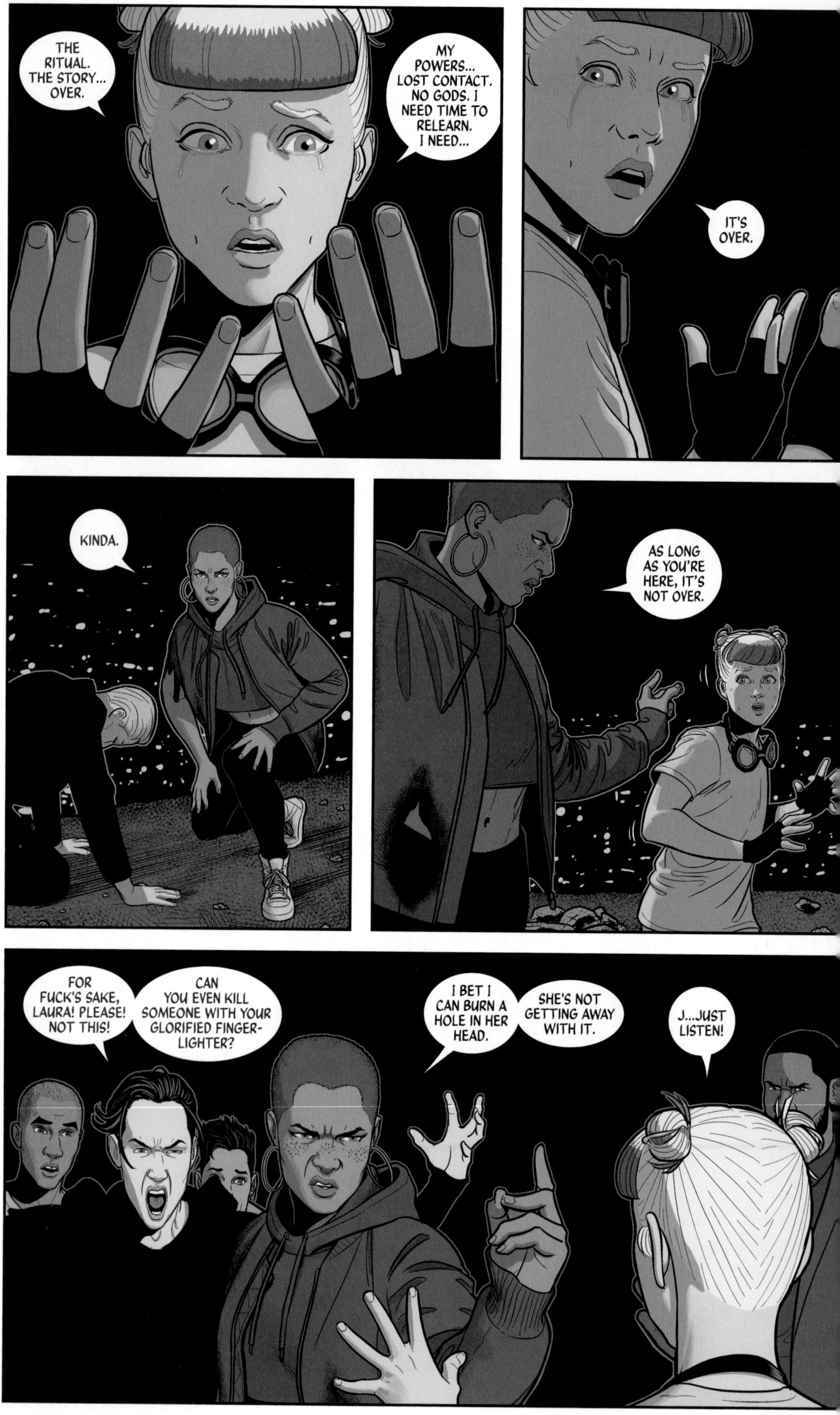
THE RITUAL. THE STORY... OVER.
MY POWERS... LOST CONTACT. NO GODS. I NEED TIME TO RELEARN. I NEED...
IT'S OVER.
KINDA.
AS LONG AS YOU'RE HERE, IT'S NOT OVER.
FOR FUCK'S SAKE, LAURA! PLEASE! NOT THIS!
CAN YOU EVEN KILL SOMEONE WITH YOUR GLORIFIED FINGER-LIGHTER?
I BET I CAN BURN A HOLE IN HER HEAD.
SHE'S NOT GETTING AWAY WITH IT.
J...JUST LISTEN!

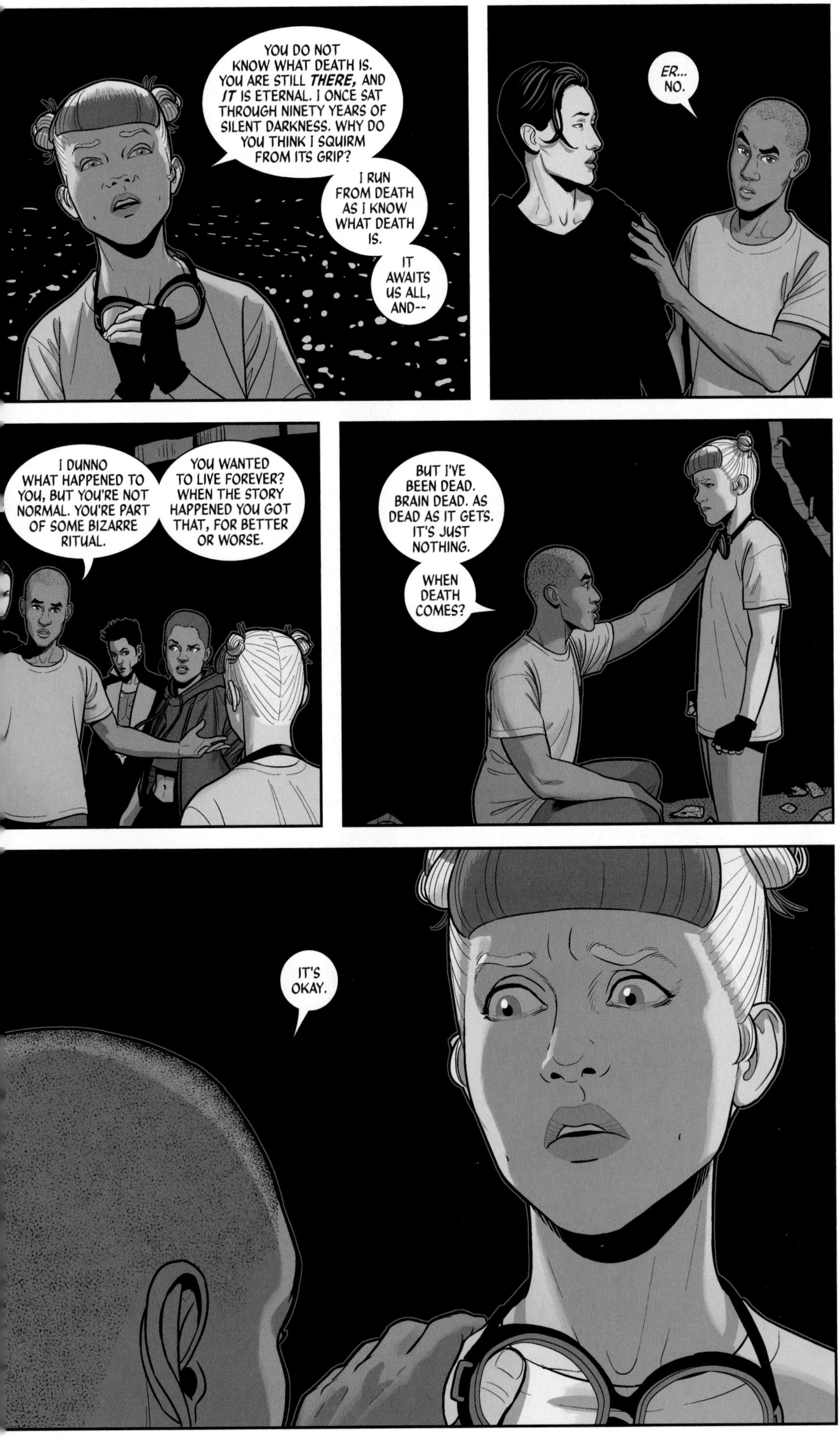

YOU DO NOT KNOW WHAT DEATH IS. YOU ARE STILL *THERE,* AND *IT* IS ETERNAL. I ONCE SAT THROUGH NINETY YEARS OF SILENT DARKNESS. WHY DO YOU THINK I SQUIRM FROM ITS GRIP?
I RUN FROM DEATH AS I KNOW WHAT DEATH IS.
IT AWAITS US ALL, AND--
ER... NO.
I DUNNO WHAT HAPPENED TO YOU, BUT YOU'RE NOT NORMAL. YOU'RE PART OF SOME BIZARRE RITUAL.
YOU WANTED TO LIVE FOREVER? WHEN THE STORY HAPPENED YOU GOT THAT, FOR BETTER OR WORSE.
BUT I'VE BEEN DEAD. BRAIN DEAD. AS DEAD AS IT GETS. IT'S JUST NOTHING.
WHEN DEATH COMES?
IT'S OKAY.

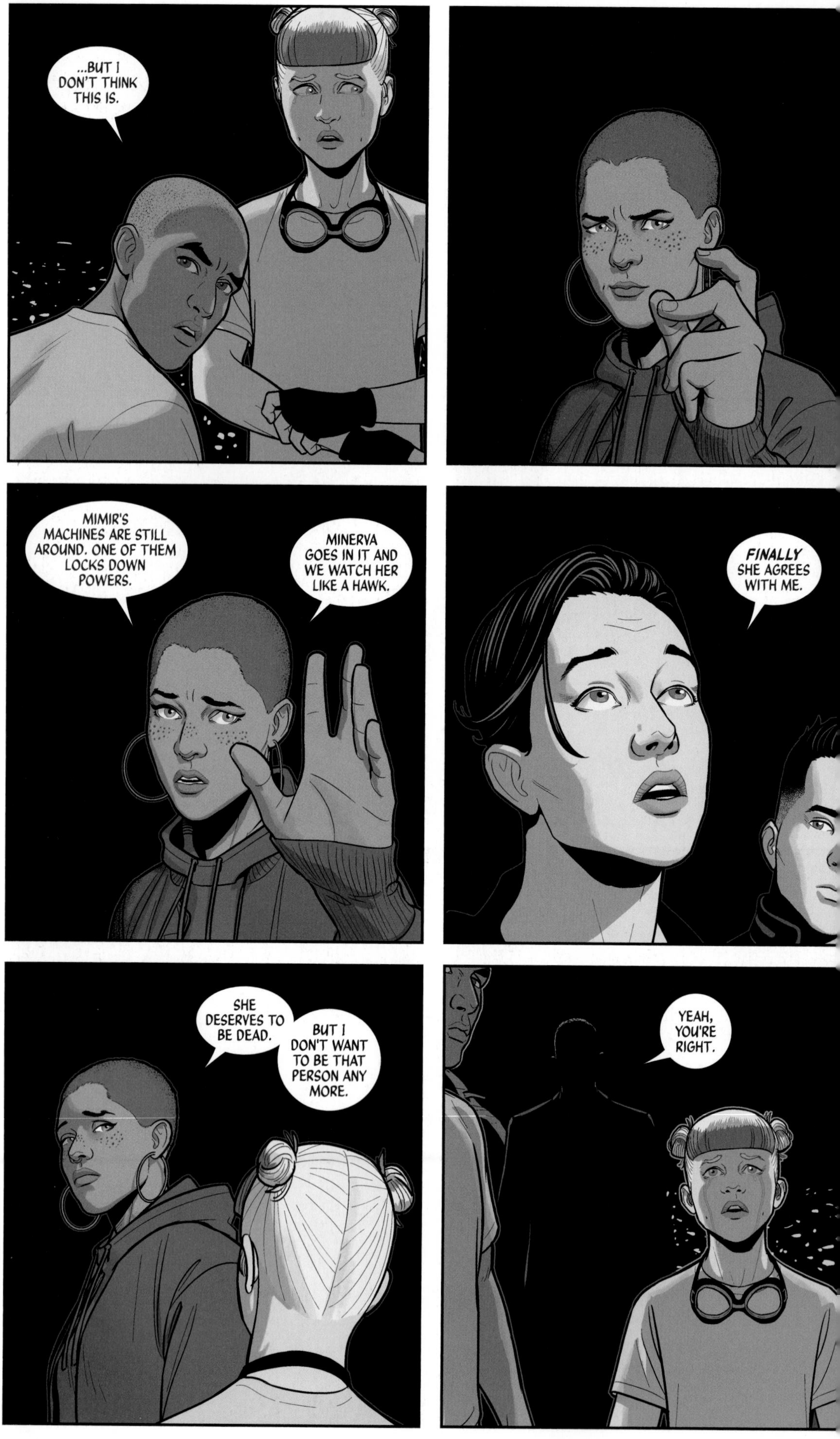

...BUT I DON'T THINK THIS IS.
MIMIR'S MACHINES ARE STILL AROUND. ONE OF THEM LOCKS DOWN POWERS.
MINERVA GOES IN IT AND WE WATCH HER LIKE A HAWK.
FINALLY SHE AGREES WITH ME.
SHE DESERVES TO BE DEAD.
BUT I DON'T WANT TO BE THAT PERSON ANY MORE.
YEAH, YOU'RE RIGHT.

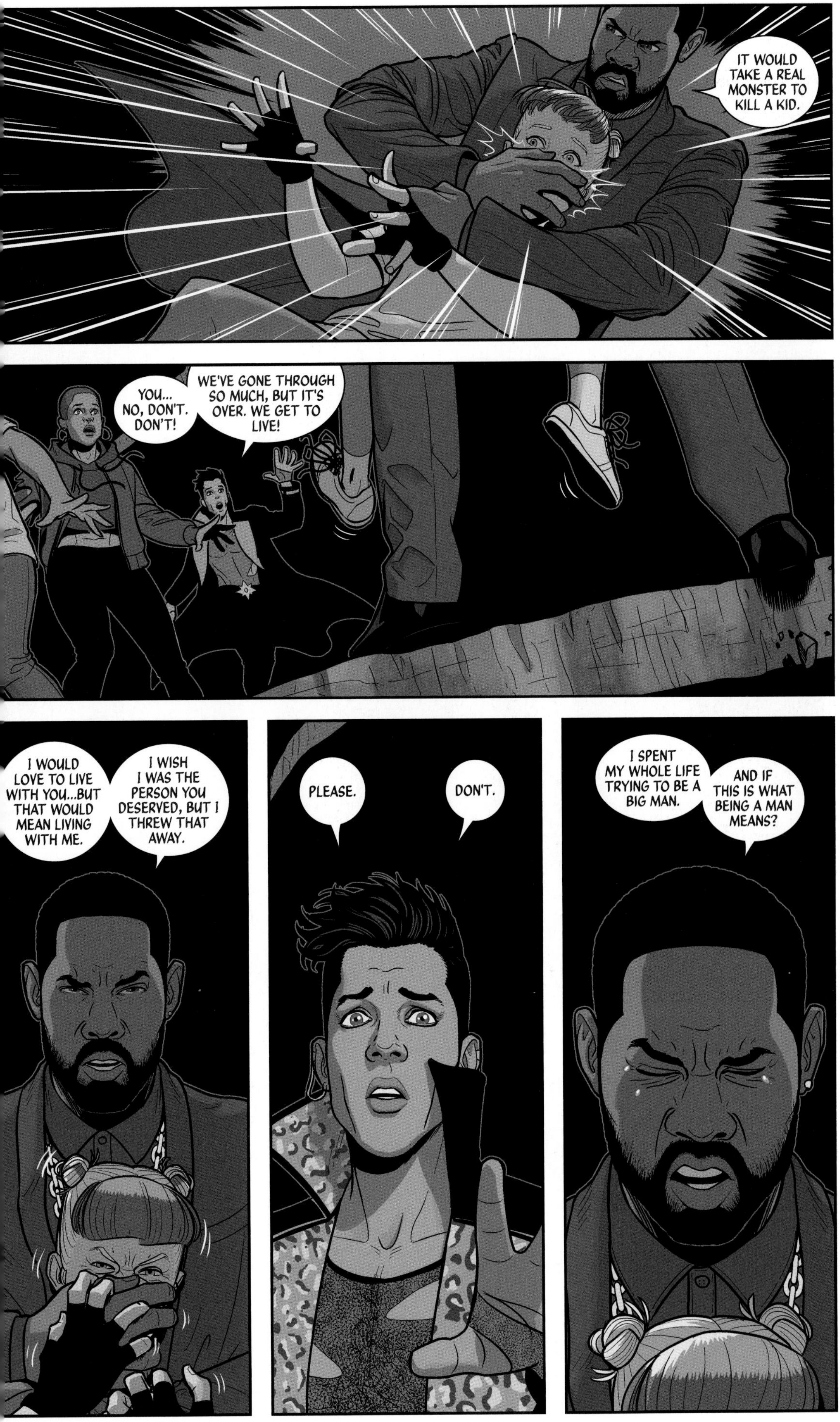
IT WOULD TAKE A REAL MONSTER TO KILL A KID.
YOU... NO, DON'T. DON'T!
WE'VE GONE THROUGH SO MUCH, BUT IT'S OVER. WE GET TO LIVE!
I WOULD LOVE TO LIVE WITH YOU...BUT THAT WOULD MEAN LIVING WITH ME.
I WISH I WAS THE PERSON YOU DESERVED, BUT I THREW THAT AWAY.
PLEASE.
DON'T.
I SPENT MY WHOLE LIFE TRYING TO BE A BIG MAN.
AND IF THIS IS WHAT BEING A MAN MEANS?

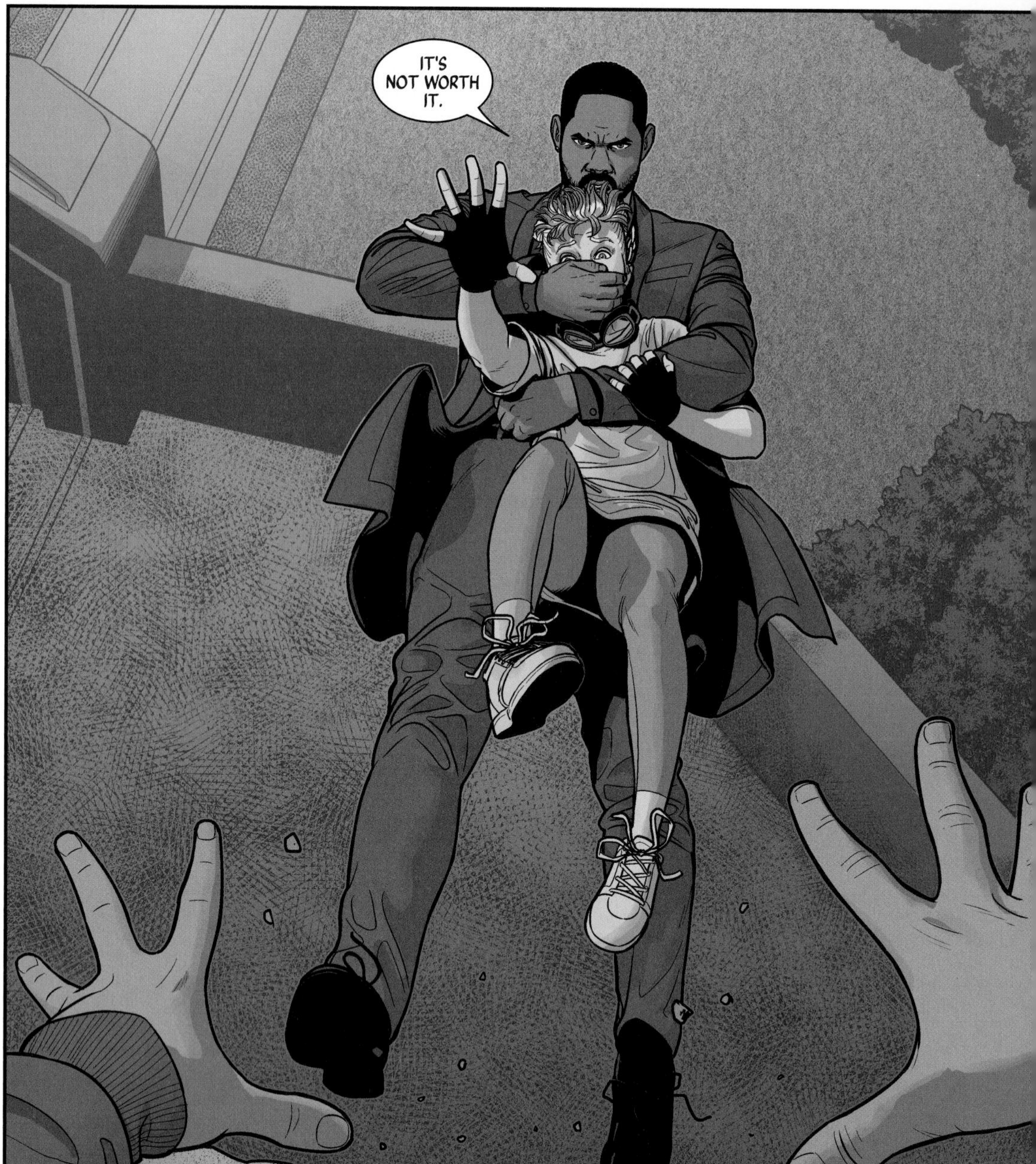
IT'S NOT WORTH IT.

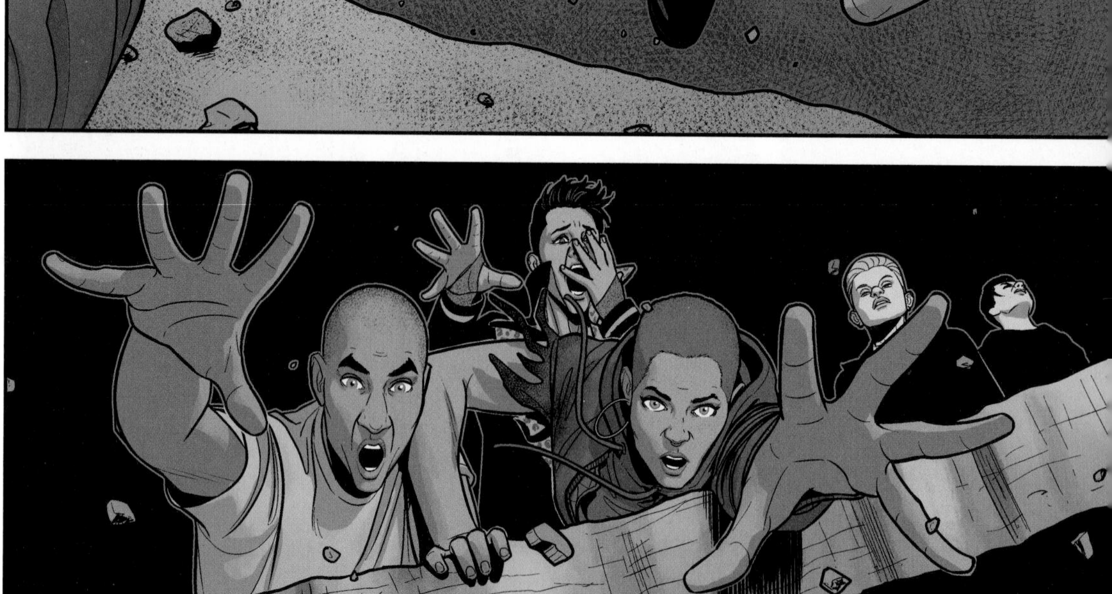

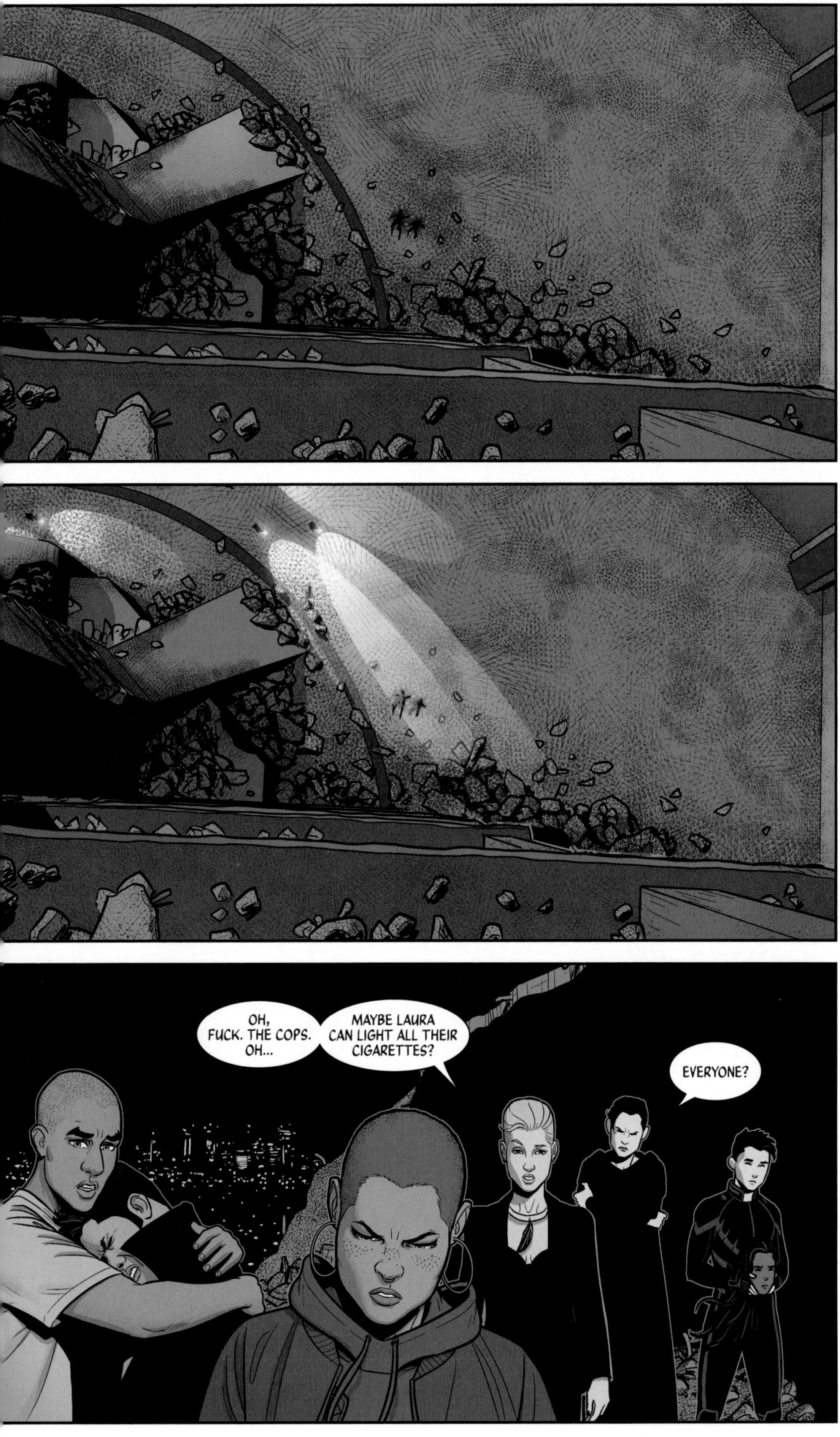
OH, FUCK. THE COPS. OH...
MAYBE LAURA CAN LIGHT ALL THEIR CIGARETTES?
EVERYONE?

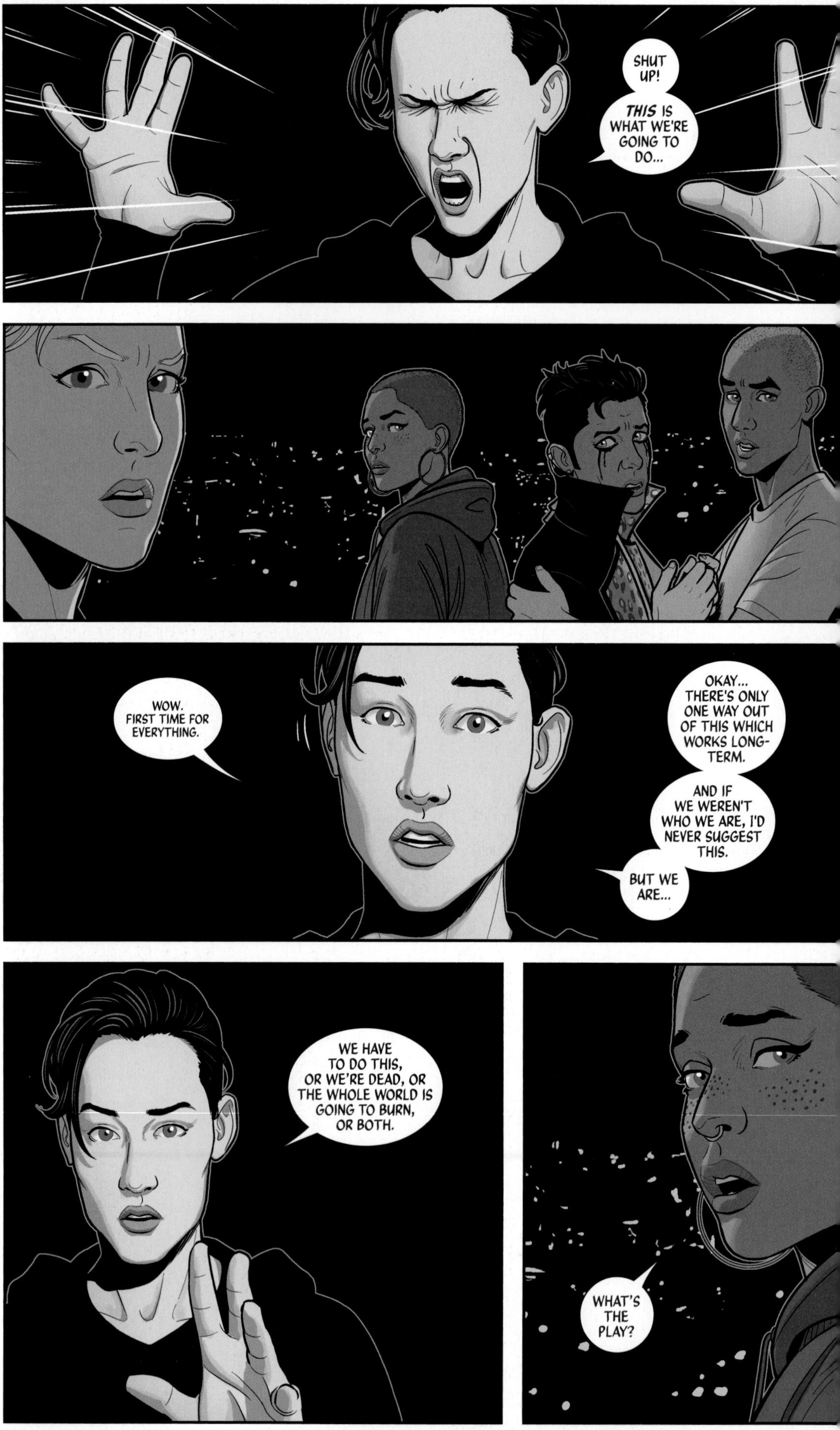
SHUT UP!
THIS IS WHAT WE'RE GOING TO DO...
WOW. FIRST TIME FOR EVERYTHING.
OKAY... THERE'S ONLY ONE WAY OUT OF THIS WHICH WORKS LONG-TERM.
AND IF WE WEREN'T WHO WE ARE, I'D NEVER SUGGEST THIS.
BUT WE ARE...
WE HAVE TO DO THIS, OR WE'RE DEAD, OR THE WHOLE WORLD IS GOING TO BURN, OR BOTH.
WHAT'S THE PLAY?

VOLUNTARYISM

2 MAY 2015

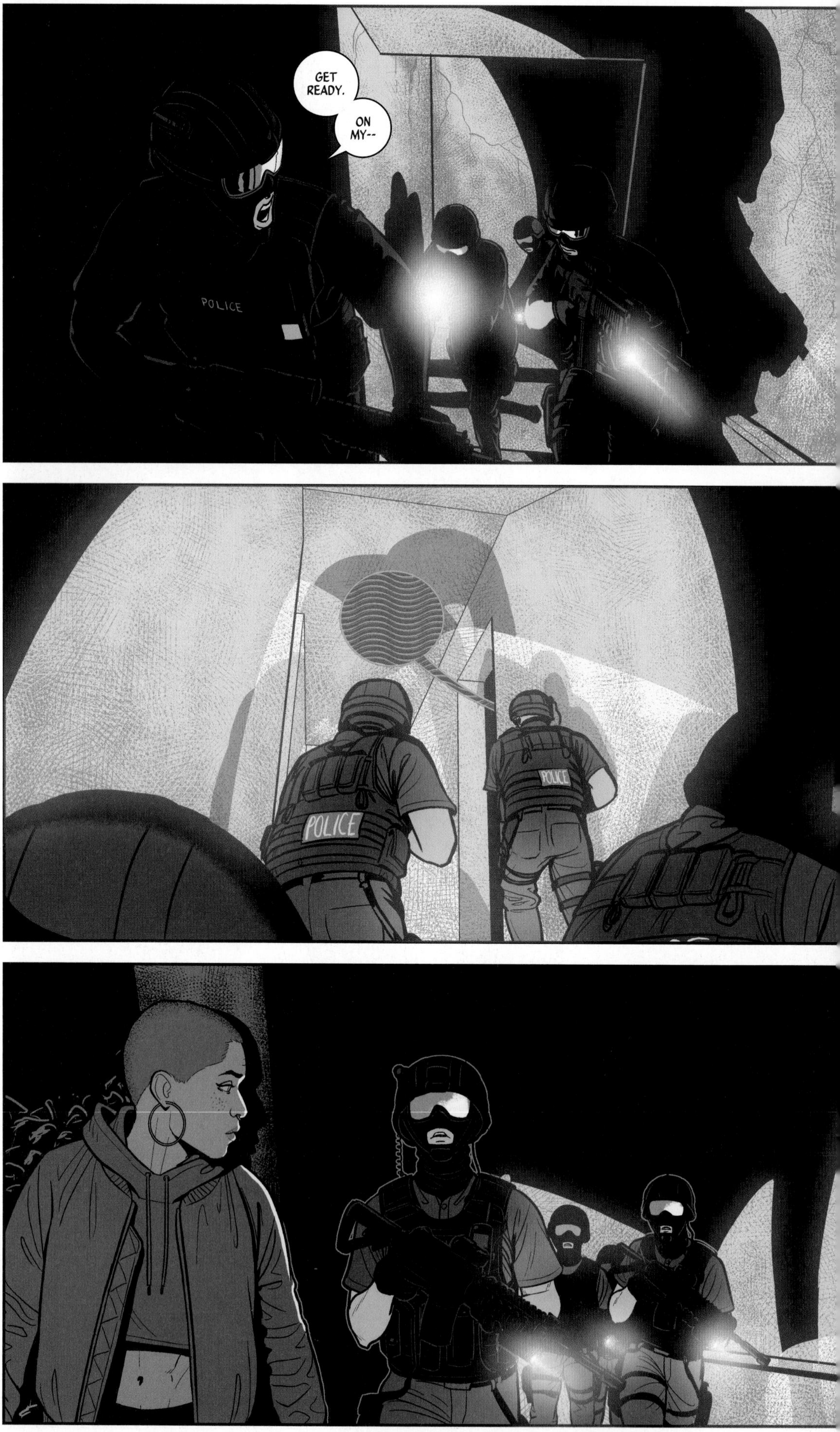
GET READY.
ON MY--
POLICE
POLICE
POLICE

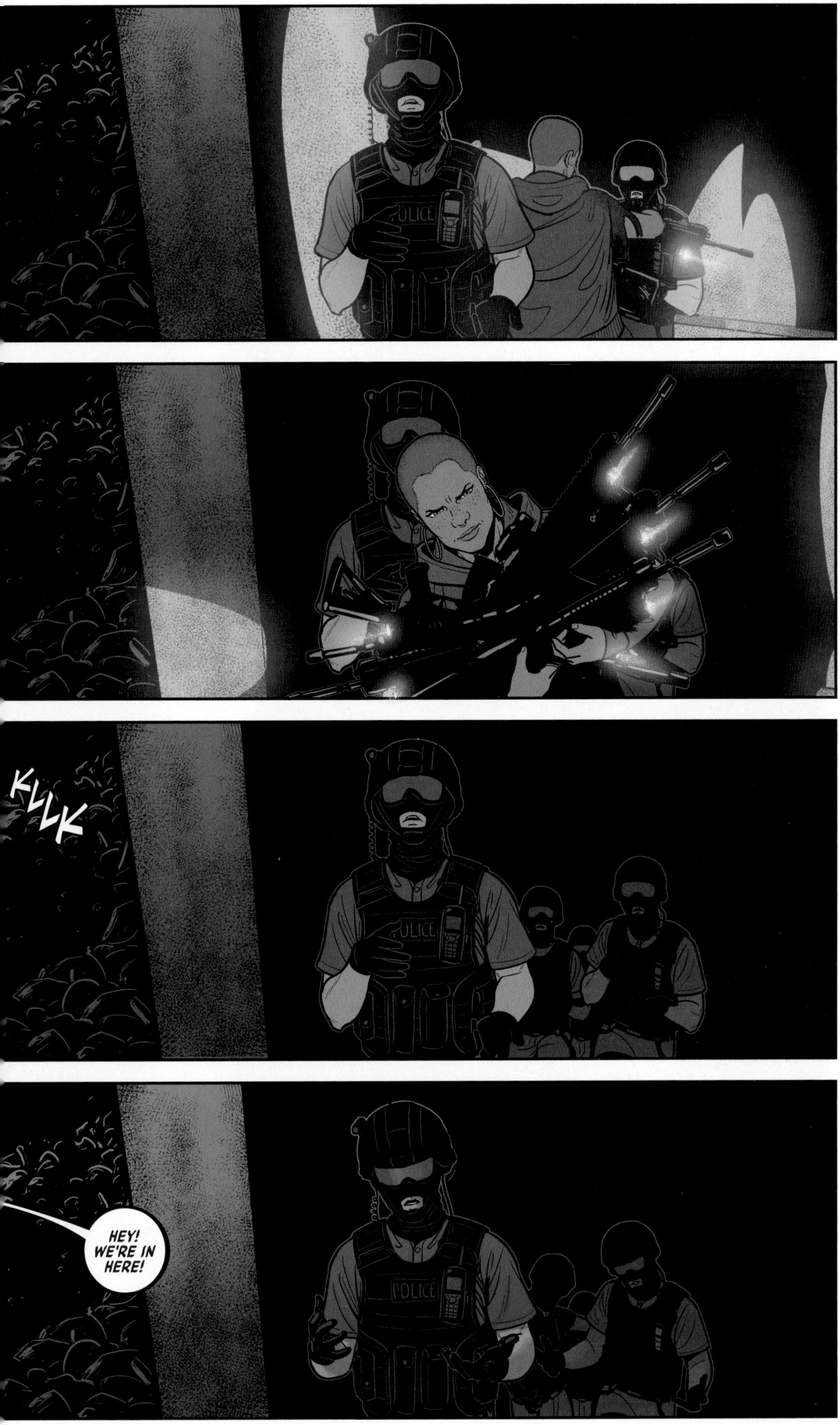
POLICE
KLLK
HEY! WE'RE IN HERE!

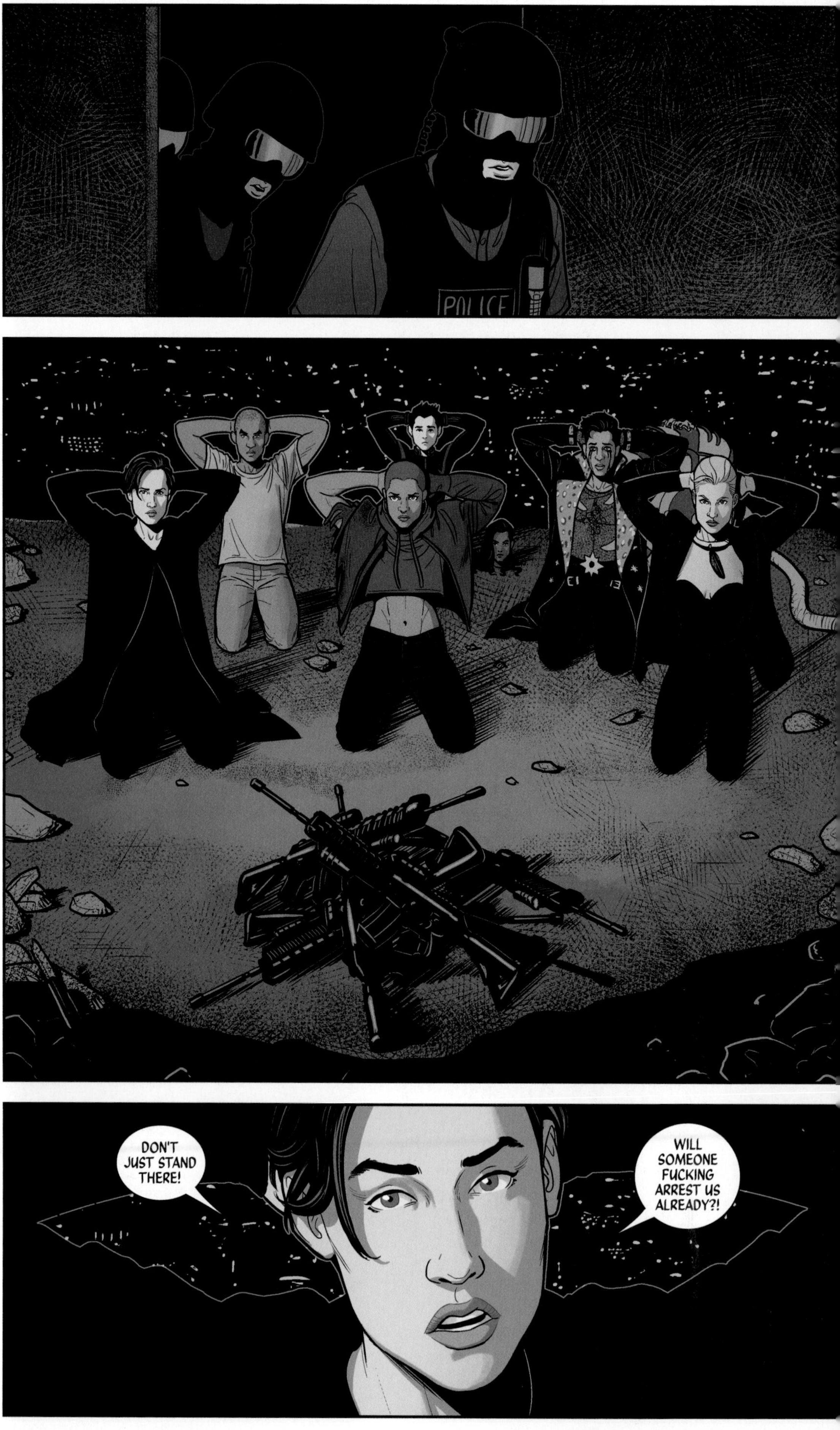
POLICE
DON'T JUST STAND THERE!
WILL SOMEONE FUCKING ARREST US ALREADY?!

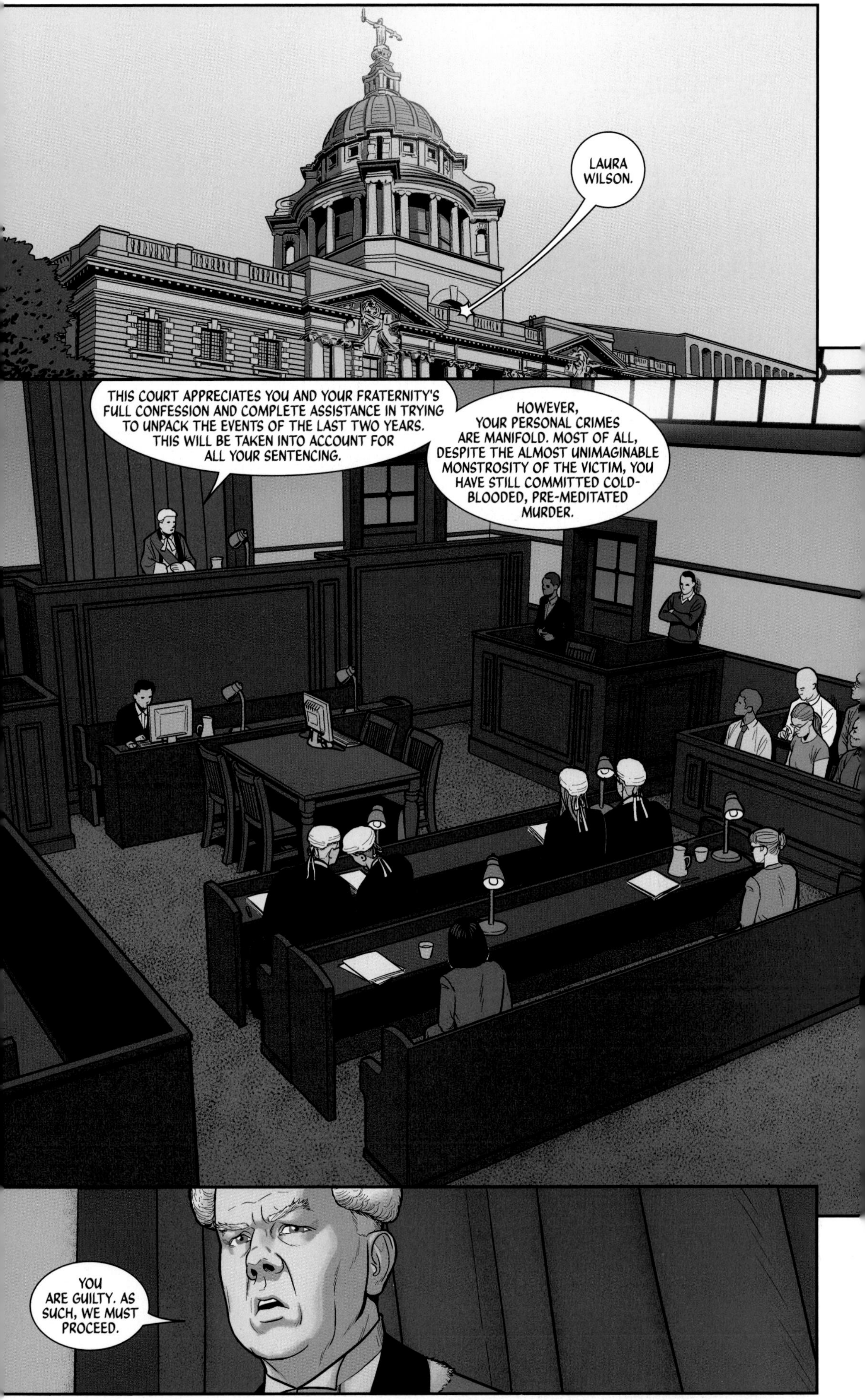
LAURA WILSON.
THIS COURT APPRECIATES YOU AND YOUR FRATERNITY'S FULL CONFESSION AND COMPLETE ASSISTANCE IN TRYING TO UNPACK THE EVENTS OF THE LAST TWO YEARS. THIS WILL BE TAKEN INTO ACCOUNT FOR ALL YOUR SENTENCING.
HOWEVER, YOUR PERSONAL CRIMES ARE MANIFOLD. MOST OF ALL, DESPITE THE ALMOST UNIMAGINABLE MONSTROSITY OF THE VICTIM, YOU HAVE STILL COMMITTED COLD-BLOODED, PRE-MEDITATED MURDER.
YOU ARE GUILTY. AS SUCH, WE MUST PROCEED.

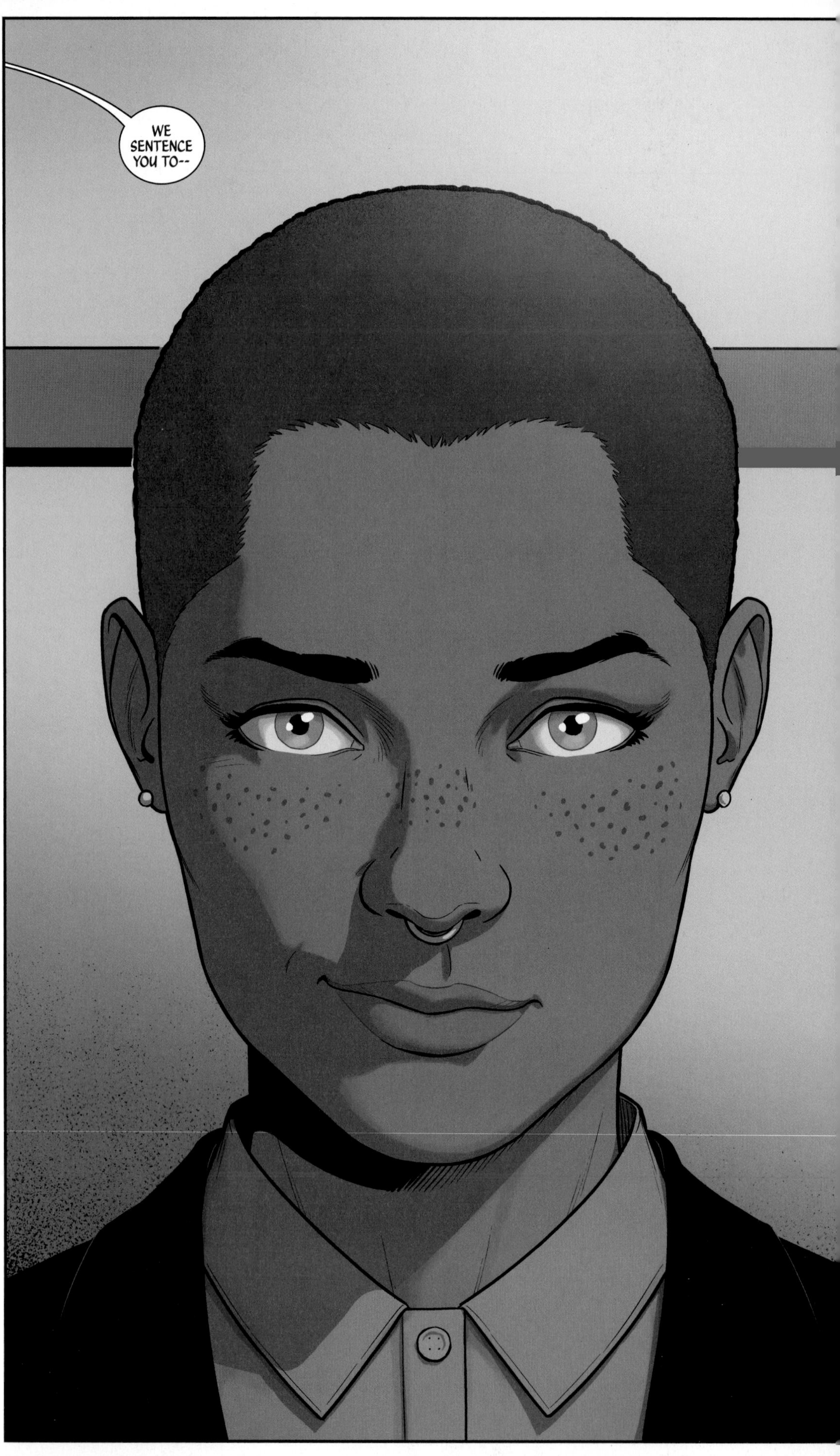
WE SENTENCE YOU TO--

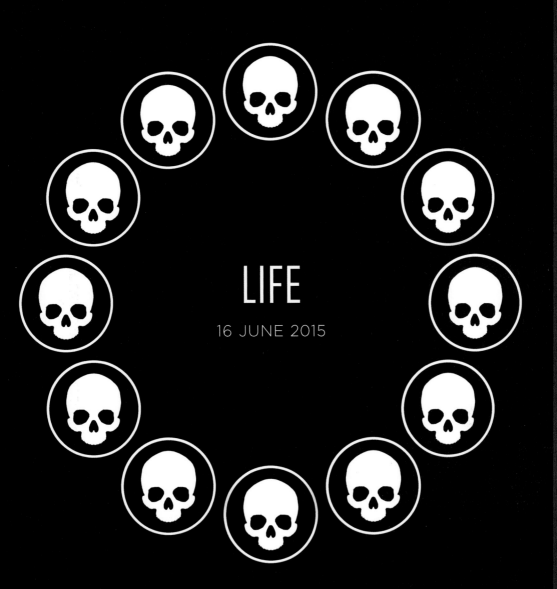

LIFE

16 JUNE 2015

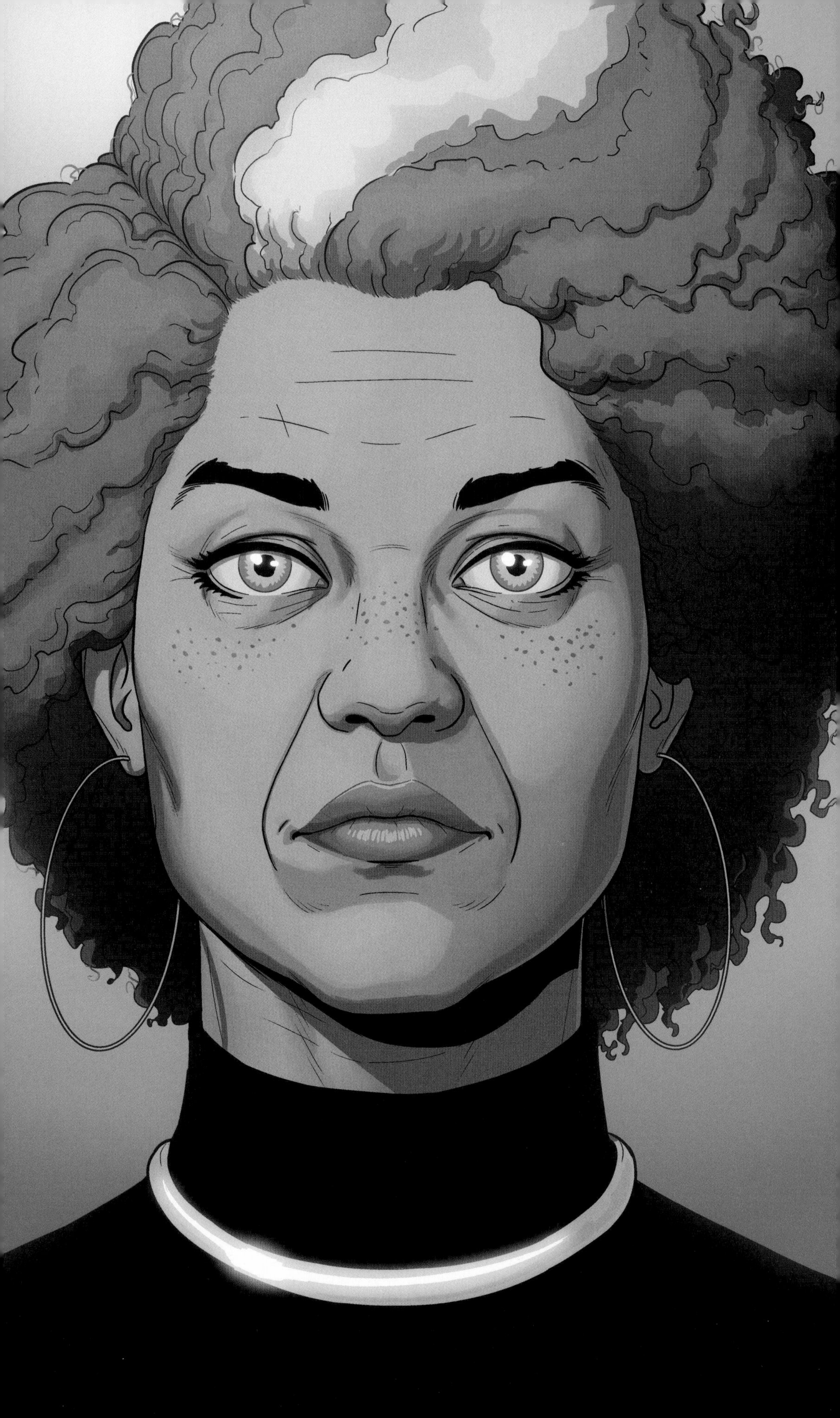

THE
WICKED
+
ƎNIΛIᗡ
ƎHⱢ

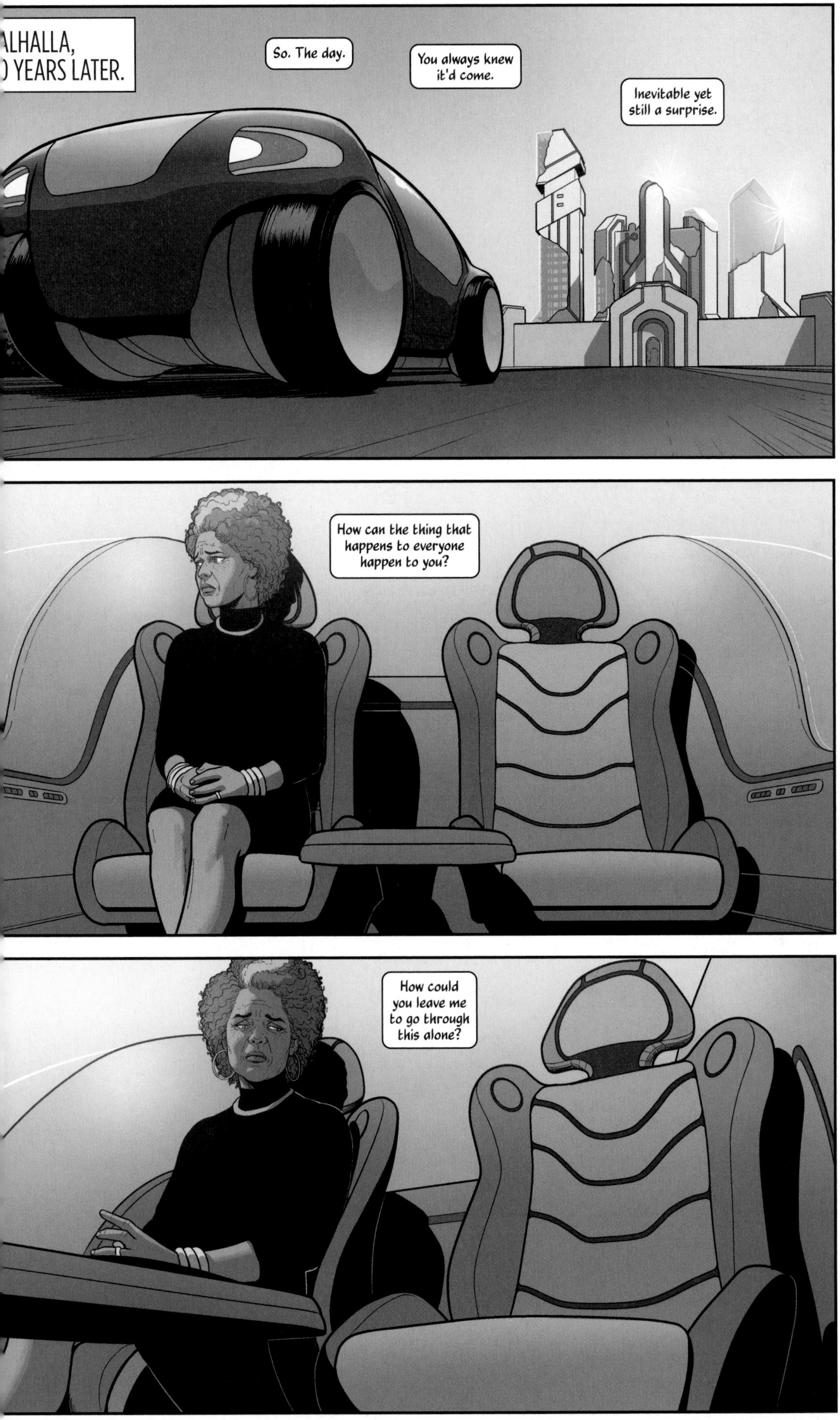
ALHALLA,
YEARS LATER.
So. The day.
You always knew it'd come.
Inevitable yet still a surprise.
How can the thing that happens to everyone happen to you?
How could you leave me to go through this alone?

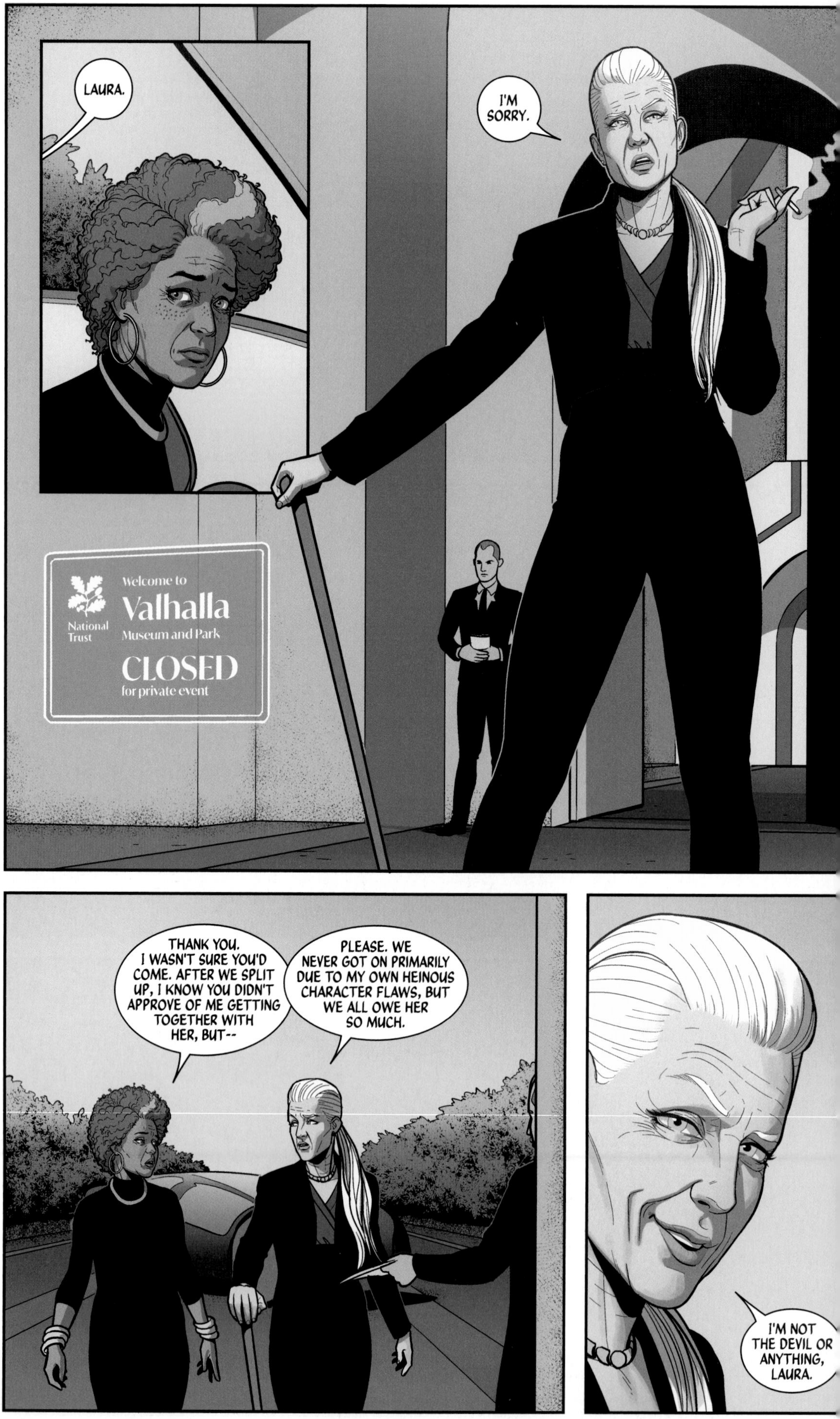
LAURA.
I'M SORRY.
Welcome to
Valhalla
Museum and Park
National Trust
CLOSED
for private event
THANK YOU. I WASN'T SURE YOU'D COME. AFTER WE SPLIT UP, I KNOW YOU DIDN'T APPROVE OF ME GETTING TOGETHER WITH HER, BUT--
PLEASE. WE NEVER GOT ON PRIMARILY DUE TO MY OWN HEINOUS CHARACTER FLAWS, BUT WE ALL OWE HER SO MUCH.
I'M NOT THE DEVIL OR ANYTHING, LAURA.

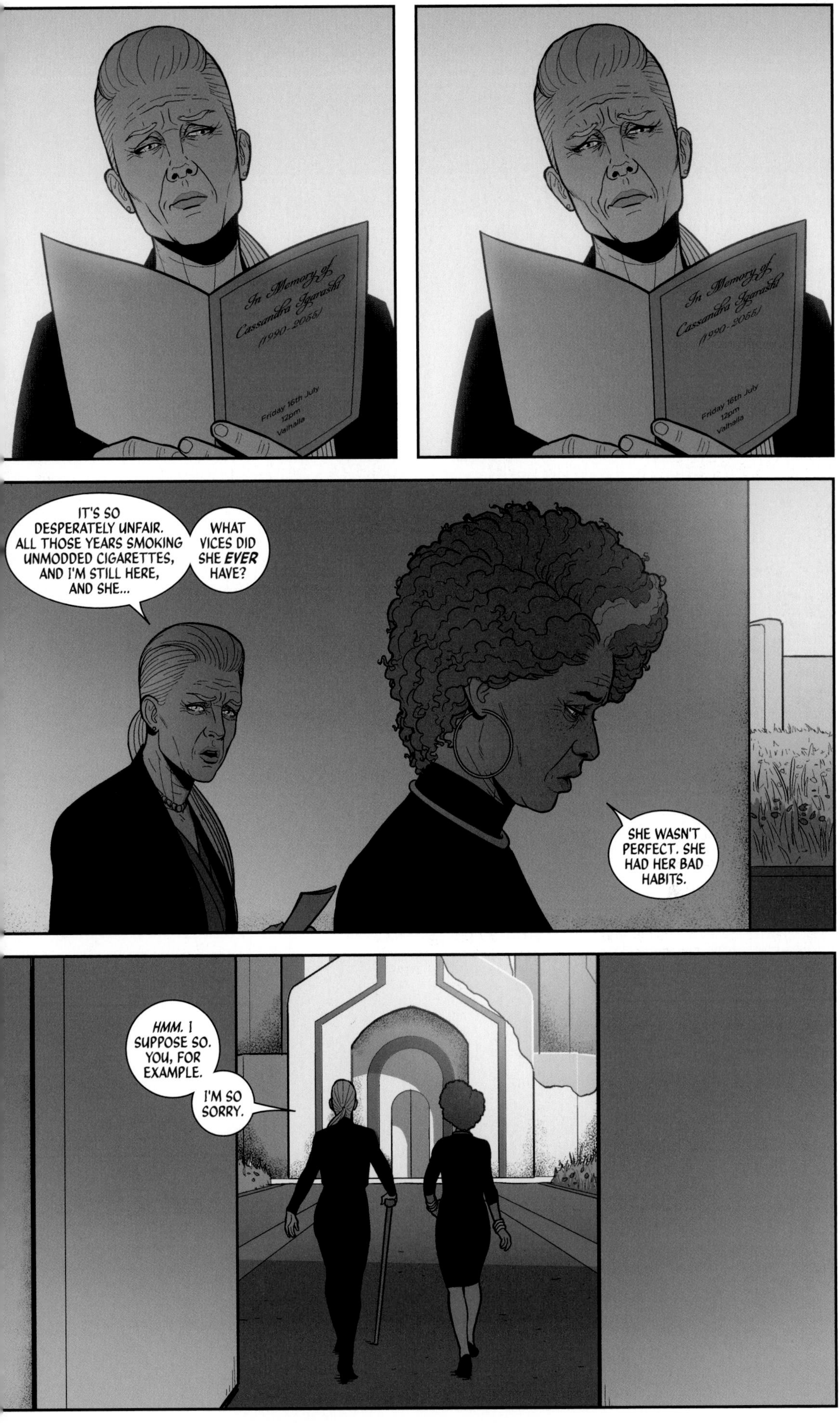

In Memory of Cassandra Igarashi (1990–2055)
Friday 16th July 12pm Valhalla
In Memory of Cassandra Igarashi (1990–2055)
Friday 16th July 12pm Valhalla
IT'S SO DESPERATELY UNFAIR. ALL THOSE YEARS SMOKING UNMODDED CIGARETTES, AND I'M STILL HERE, AND SHE...
WHAT VICES DID SHE *EVER* HAVE?
SHE WASN'T PERFECT. SHE HAD HER BAD HABITS.
HMM. I SUPPOSE SO. YOU, FOR EXAMPLE.
I'M SO SORRY.

IN MEMORIAM

16 JULY 2055

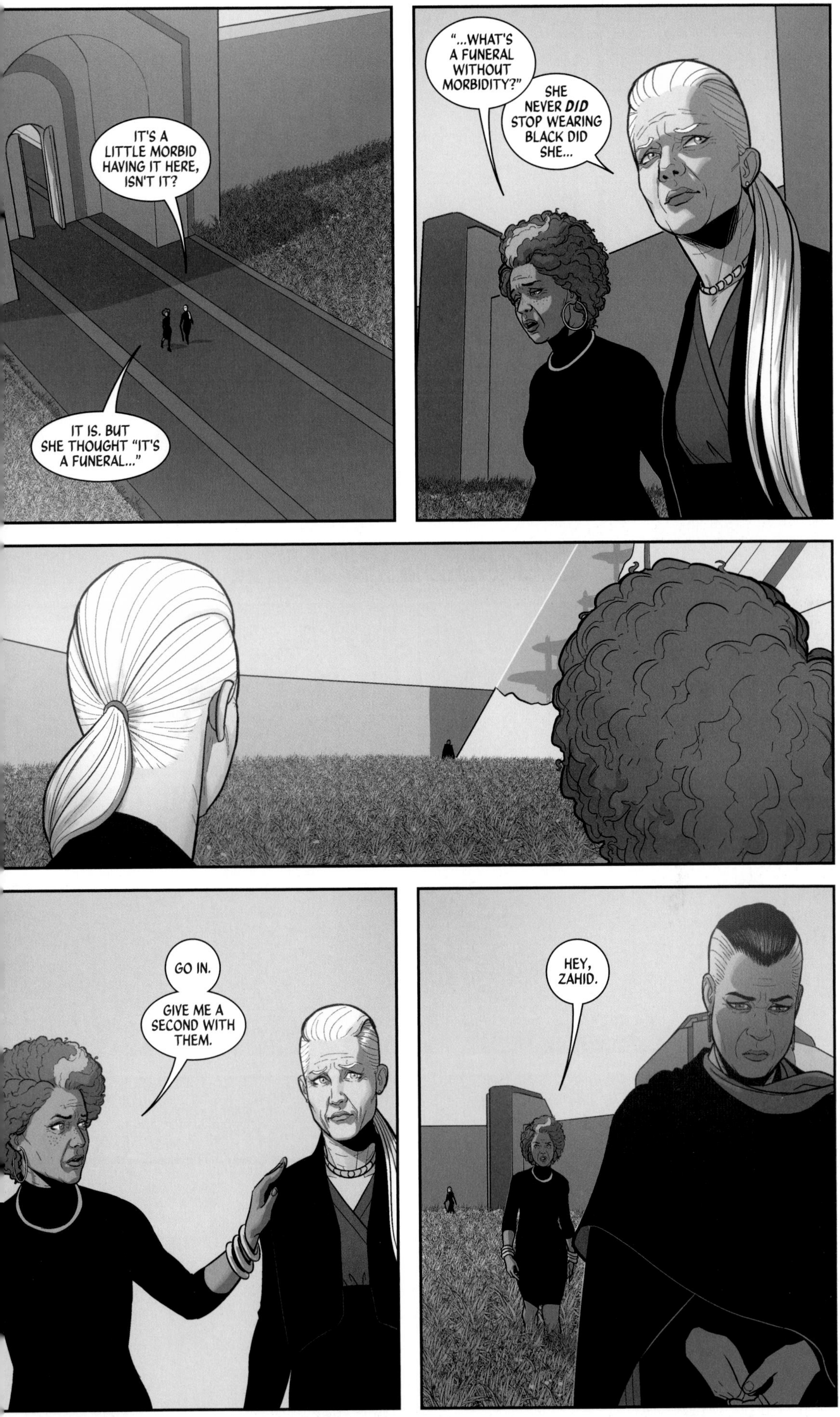
IT'S A LITTLE MORBID HAVING IT HERE, ISN'T IT?
IT IS. BUT SHE THOUGHT "IT'S A FUNERAL..."
"...WHAT'S A FUNERAL WITHOUT MORBIDITY?"
SHE NEVER DID STOP WEARING BLACK DID SHE...
GO IN.
GIVE ME A SECOND WITH THEM.
HEY, ZAHID.

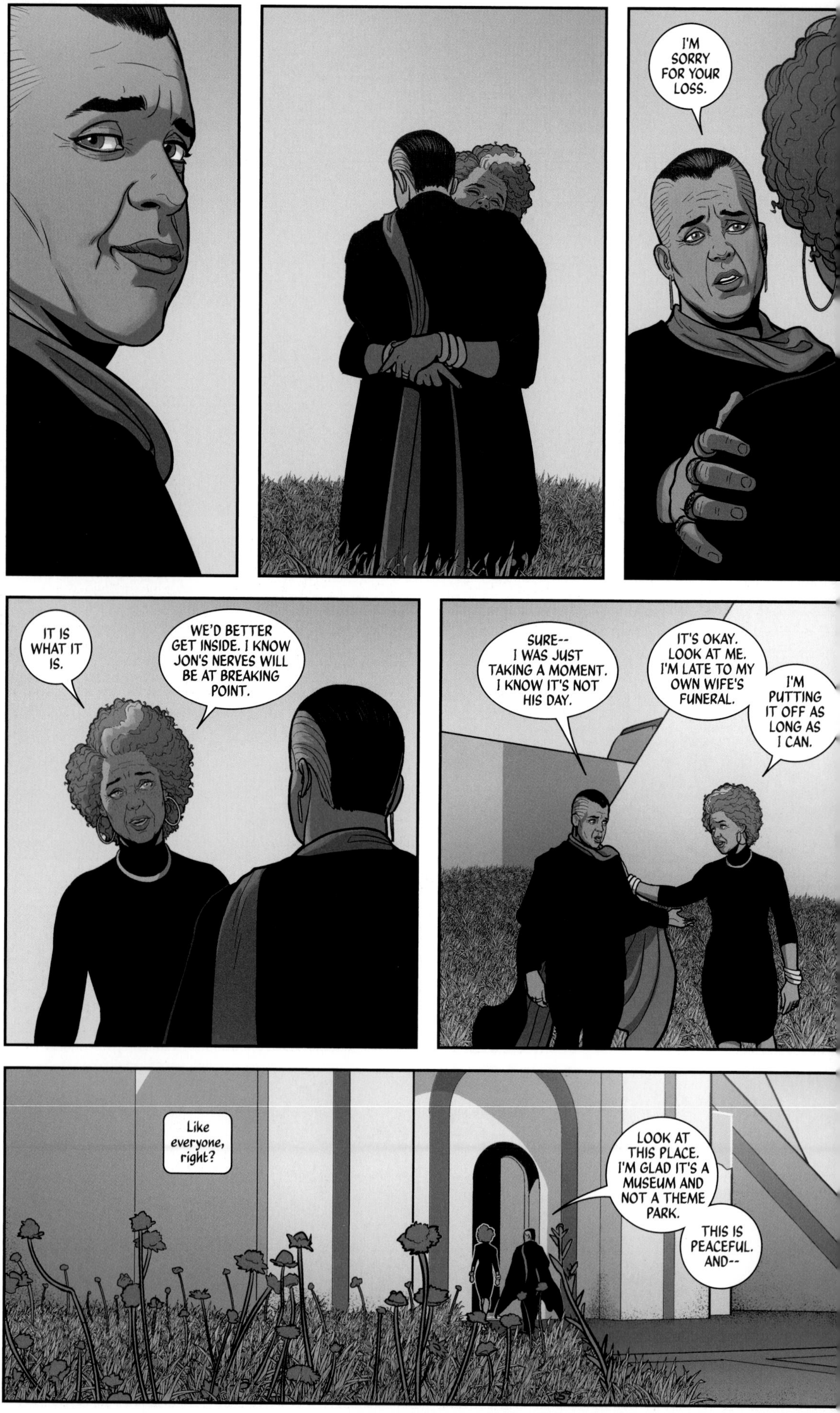
I'M SORRY FOR YOUR LOSS.
IT IS WHAT IT IS.
WE'D BETTER GET INSIDE. I KNOW JON'S NERVES WILL BE AT BREAKING POINT.
SURE-- I WAS JUST TAKING A MOMENT. I KNOW IT'S NOT HIS DAY.
IT'S OKAY. LOOK AT ME. I'M LATE TO MY OWN WIFE'S FUNERAL.
I'M PUTTING IT OFF AS LONG AS I CAN.
Like everyone, right?
LOOK AT THIS PLACE. I'M GLAD IT'S A MUSEUM AND NOT A THEME PARK.
THIS IS PEACEFUL. AND--

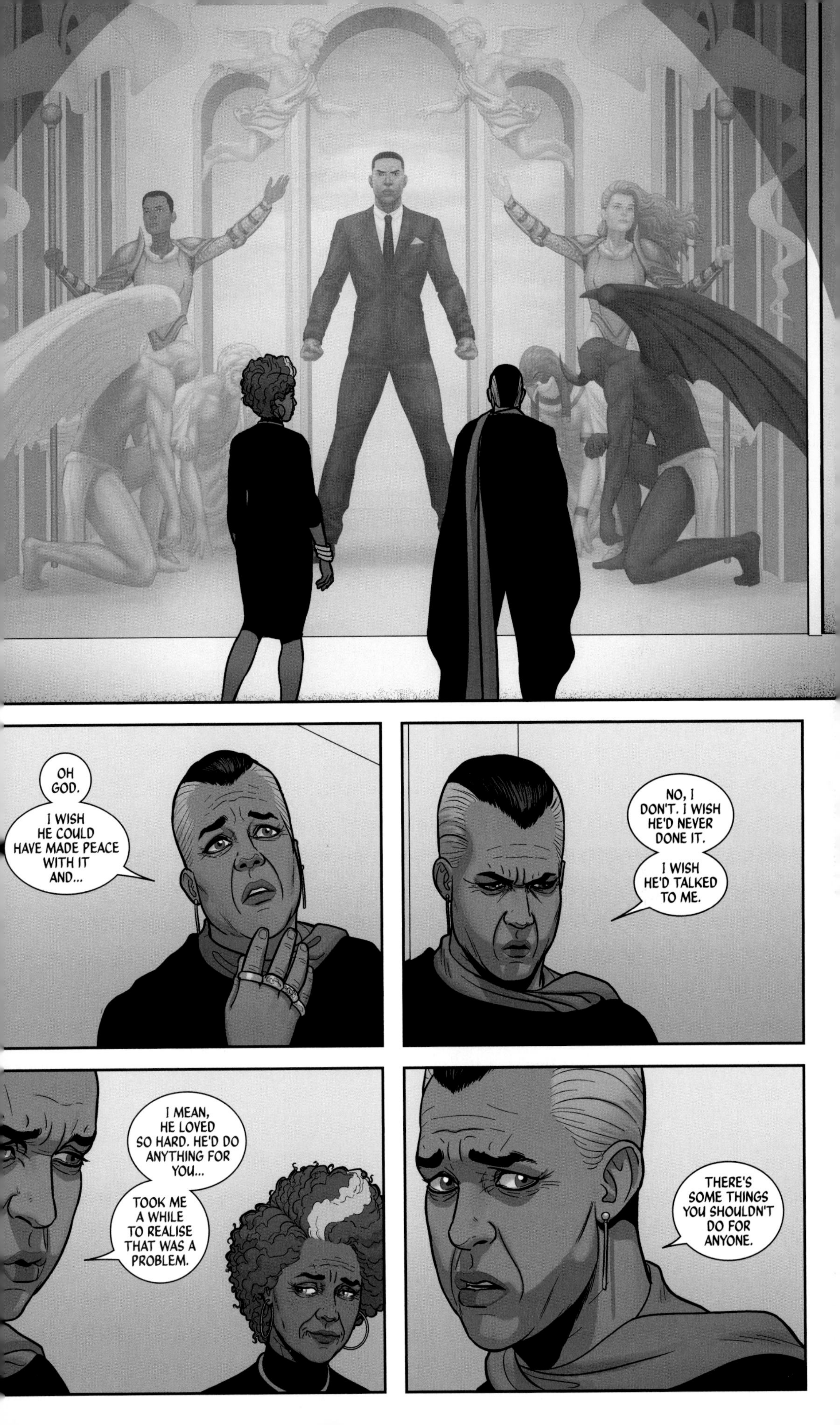
OH GOD.
I WISH HE COULD HAVE MADE PEACE WITH IT AND...
NO, I DON'T. I WISH HE'D NEVER DONE IT.
I WISH HE'D TALKED TO ME.
I MEAN, HE LOVED SO HARD. HE'D DO ANYTHING FOR YOU...
TOOK ME A WHILE TO REALISE THAT WAS A PROBLEM.
THERE'S SOME THINGS YOU SHOULDN'T DO FOR ANYONE.

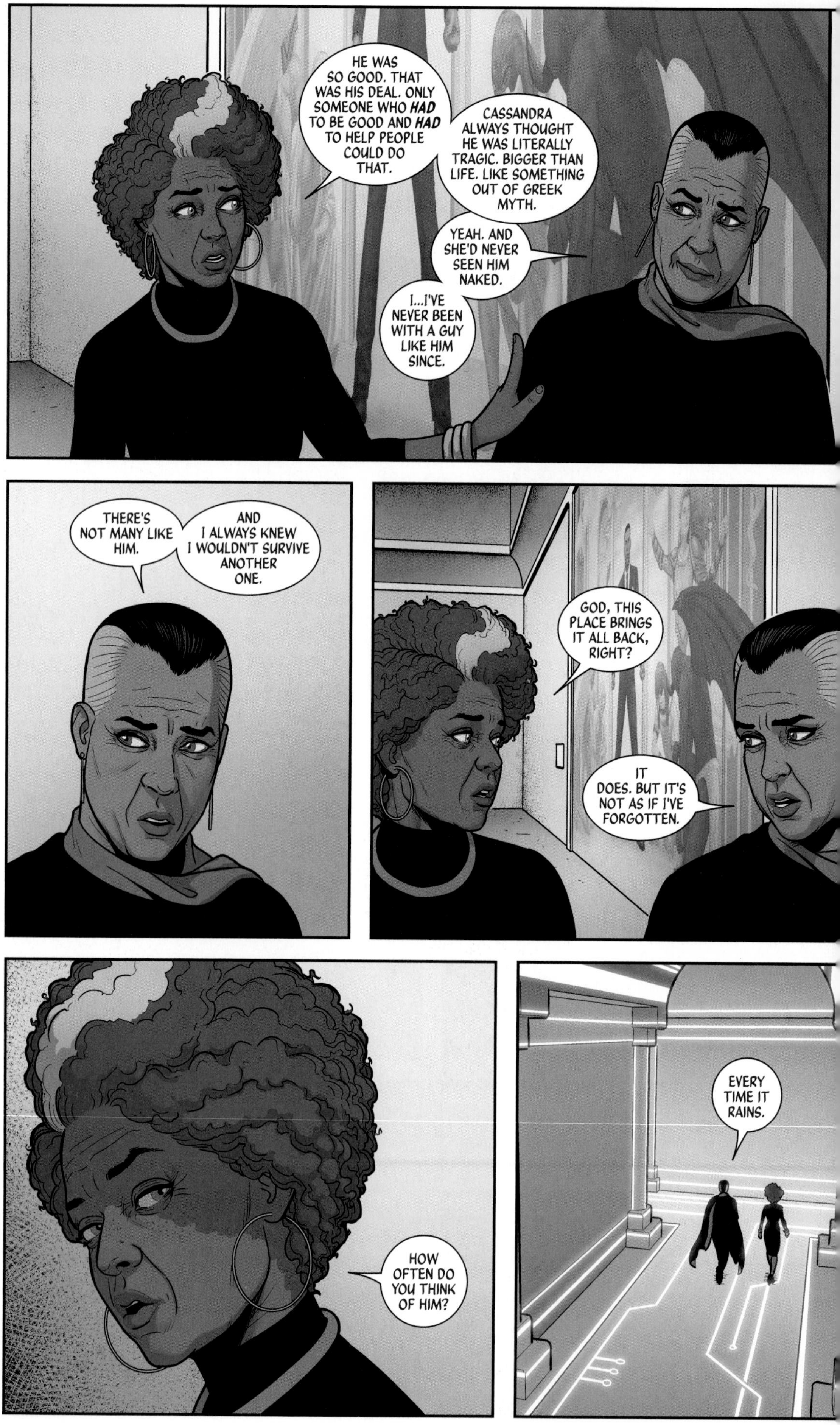
HE WAS SO GOOD. THAT WAS HIS DEAL. ONLY SOMEONE WHO *HAD* TO BE GOOD AND *HAD* TO HELP PEOPLE COULD DO THAT.
CASSANDRA ALWAYS THOUGHT HE WAS LITERALLY TRAGIC. BIGGER THAN LIFE. LIKE SOMETHING OUT OF GREEK MYTH.
YEAH. AND SHE'D NEVER SEEN HIM NAKED.
I...I'VE NEVER BEEN WITH A GUY LIKE HIM SINCE.
THERE'S NOT MANY LIKE HIM.
AND I ALWAYS KNEW I WOULDN'T SURVIVE ANOTHER ONE.
GOD, THIS PLACE BRINGS IT ALL BACK, RIGHT?
IT DOES. BUT IT'S NOT AS IF I'VE FORGOTTEN.
HOW OFTEN DO YOU THINK OF HIM?
EVERY TIME IT RAINS.

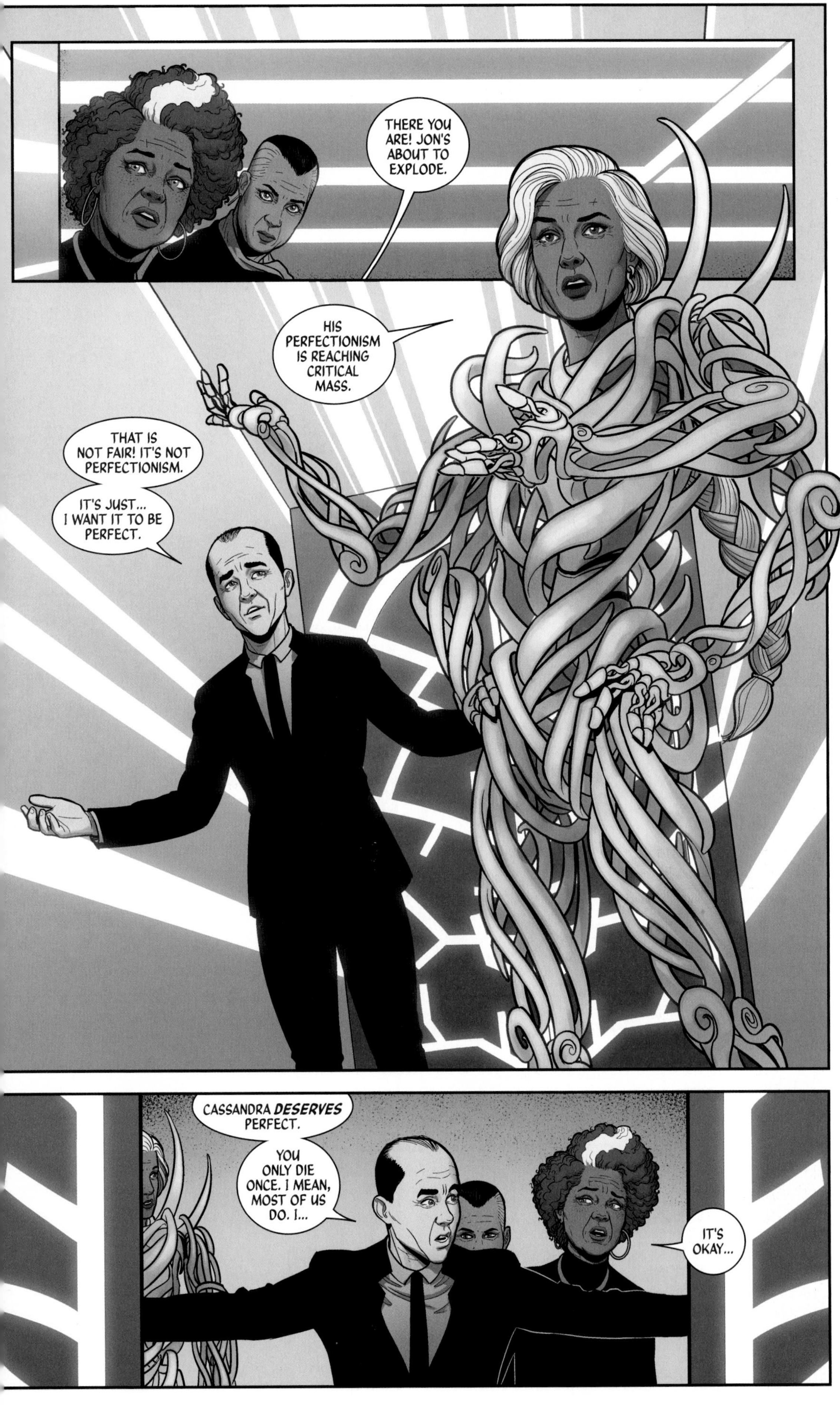
THERE YOU ARE! JON'S ABOUT TO EXPLODE.
HIS PERFECTIONISM IS REACHING CRITICAL MASS.
THAT IS NOT FAIR! IT'S NOT PERFECTIONISM.
IT'S JUST... I WANT IT TO BE PERFECT.
CASSANDRA DESERVES PERFECT.
YOU ONLY DIE ONCE. I MEAN, MOST OF US DO. I...
IT'S OKAY...

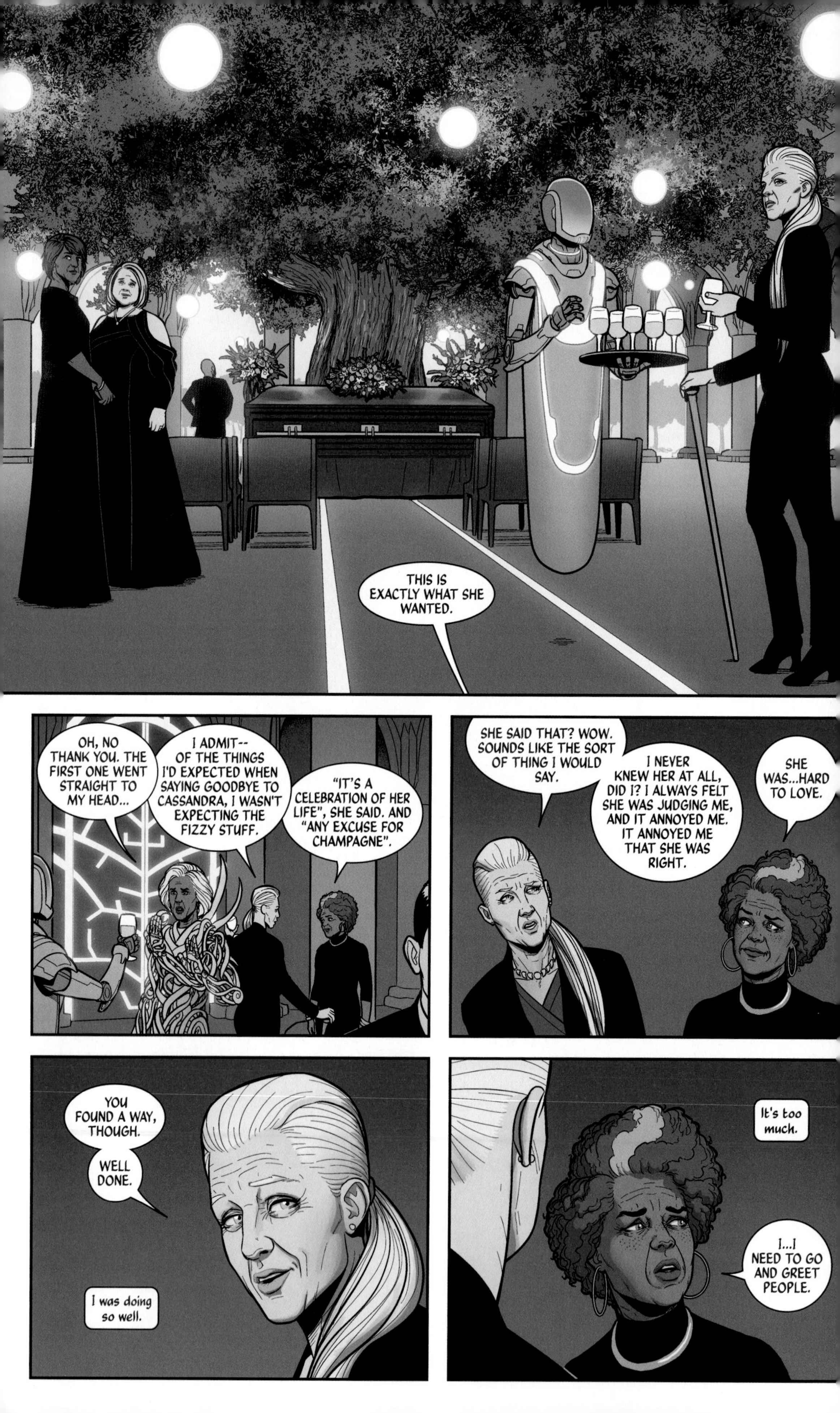
THIS IS EXACTLY WHAT SHE WANTED.
OH, NO THANK YOU. THE FIRST ONE WENT STRAIGHT TO MY HEAD...
I ADMIT-- OF THE THINGS I'D EXPECTED WHEN SAYING GOODBYE TO CASSANDRA, I WASN'T EXPECTING THE FIZZY STUFF.
"IT'S A CELEBRATION OF HER LIFE", SHE SAID. AND "ANY EXCUSE FOR CHAMPAGNE".
SHE SAID THAT? WOW. SOUNDS LIKE THE SORT OF THING I WOULD SAY.
I NEVER KNEW HER AT ALL, DID I? I ALWAYS FELT SHE WAS JUDGING ME, AND IT ANNOYED ME. IT ANNOYED ME THAT SHE WAS RIGHT.
SHE WAS...HARD TO LOVE.
YOU FOUND A WAY, THOUGH.
WELL DONE.
I was doing so well.
It's too much.
I...I NEED TO GO AND GREET PEOPLE.

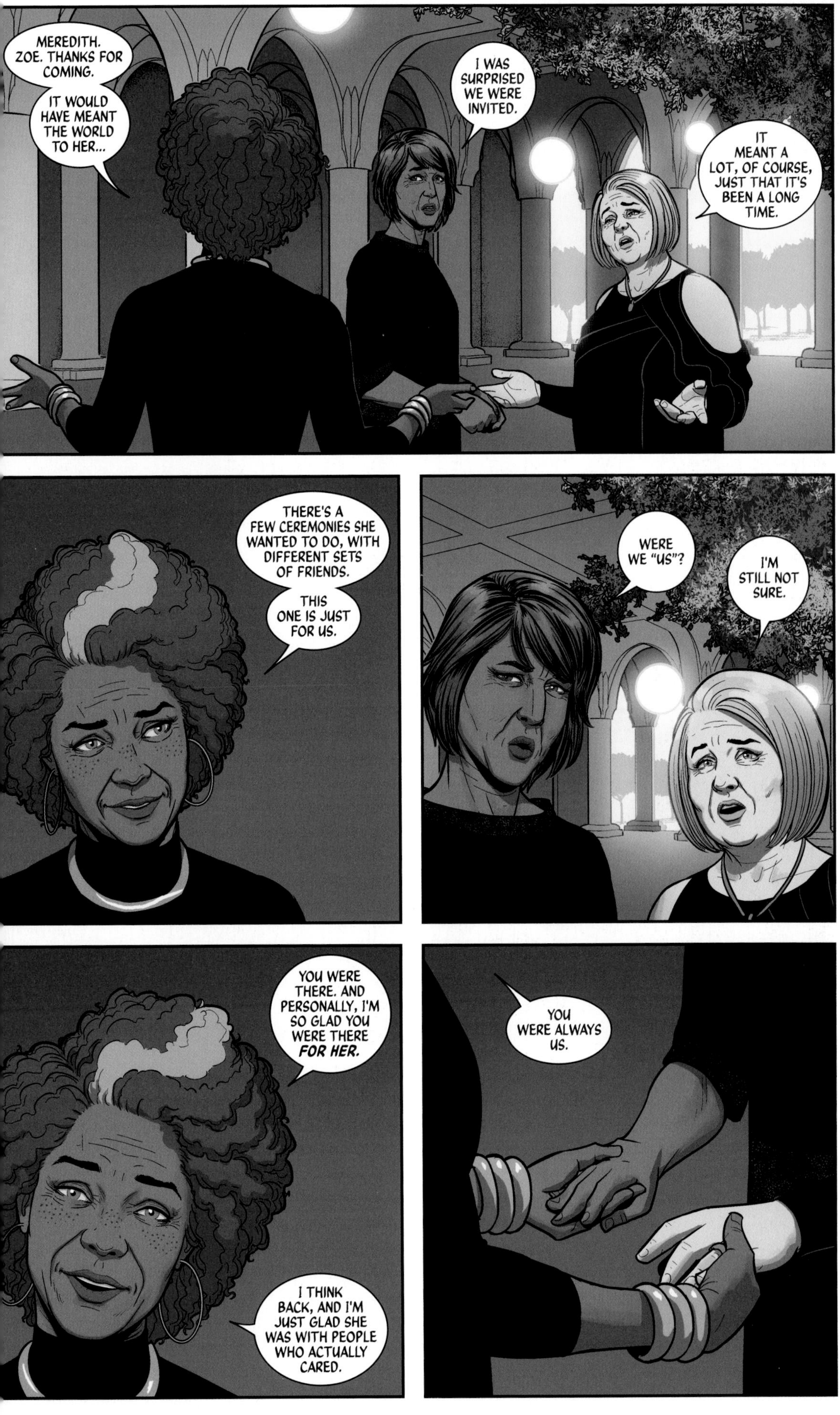
MEREDITH. ZOE. THANKS FOR COMING.
IT WOULD HAVE MEANT THE WORLD TO HER...
I WAS SURPRISED WE WERE INVITED.
IT MEANT A LOT, OF COURSE, JUST THAT IT'S BEEN A LONG TIME.
THERE'S A FEW CEREMONIES SHE WANTED TO DO, WITH DIFFERENT SETS OF FRIENDS.
THIS ONE IS JUST FOR US.
WERE WE "US"?
I'M STILL NOT SURE.
YOU WERE THERE. AND PERSONALLY, I'M SO GLAD YOU WERE THERE ***FOR HER.***
I THINK BACK, AND I'M JUST GLAD SHE WAS WITH PEOPLE WHO ACTUALLY CARED.
YOU WERE ALWAYS US.

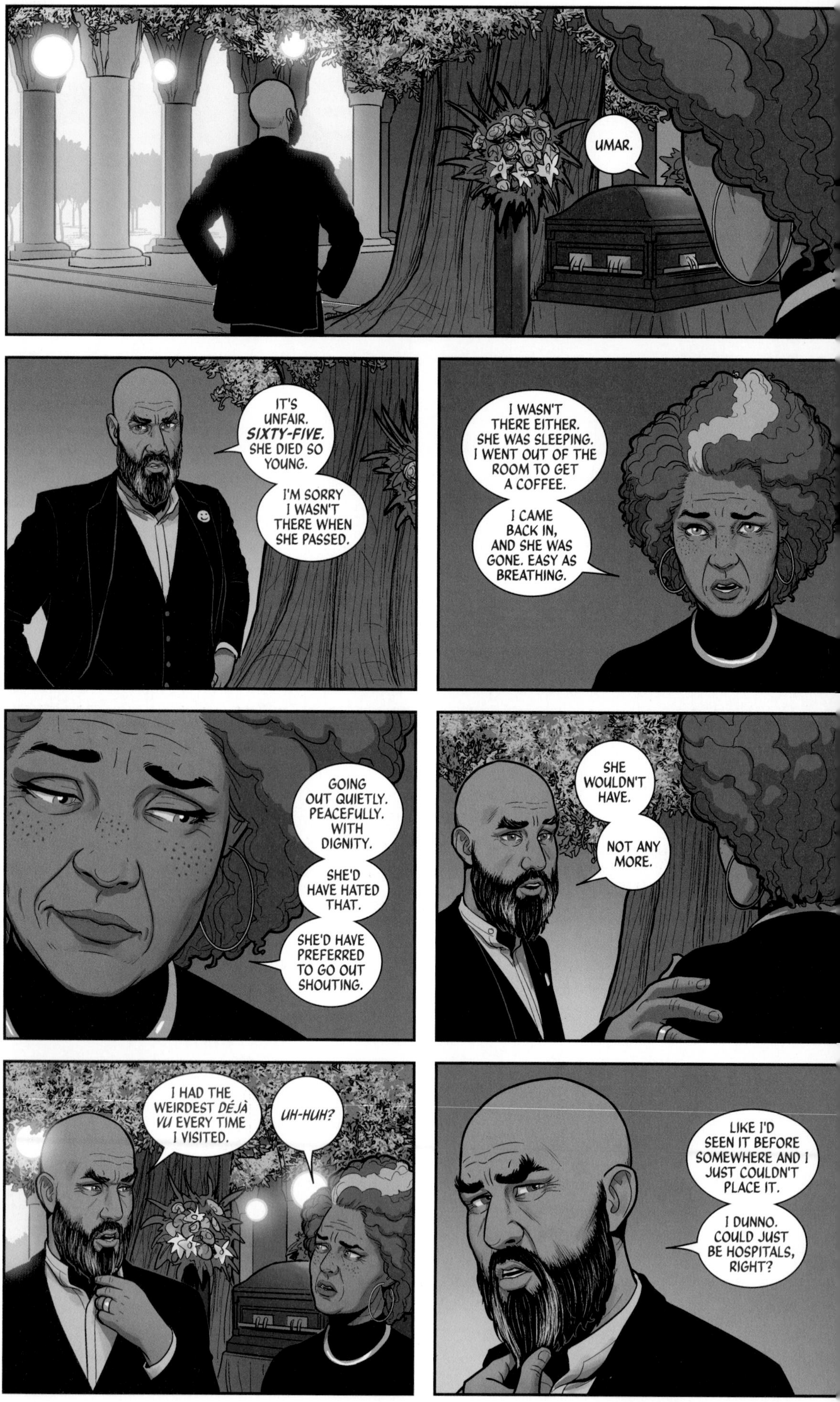
UMAR.
IT'S UNFAIR. *SIXTY-FIVE.* SHE DIED SO YOUNG.
I'M SORRY I WASN'T THERE WHEN SHE PASSED.
I WASN'T THERE EITHER. SHE WAS SLEEPING. I WENT OUT OF THE ROOM TO GET A COFFEE.
I CAME BACK IN, AND SHE WAS GONE. EASY AS BREATHING.
GOING OUT QUIETLY. PEACEFULLY. WITH DIGNITY.
SHE'D HAVE HATED THAT.
SHE'D HAVE PREFERRED TO GO OUT SHOUTING.
SHE WOULDN'T HAVE.
NOT ANY MORE.
I HAD THE WEIRDEST *DÉJÀ VU* EVERY TIME I VISITED.
UH-HUH?
LIKE I'D SEEN IT BEFORE SOMEWHERE AND I JUST COULDN'T PLACE IT.
I DUNNO. COULD JUST BE HOSPITALS, RIGHT?

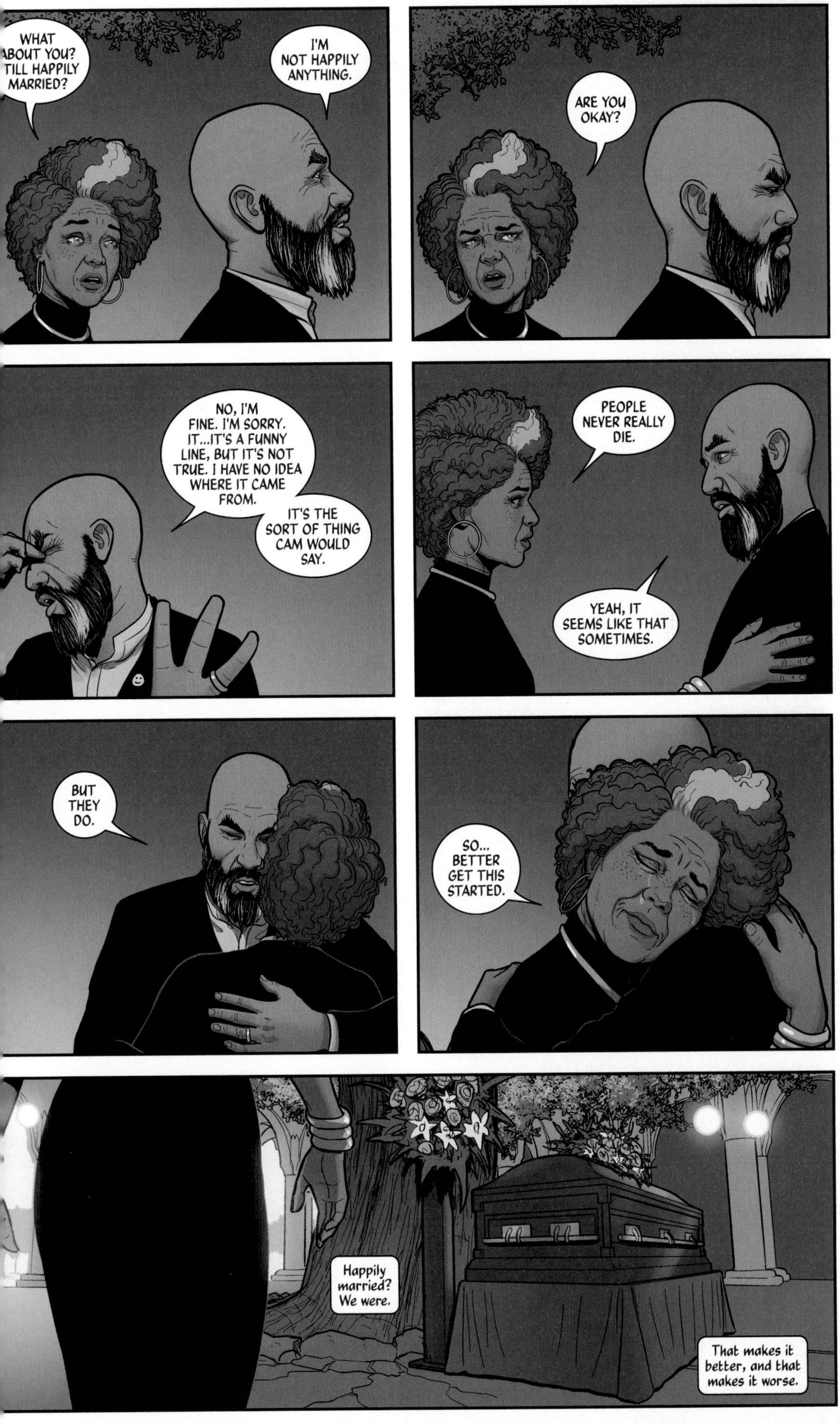
WHAT ABOUT YOU? STILL HAPPILY MARRIED?
I'M NOT HAPPILY ANYTHING.
ARE YOU OKAY?
NO, I'M FINE. I'M SORRY. IT...IT'S A FUNNY LINE, BUT IT'S NOT TRUE. I HAVE NO IDEA WHERE IT CAME FROM.
IT'S THE SORT OF THING CAM WOULD SAY.
PEOPLE NEVER REALLY DIE.
YEAH, IT SEEMS LIKE THAT SOMETIMES.
BUT THEY DO.
SO... BETTER GET THIS STARTED.
Happily married? We were.
That makes it better, and that makes it worse.

CODA

16 JULY 2055

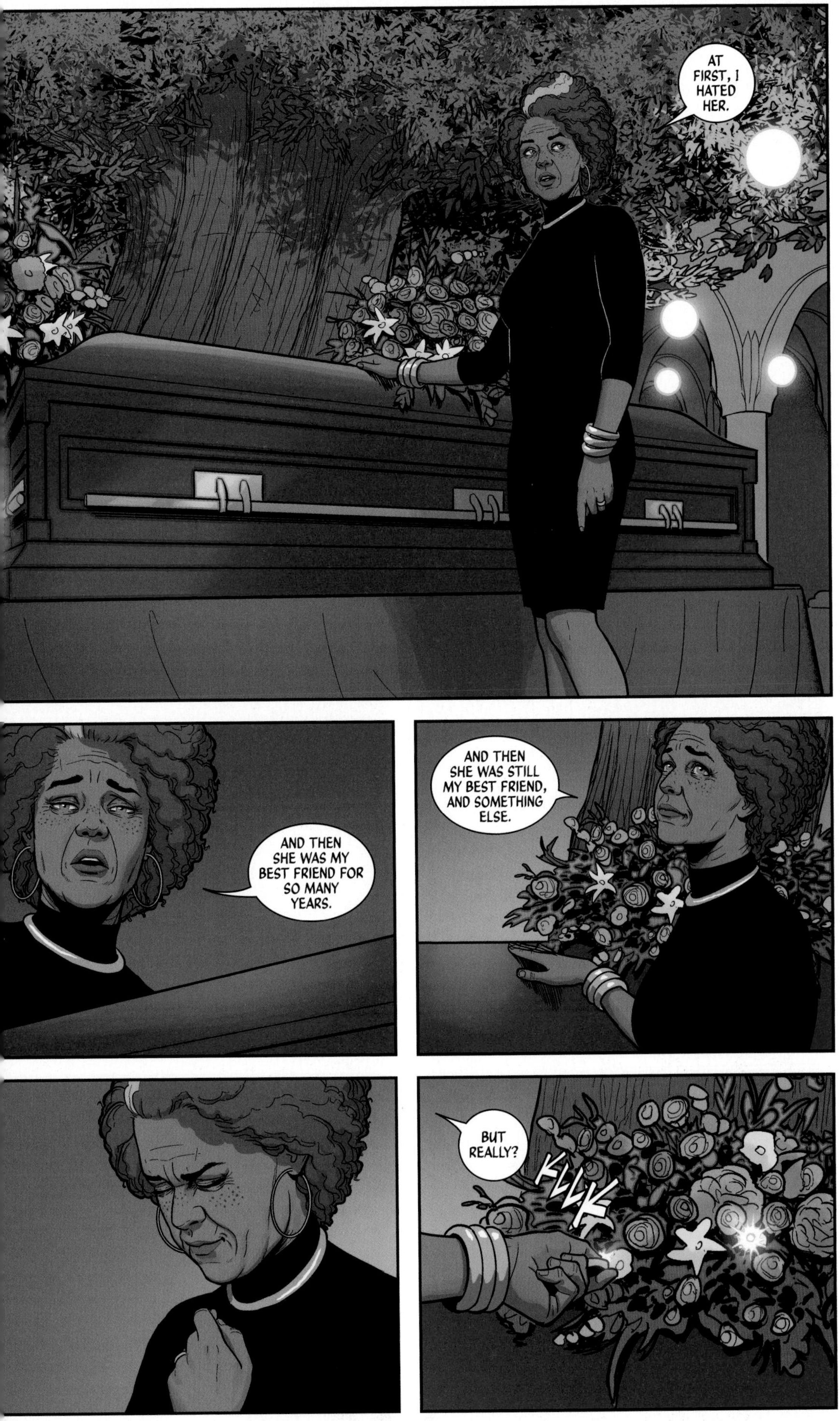
AT FIRST, I HATED HER.
AND THEN SHE WAS MY BEST FRIEND FOR SO MANY YEARS.
AND THEN SHE WAS STILL MY BEST FRIEND, AND SOMETHING ELSE.
BUT REALLY?
KLIK

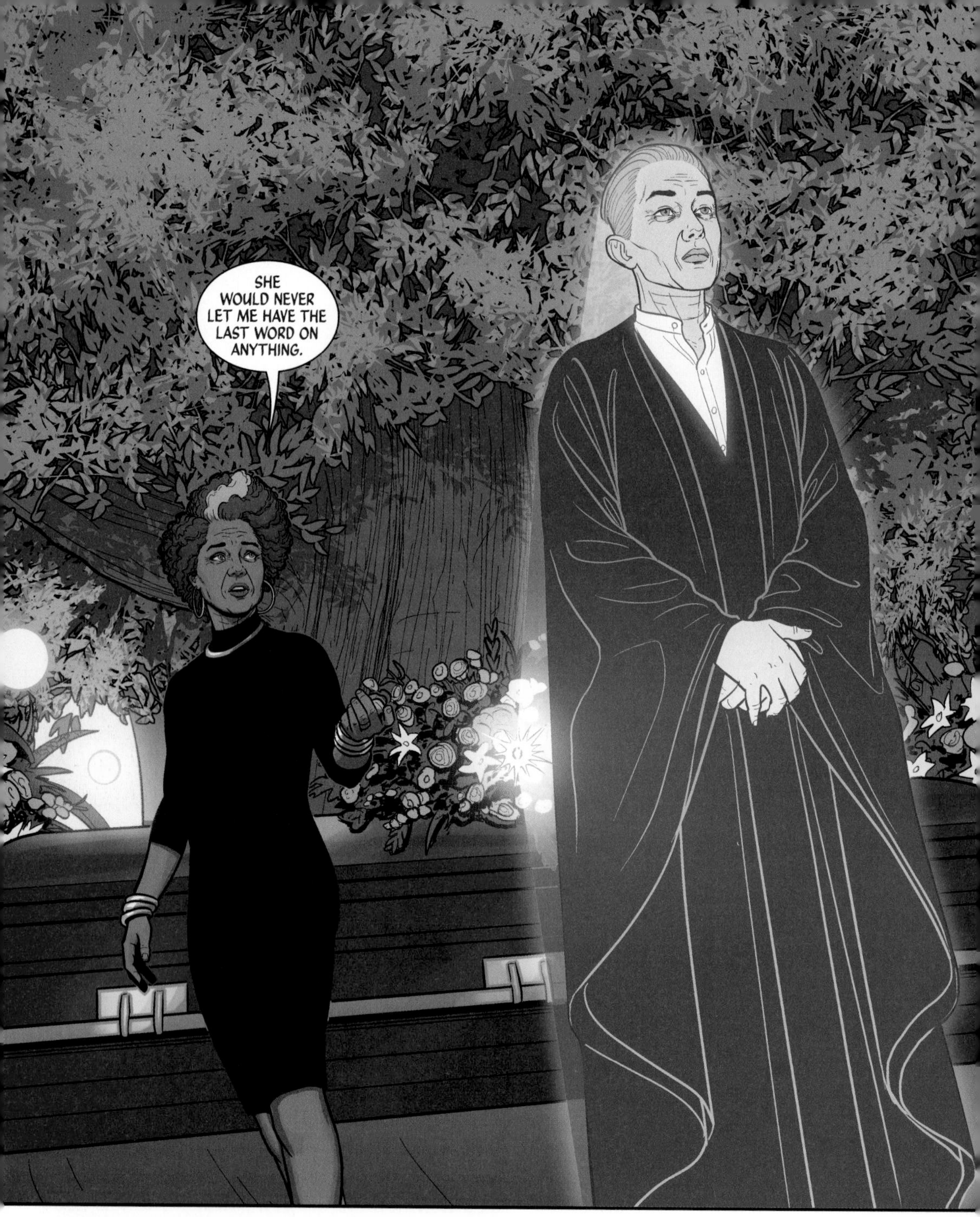
SHE WOULD NEVER LET ME HAVE THE LAST WORD ON ANYTHING.

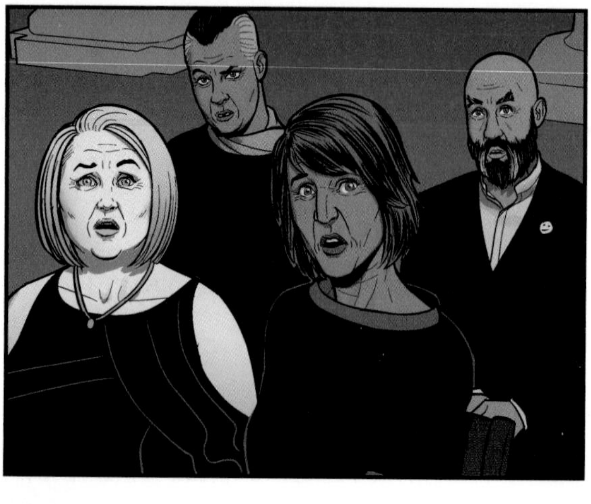

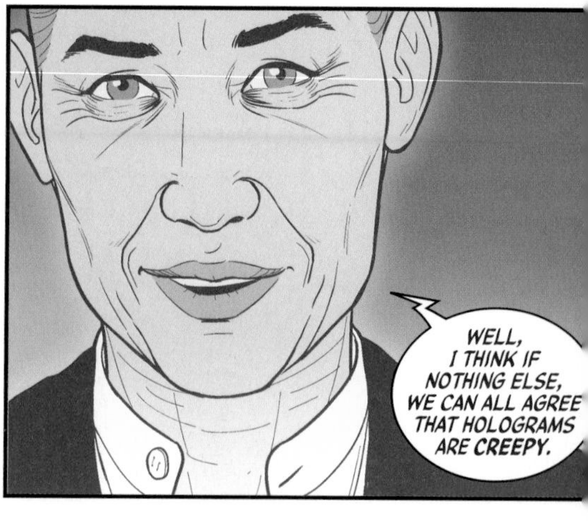
WELL, I THINK IF NOTHING ELSE, WE CAN ALL AGREE THAT HOLOGRAMS ARE CREEPY.

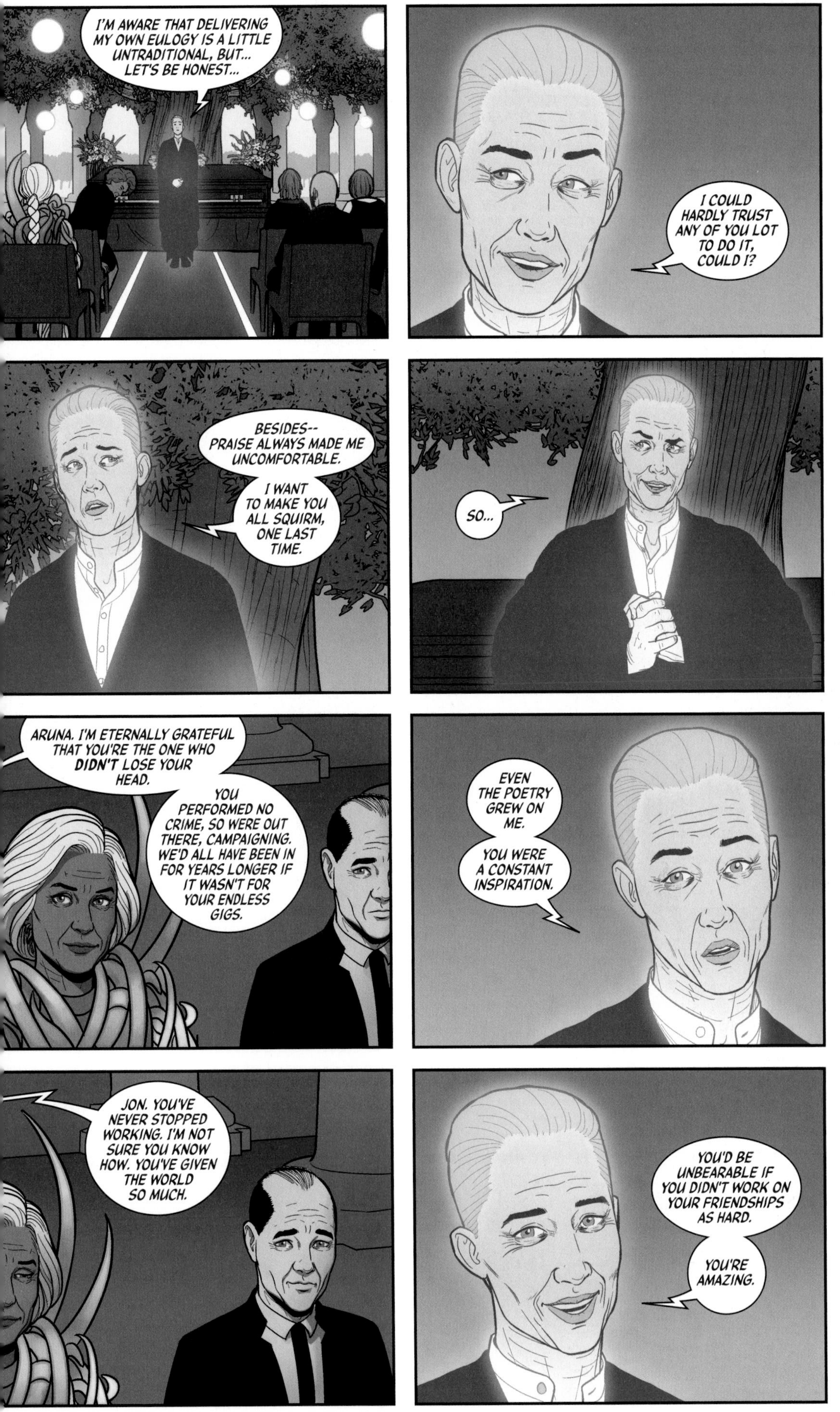
I'M AWARE THAT DELIVERING MY OWN EULOGY IS A LITTLE UNTRADITIONAL, BUT... LET'S BE HONEST...
I COULD HARDLY TRUST ANY OF YOU LOT TO DO IT, COULD I?
BESIDES-- PRAISE ALWAYS MADE ME UNCOMFORTABLE.
I WANT TO MAKE YOU ALL SQUIRM, ONE LAST TIME.
SO...
ARUNA. I'M ETERNALLY GRATEFUL THAT YOU'RE THE ONE WHO **DIDN'T** LOSE YOUR HEAD.
YOU PERFORMED NO CRIME, SO WERE OUT THERE, CAMPAIGNING. WE'D ALL HAVE BEEN IN FOR YEARS LONGER IF IT WASN'T FOR YOUR ENDLESS GIGS.
EVEN THE POETRY GREW ON ME.
YOU WERE A CONSTANT INSPIRATION.
JON. YOU'VE NEVER STOPPED WORKING. I'M NOT SURE YOU KNOW HOW. YOU'VE GIVEN THE WORLD SO MUCH.
YOU'D BE UNBEARABLE IF YOU DIDN'T WORK ON YOUR FRIENDSHIPS AS HARD.
YOU'RE AMAZING.

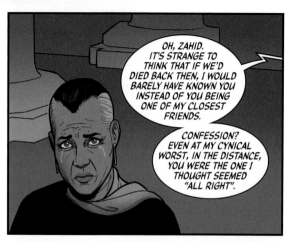

OH, ZAHID. IT'S STRANGE TO THINK THAT IF WE'D DIED BACK THEN, I WOULD BARELY HAVE KNOWN YOU INSTEAD OF YOU BEING ONE OF MY CLOSEST FRIENDS.

CONFESSION? EVEN AT MY CYNICAL WORST, IN THE DISTANCE, YOU WERE THE ONE I THOUGHT SEEMED "ALL RIGHT".

UNDERSTATEMENT OF A LIFETIME.

ELEANOR. WE...WELL, WE'VE NEVER BEEN CLOSE.

BUT I'LL SAY THIS.

IF YOU WEREN'T LUCIFER, IT WASN'T FOR LACK OF TRYING.

NOBODY DID WORSE BETTER THAN YOU.

UMAR, YOU DUMB SWEETHEART, YOU HAVE ALWAYS BEEN TOO KIND.

YOU ALWAYS MADE ME WANT TO BE KINDER, BUT IF I'M GOING OUT, I'M GOING OUT LIKE I'VE ALWAYS PLAYED THIS GAME: WITH BRUTAL HONESTY.

YOU WERE THE BEST PERSON I EVER MET.

MEREDITH. ZOE. I DON'T KNOW. WHAT CAN I SAY?

EVERY DAY I WAS WITH YOU?

YOU LEFT ME SPEECHLESS.

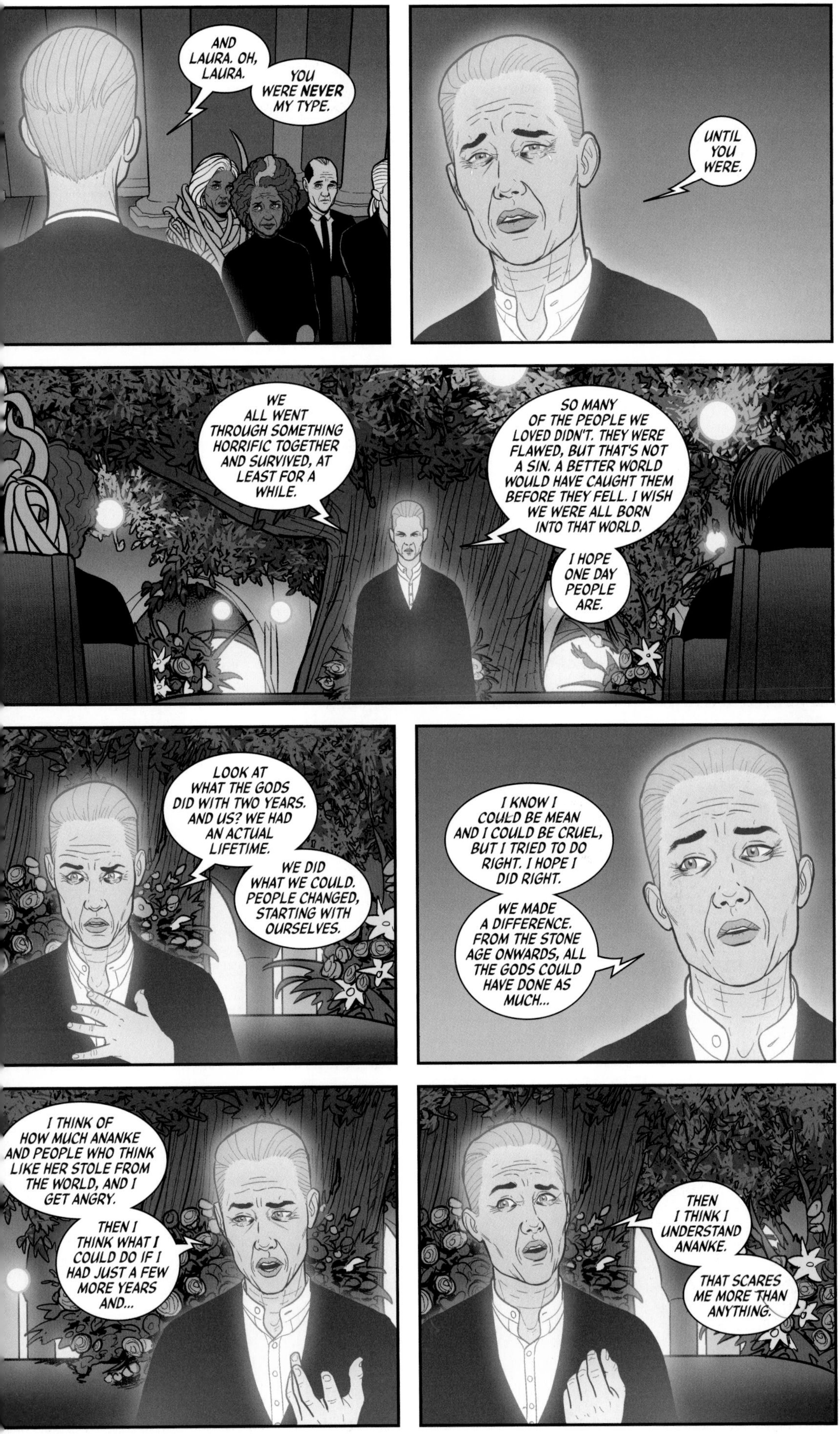
AND LAURA. OH, LAURA.
YOU WERE NEVER MY TYPE.
UNTIL YOU WERE.
WE ALL WENT THROUGH SOMETHING HORRIFIC TOGETHER AND SURVIVED, AT LEAST FOR A WHILE.
SO MANY OF THE PEOPLE WE LOVED DIDN'T. THEY WERE FLAWED, BUT THAT'S NOT A SIN. A BETTER WORLD WOULD HAVE CAUGHT THEM BEFORE THEY FELL. I WISH WE WERE ALL BORN INTO THAT WORLD.
I HOPE ONE DAY PEOPLE ARE.
LOOK AT WHAT THE GODS DID WITH TWO YEARS. AND US? WE HAD AN ACTUAL LIFETIME.
WE DID WHAT WE COULD. PEOPLE CHANGED, STARTING WITH OURSELVES.
I KNOW I COULD BE MEAN AND I COULD BE CRUEL, BUT I TRIED TO DO RIGHT. I HOPE I DID RIGHT.
WE MADE A DIFFERENCE. FROM THE STONE AGE ONWARDS, ALL THE GODS COULD HAVE DONE AS MUCH...
I THINK OF HOW MUCH ANANKE AND PEOPLE WHO THINK LIKE HER STOLE FROM THE WORLD, AND I GET ANGRY.
THEN I THINK WHAT I COULD DO IF I HAD JUST A FEW MORE YEARS AND...
THEN I THINK I UNDERSTAND ANANKE.
THAT SCARES ME MORE THAN ANYTHING.

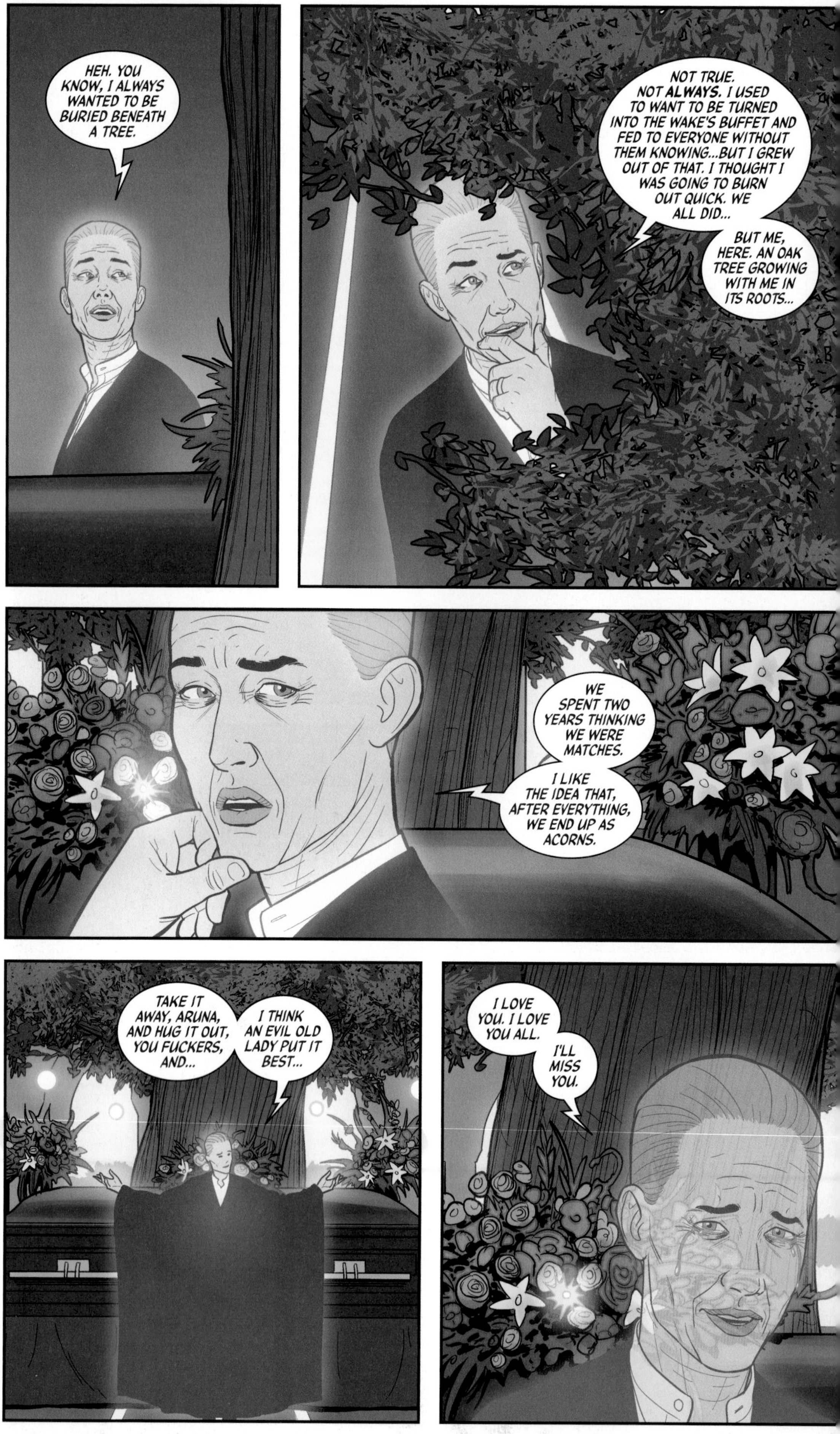
HEH. YOU KNOW, I ALWAYS WANTED TO BE BURIED BENEATH A TREE.
NOT TRUE. NOT ALWAYS. I USED TO WANT TO BE TURNED INTO THE WAKE'S BUFFET AND FED TO EVERYONE WITHOUT THEM KNOWING...BUT I GREW OUT OF THAT. I THOUGHT I WAS GOING TO BURN OUT QUICK. WE ALL DID...
BUT ME, HERE. AN OAK TREE GROWING WITH ME IN ITS ROOTS...
WE SPENT TWO YEARS THINKING WE WERE MATCHES.
I LIKE THE IDEA THAT, AFTER EVERYTHING, WE END UP AS ACORNS.
I THINK AN EVIL OLD LADY PUT IT BEST...
TAKE IT AWAY, ARUNA, AND HUG IT OUT, YOU FUCKERS, AND...
I LOVE YOU. I LOVE YOU ALL.
I'LL MISS YOU.

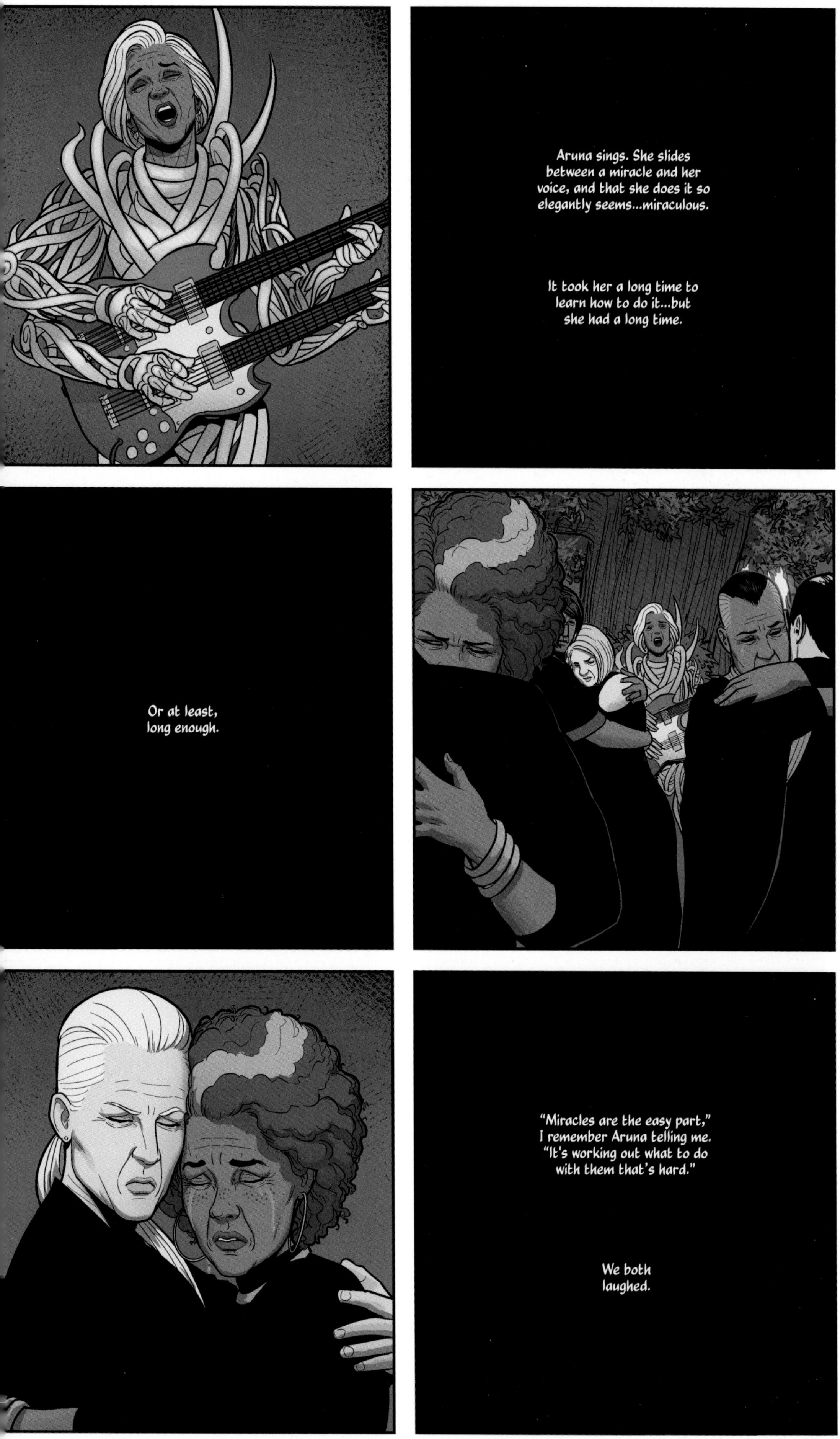
Aruna sings. She slides between a miracle and her voice, and that she does it so elegantly seems...miraculous.
It took her a long time to learn how to do it...but she had a long time.
Or at least, long enough.
"Miracles are the easy part," I remember Aruna telling me. "It's working out what to do with them that's hard."
We both laughed.

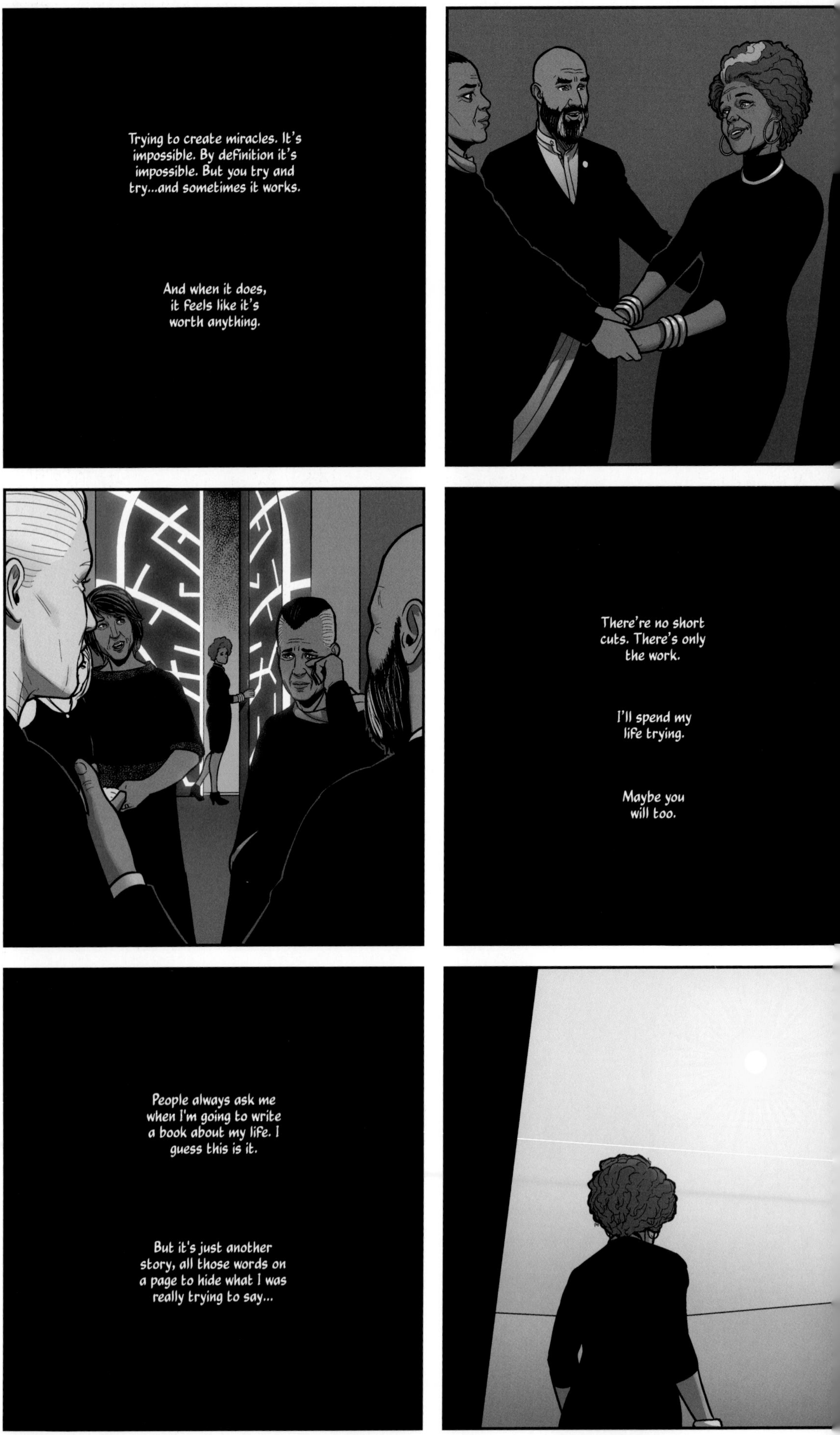
Trying to create miracles. It's impossible. By definition it's impossible. But you try and try...and sometimes it works.
And when it does, it feels like it's worth anything.
There're no short cuts. There's only the work.
I'll spend my life trying.
Maybe you will too.
People always ask me when I'm going to write a book about my life. I guess this is it.
But it's just another story, all those words on a page to hide what I was really trying to say...

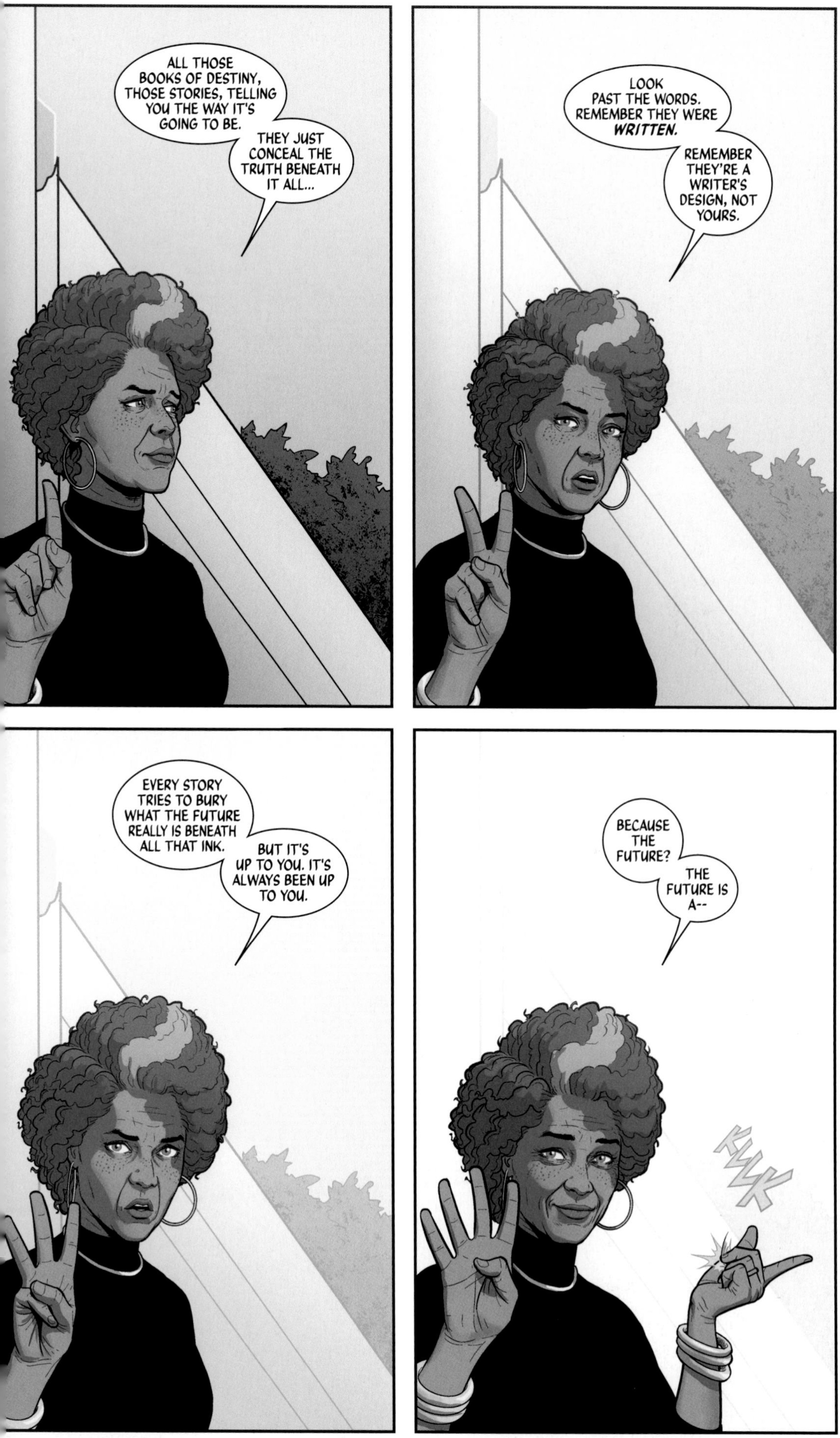
ALL THOSE BOOKS OF DESTINY, THOSE STORIES, TELLING YOU THE WAY IT'S GOING TO BE.
THEY JUST CONCEAL THE TRUTH BENEATH IT ALL...
LOOK PAST THE WORDS. REMEMBER THEY WERE ***WRITTEN.***
REMEMBER THEY'RE A WRITER'S DESIGN, NOT YOURS.
EVERY STORY TRIES TO BURY WHAT THE FUTURE REALLY IS BENEATH ALL THAT INK.
BUT IT'S UP TO YOU. IT'S ALWAYS BEEN UP TO YOU.
BECAUSE THE FUTURE?
THE FUTURE IS A--
KWK